POWER HANDTOOL HANDBOOK

by Dave Case

Publisher: Jonathan Latimer; Editor: Ted DiSante;
Art Director: Don Burton; Design & Assembly: George Haigh;
Typography: Cindy Coatsworth, Joanne Nociti, Kris Spitler

Published by **H.P. Books**, P.O. Box 5367, Tucson, AZ 85703   602/888-2150
ISBN: 0-89586-027-9
Library of Congress Catalog Card Number: 80-80172
© 1980 Fisher Publishing, Inc.
Printed in USA

Contents

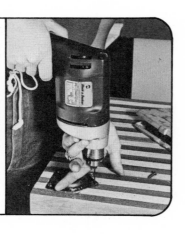
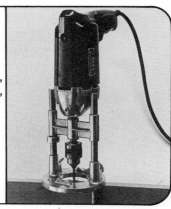

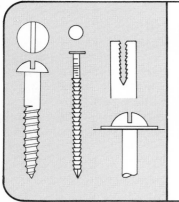

1
Getting Started

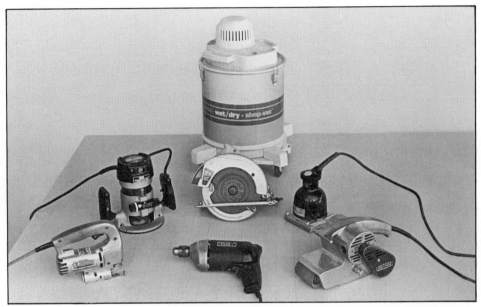

This is my personal power tool selection. I can accomplish almost any woodworking task I need, from building a small toy to a complete house.

There are not many ways you can save money today and still have fun. Making things with power tools is one of the best. You can build useful projects for indoors or out, do home repairs or even start a new hobby by making a project like the boat in this book. Working with your hands is a relaxing alternative to the nine-to-five grind. And you can discover the joys of making your own furniture, your own designs, and your own things. Both men and women are finding out how much fun it is to make something, and how much they can save. So, come on in. The water's fine, and there is plenty of room for more.

WELCOME

Woodworking can be one of the most satisfying ways to spend your time. It's fun to hear the sound of a drill or watch the ease with which a saber saw cuts a random scroll through a piece of plywood. And there *is* a sense of pride and accomplishment in looking at something you created out of a few scraps of raw wood or metal. However, the number of people using power tools who don't really have an understanding of what they are doing is amazing. Sure, anyone can plug in a cord and squeeze a trigger. But there is much more to operating power tools than just those two steps. On the other hand, you don't *have* to be a combination engineer/master mechanic to enjoy the fun of power tools.

WHY THIS BOOK?

Most of the books I've read on power tools are so technical they either confuse me or put me to sleep. This book is designed to cut through this technical confusion. It is directed at the beginner or the person with some familiarity with power tools. I want to teach you as much as you'll need to know to get started in this rewarding hobby with safety and confidence.

I've described the latest products on the market: what they are; what they do; and how they work. There are detailed instructions, tips and short cuts to save you time and improve your tool-handling technique. Finally, some plans are included to get you started. A few may appear too simple, but use them to improve your skills before tackling larger, more complex and expensive projects.

COMING TO TERMS

Every field has its own language. And so it is with the home craftsman. Because most of the work done by you will be with wood, I want to familiarize you with a few words that are part of the language used in this book. Most of them are merely a different way of saying what you already know.

A *drill* is an electrical power tool. The actual thing that drills the hole is called a *bit*. The bit is held in the drill by an adjustable, circular vise called a *chuck*. A *chuck key* tightens the chuck jaws around the shank of the bit to hold the bit securely in the chuck. The tip of the bit does the cutting. Grooves in the shank called *flutes* carry waste material up and out the hole.

On a router the chuck is called a *collet* and is designed to take only one size bit, usually with a 1/4-inch

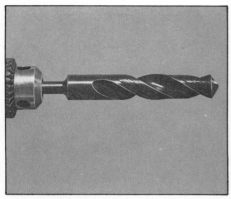

You're looking at a close-up of a 1/4-inch chuck holding a reduced shank 1/2-inch bit. The chuck is driven by a drill motor through a gear train in the drill casing.

The *kerf*, the cut made by a sawblade, should always be made on the waste side of the lined measurement.

Rip sawing always indicates you are cutting parallel to the grain of the wood. Here you can see how an edge guide or *rip fence* is a help in making an accurate long cut.

A router collet looks similar to a drill chuck but only takes one size bit.

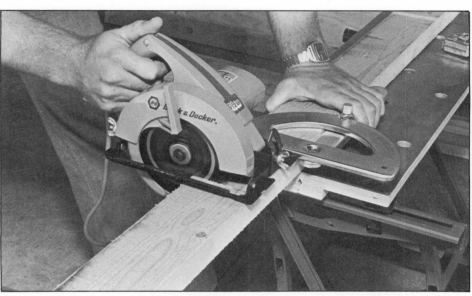

Crosscutting is sawing at an angle of 90 degrees to the grain. Use a protractor guide with the saw to assure a clean precise cut.

shank. Router cutting tools are also called *bits*.

Whenever you use a saw, the cut made by the blade as it slices through the wood is called the *kerf*. For an accurate cut, guide the saw so only one side of the kerf touches the pencil line on the stock, with the rest of the kerf cut on the waste side.

Any sawing done parallel to the wood grain is called *ripping*. If you have a 1-inch-thick board which is 6 inches wide by 8 feet long and wish to reduce its width to 4 inches, you'll make a rip cut with either a *rip* or *combination blade*.

Now that the board is 4 inches wide, let's say the next step is to cut it into 2-foot lengths. This means sawing at a right angle to the grain of the wood, called *crosscutting*. Use a *crosscut* or *combination blade* for this job.

A *combination blade* is a compromise between the crosscut and the rip sawblades. It won't do either job quite as well, but a rip blade won't crosscut and the crosscut won't rip efficiently. A combination blade handles both chores acceptably. It is the all-around utility blade that can do 85 to 90 percent of your sawing.

Miter and *bevel* cuts are fairly common when working with wood and they are similar in appearance. You are making a miter cut anytime you *crosscut* at less than a 90-degree *angle to the grain*. For instance, a picture frame is made by using 45-degree miter cuts at each corner.

A miter cut is any cut more *or less* than 90 degrees to the wood grain with the saw blade perpendicular to the surface.

A bevel is made anytime the sawblade is tilted away from 90 degrees *to the surface to be cut.* Joining two long boards with a 45-degree bevel cut works well because each board overlaps the other. *Compound* or *combination bevel/miter* cuts are commonly used in cabinet work and boatbuilding.

Chamfer is another word for a bevel cut. While a bevel generally goes from surface to surface, a chamfer is cut only part of the way down the side. If you have a square piece of wood and wish to make it an octagon, you would make four 45-degree chamfer cuts down the length of the stock.

When the ends or side of a board are notched, the joint is called a *rabbet.* You can see a rabbet by opening a kitchen cabinet and looking at the edges. The rabbet joint is used extensively on cabinet doors and occasionally to splice two boards together.

A *dado* is merely notching a board somewhere between, but not on, the ends. Dadoing is often used where two boards cross at right angles and a strong joint is required. One board is dadoed, or notched, to accept the other where they cross. Once the dado is made, the boards are joined together, forming a very strong support joint.

THE RIGHT TOOL

Tools themselves are another thing to think a bit about. Not only do you need the right attitude and patience to build a successful project, you need the right tools. The old saying, *the right tool for the right job,* is certainly true, although there *are* times when one tool will do more than just one job.

Not only do you want the right tool, the machine should be the *best* quality you can afford. Buying second- or third-best is usually more expensive in the long run. Second-rate tools usually don't last long enough for you to get your money's worth out of them. Even if you have to wait and save for it, buy the best tool. Now don't misunderstand. I said buy the *best,* which is not always the most expensive. I have definite opinions on which tools are the best. Combining the information in this book and some conversation with your local hardware dealer or a knowledgeable friend should give you a pretty fair idea of what is best for you.

COST

Cost is a factor in everything you do today, and it's no different with shop tools. What will they cost? By watching for sales and even checking with factory repair outlets, you can purchase a good quality drill and saber or circular saw for under $60. Combined with your hand tools, these two basic items will give you the capability to make a multitude of repairs and projects. As a matter of fact, I heartily recommend you start small and add to your shop only after you've learned to use what you already own. By that time you'll have a good idea of what you're going to need next.

A drill, saber and circular saws, router, belt and vibrator sanders and related attachments can all be purchased for a reasonable amount by watching for sales. These tools not only give you a very wide range of possibilities, but also get the job done with ease and professional appearance.

Bevel cuts are crosscuts with the sawblade tilted less than 90 degrees from the baseplate and therefore the surface of the wood.

A compound-bevel cut is merely a combination of miter and bevel cuts. The kerf is more *or less* than 90 degrees to the grain *and* the blade is tilted less than perpendicular to the surface. Two operations are performed with one slice.

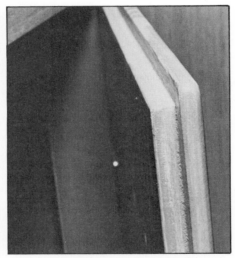

A close-up of a cabinet door reveals a rabbet cut. This type of joint makes a thinner facing, while still maintaining the strength of the door panel.

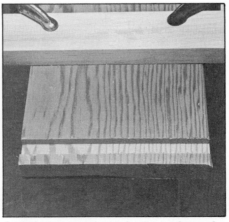

A *dado* is a notch cut in the surface of a board which will hold the end of another board.

CLAMPS

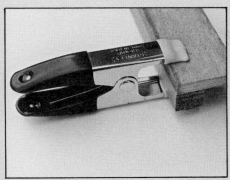

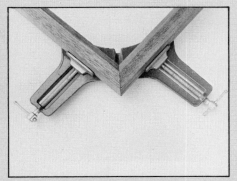

A *pipe clamp* runs the length of my tired sawhorse. Below that a *web clamp* holds the legs together. Then from left to right are: an *edge clamp*, a *C-clamp*, a *bar clamp*, and a *wand screw wood clamp*.

This tough little *spring clamp* is just right for holding small parts.

A *miter clamp* holds both parts at a perfect 90° angle. You should get a good glue joint and a square picture frame if you cut each corner exactly.

Throughout the book I keep telling you to "clamp it." I guess if I put so much emphasis on clamping, I should take a little time to explain what's available when you need to "clamp it."

The *C-clamp* will probably perform the lion's share of your holding operations. They're inexpensive (I buy mine at swap meets and garage sales), plentiful and can be used in a wide variety of ways. C-clamps come in sizes from 1 to 8 inches, which is the measure of the maximum width of the opening. Normally the C-shape will provide a depth of 1 to 4 inches, depending upon the size of the clamp. Always use scraps of wood to pad and protect your work from the steel jaws of the clamps.

If the project calls for something that needs a wider opening you might consider a *bar clamp*. They come in sizes from 12 to 48 inches and are fully adjustable from the smallest opening to the full length of their bar. Padded protection is also required.

For a super-wide job, *pipe clamps* are the answer. A hardware store will sell you two end mounts as a unit. The pipe must be purchased separately. But that's really not a bad idea, because you can buy whatever length pipe you need to anchor your project. Pipe clamps are adjustable like bar clamps—from zero to the maximum length of the pipe you bought. By getting different lengths of pipe, say 2-foot, 4-foot and 6-foot lengths, you can interchange the end brackets and have clamps for a variety of needs. Pipe clamps are made to accept either 1/2-inch or 3/4-inch steel pipe. One end of the pipe must be threaded to attach the base clamp. The other part slides down the pipe to adjust to your requirements. Padding is a must.

We've talked about big clamps, but how about those small projects? Hand *spring clamps* will work on most of your lighter chores. They look a little like giant metal clothes pins. Squeezing the handle opens the vinyl-coated jaws. Depending upon the size, the jaw depth is from 4 to 8 inches with an opening of 7/8 to 3 inches. The bigger models are quite strong and require two hands to overcome the spring pressure.

So far, all the compression devices I've discussed work equally well for wood or metal. This next one is strictly a wood clamp and no padding is necessary. It's called an *adjustable hand screw clamp*. The maple jaws will hold to a depth of 6 to 14 inches and they'll open from 3 to 10 inches, depending on the size used. The jaws operate on two worm screws that are individually adjustable. So instead of re- maining parallel to each other, they can form angles. This allows the clamp to clasp irregular shapes. They are relatively expensive, but are worth it if you're going to do a lot of woodworking.

Here are a couple of specialty clamps: The *web clamp* works like a gigantic rubber band. It goes around the circumference of an object—say four chair legs—and is cinched up by hand and finally tightened with a wrench. The web belt will take a tremendous amount of pressure, keeping everything within its grip squeezed tight. The other specialty item is a *miter clamp*. This unit works well when you're making picture frames and are using a 45° miter butt joint. Two sets of jaws at right angles let you hold the two pieces to be glued at a perfect 90° angle, thereby giving you a frame that is square and not a parallelogram.

A last note on clamps: If all else fails, try using your workbench to hold the stock. A couple of scrap 2x4s, some C-clamps, and some wedges can be used to hold oversize material. I used this arrangement while making the table top of the Picnic Table in Chapter 11. Check the photos on page 119 for details on how to hold a piece that won't fit conventional clamps.

Remember—where ther's a will, there's a way to "clamp it."

JOINTS

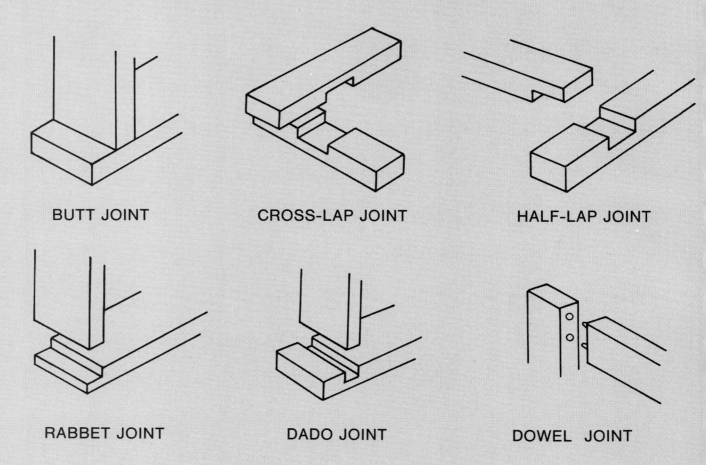

BUTT JOINT   CROSS-LAP JOINT   HALF-LAP JOINT

RABBET JOINT   DADO JOINT   DOWEL JOINT

Anytime two pieces of wood are attached to each other you have a joint. Whether it's a simple *butt joint* held together by nails, or the beautiful *dovetail* requiring only a few drops of glue to maintain its position, you have to make a joint to join two pieces of wood. Fortunately, most joints are fairly easy to make and many are interchangeable. So it becomes the builder's prerogative to choose whatever he wants for the given situation. The following discussion offers guidelines for selecting the best joint.

BUTT JOINT

Used extensively in rough construction. Simple, but only as strong as the fasteners. Nails or screws must be used to hold the pieces together. Glue will provide additional strength.

LAP JOINT

Uses include frames, shelves, chairs, cabinets, easels, fencing, decking and general construction. Probably the most common joint after the butt, it is relatively easy to make and gets much of its strength from interlocking the stock. If you own a saber saw, circular saw or router, you'll have no difficulty making this joint. Nails or screws and glue make the tightest joint. In assembling the half lap use clamps to ensure the proper angle.

RABBET

Used extensively in cabinets, tables and shelving, rabbets are strong and make a neat corner. They can be made with a circular saw but a router works best. Nails or screws and glue are required.

DADO

A dado is similar to the rabbet except it's made anywhere except the end of the board. The joint is excellent when making shelving. It may also be used in tables and general cabinetry. A circular saw or router with a rip fence will easily make this joint. The dado can be held together with glue only, but screws or nails help if it won't spoil the outside face.

MITER

Picture frames, door moldings and screens are but a few uses. Miter joints usually require the

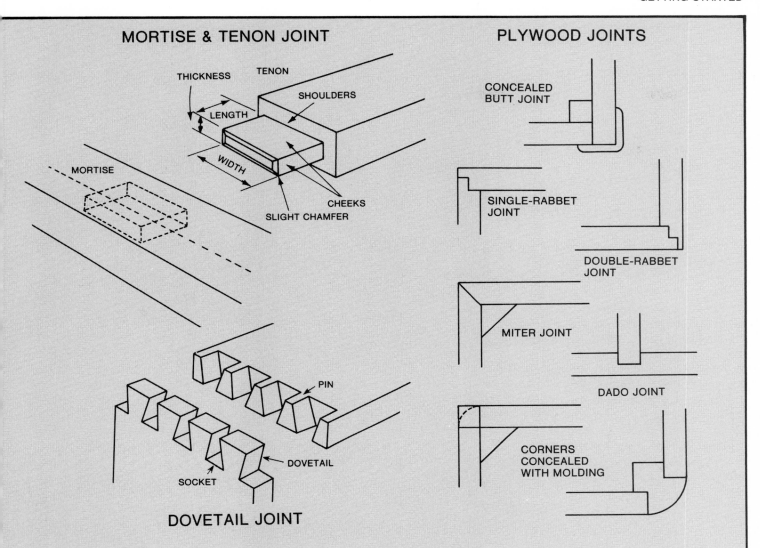

MORTISE & TENON JOINT

PLYWOOD JOINTS

DOVETAIL JOINT

baseplate to be perpendicular to the work with the saw crosscutting at a 45° angle. Generally, the joint is a butt type. Where strength is required, use dowels or corrugated fasteners to do the job.

MORTISE & TENON

Used in chairs and fencing, it provides excellent strength. Cut the tenon first, making sure the tongue is not more than 1/3 of the width of the stock. Lay out the mortise using the tongue of the tenon as a pattern. Use a drill to remove the majority of the stock from the mortise. Use a sharp chisel to clean the sides and make the corners. Glue and wedge if necessary with a tapered piece of stock tapped in with a mallet.

DOVETAIL

Used for drawers and fine furniture, the dovetail is the "classy" joint. Made with a router and a template, a well-made dovetail will actually hold without using any fasteners, including glue! However, I prefer to use a few drops to ensure against loosening due to shrinkage.

PLYWOOD JOINTS

Working with plywood can present special joint-making problems because the end grain shows on the corners. Here are a few easy ways you can solve this problem.

Butt Joint—Simple, but end grain shows. The end grain can be concealed with molding. Also, a butt joint can be supported on the inside with a cleat.

Single-Rabbet Joint—Stronger than a butt joint and simple to make. Most of the end grain is covered.

Double-Rabbet Joint—Rabbets are cut in both pieces which creates a large gluing surface.

Miter Joint—Miter cut must be very accurate. Both end grains hidden.

Dado Joint—Ideal for shelving. Easy to make, and holds with glue alone. End grain is concealed.

Using Molding—A corner can be made with two pieces of molding. The end grain is covered, but finishing can be a problem.

The same type of corner as above except the corner post is rabbeted on two sides and rounded on the edge. This is used where the posts are the actual frame. No end grain shows.

SAVE WITH POWER TOOLS

When you start using portable power tools, one of the first things you will realize is their tremendous value as time savers. About 95 percent of all fix-it jobs around the house can be accomplished faster and cheaper with power tools than by any other method. Home repairs using only hand tools are slow, and sometimes impossible. But hiring an electrician or a carpenter can be a little like making interest payments on the national debt.

With just a drill and a saw you can really save on run-of-the-mill home projects. For example, with a power drill, boring a hole in the ceiling for a hanging lamp or planter takes effortless seconds, compared to standing on a chair trying to make an old hand-crank drill work. Or, correcting a door that drags on the rug, is a few minutes' work with a power saw. Compare that with trying to make a smooth cut with a hand saw and then finishing it with a plane. So, not only will you enjoy power tools, they'll also save you time and money.

THE RIGHT ATTITUDE

Something you should begin to think about as you read this book, and particularly as you begin to work with power tools, is the Philosophy of Working: *Anything worth doing is worth doing right.* This is certainly true when you're working for yourself. So, anything you build, any line you saw, any hole you drill should be the best you can do. If you start with this attitude in mind, your whole learning experience will accelerate—just because of your inner *desire to do your best* on each and everything you undertake. As a result, the finished work will be something you are proud of—something you will be proud to give or display. And your friends will see it in your work too, only they will call it *craftsmanship.*

Don't hurry to finish the job. Take your time. After all, you are doing this for yourself. There's no foreman or supervisor breathing

Power tools make common, but difficult jobs easy. Even someone as small as my wife can easily install a hanging basket for plants.

down your neck pushing you for more production. I too have suffered from the *hurry-up syndrome.* Once a project is started, it's *hurry-up* until the thing is completed. *This is wrong.* Mistakes are made, cuts aren't as accurate, joints aren't as tight, and the finish isn't as fine as it could be.

When you find yourself getting all wound up and yelling at some piece of wood that can't hear you, take a break. Sit down for a few minutes and recover your composure. The excellence of your finished product will generally reflect how *relaxed* you were when you built it, not how fast you made it. Few projects ever get done on schedule. There are always delays for the phone, friends and chasing parts. Time will slip away, but don't let it worry you. Work at a relaxed pace and you'll do a better job.

THE RIGHT SIZE TOOL

The idea that *Smaller is Better* in reference to energy conservation sounds good, but it may not be so. Buying a small drill because it won't use as much power as a bigger model seems to make sense, but unfortunately, it doesn't work that way. Often the reverse is true.

The reason it does not work is because of *time.* If a 1/4hp drill takes 30 seconds to make a hole, a 1/2hp drill will do the same job in 15 seconds. Twice the amount of energy was spent doing the second hole, but in only *half* the time. So the power use is the same for both drills.

In many instances the smaller drill will not have enough power to do the job without overextending its capacity. In that case you're actually going to use *more* power than you would with a larger model. And you run the risk of wearing out the smaller drill prematurely.

You should also know that **Volts x Amps = Watts, or V x A = W.**

This formula is very handy. If you keep tripping a circuit breaker every time you start to use that big circular saw Uncle Harry left you, take a look at the circuit breaker and read the amp rating on the switch.

Let's say the figure is 15amps. By using the above formula you multiply 110V x 15A and get 1650W. You now know that circuit is capable of handling 1650 watts. If a quick check on the saw's nameplate tells you the machine is rated at 13 amps, it uses 1430 watts: 110V x 13A = 1430W, of power. That's not enough to trip the breaker, but running two 100-watt light bulbs and the radio on the same circuit would do it for sure.

To avoid tripping the circuit breaker the next time you use the saw, don't play the radio, and you can even downgrade the lights to two 75-watt bulbs.

That's one way to make the formula work for you. Here's another even more useful example. Practically all power tool manufacturers that give horsepower ratings measure it at the blade, after going through the gear train, and with no load on the tool.

Now, how do you compare a horsepower-rated tool with one only listing voltage and amperes? Easy. Check the volts and amps on the nameplate of each tool and calculate the individual wattages. The unit with the higher wattage rating has the more powerful motor.

Another simple formula you should know is: 746 watts equal 1 horsepower, or 746W = 1hp. If you divide 746 into whatever wattage you've determined, you will find the actual horsepower of that tool's motor. A saw rated at 120 volts and 10 amps will use 1200 watts and develop 1.6hp. 120V x 10A = 1200W ÷ 746 = 1.6hp.

The calculated horsepower figure doesn't necessarily agree with the manufacturer's listed horsepower because, as I mentioned earlier, the listed horsepower is measured at the blade and is no-load, geared power. The figure we arrived at is the motor's *capable power*. When comparing models, be sure to compare the *same* horsepower rating: either the motor's or the tool's. The model with the highest motor horsepower will usually give the best performance and longest wear.

PRACTICE

There is another thing to consider before you start building your bookshelf or that house you've always dreamed of. That is *practice*. Very few people can sit down at the piano for the first time and play Rodgers & Hart. I don't know any-

one who makes a guitar sound good without practicing. So, don't expect to *play* a drill, saw or router perfectly the first time you plug them in. Just like playing the piano or the guitar, it takes practice to become a virtuoso. But it can be done, and you can do it.

With every new tool you buy, get a piece of scrap wood and practice. Check the balance, allow your fingers to locate the controls. If it's a drill, make a few holes until you can start a hole without walking the drill all over the material. Hold the drill in a manner that lets you drill 90 degrees to the stock. Do the same with a saw or a sander. Get the *feel* of the equipment. Practice until you're comfortable with the operation of the tool. This way you're in command, not vice-versa.

Keep your first projects simple. Even though you bought that saw to build a boat or a cabin, start with a picnic table or maybe some toys for the kids. This too is practice.

Those simple building projects will give you the experience you'll need to build that boat. In a sense, everything you do is practice for advancing to the next project. As you practice, put forth your best effort in every way. That way you'll constantly improve with every job you do.

MAINTAINING YOUR TOOLS

Just like the piano and guitar I mentioned earlier, your tools are your instruments. A piano sounds awful if it's not kept in tune. By the same token, an electric saw with a dull blade chews through wood like a termite with gum disease. Keeping your tools sharp, clean and in good working order will more than pay you back in the type of work you turn out. Sharp, well-tuned tools are also safer to use—something that should be at the top of your priorities when working in the shop. Chapter 10 gives more detailed information on repairs and maintenance.

PRACTICAL PRACTICE

While it's useful to practice with your tools on scrap, it is really not very satisfying. It's much more fun to learn while you make something that's useful. The project chapters are designed to let you do just that. Chapter 11 takes you through a series of projects chosen to give you experience with each of your tools. Even if you only own a drill, you can still make the die pencil holder on page 99. Other plans include a picnic table and a dog house. Not only that, you can make a special workbench for your tools as well.

The plans in Chapter 12 do not have the step-by-step narrative like the plans in Chapter 11. Instead, they are presented in the same way you will find plans in magazines or other books. You should study them carefully before you start so you can avoid costly mistakes.

BEARINGS

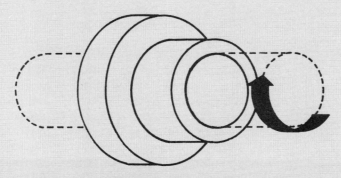

SLEEVE BEARING

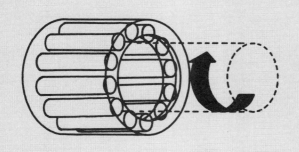

ROLLER BEARING

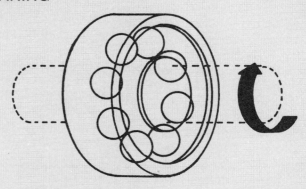

BALL BEARING

One of the important factors contributing to the service life of a power tool is the type of bearings used in its construction. Generally, an inexpensive tool will have cheap bearings and wear out sooner than a more costly model with higher priced bearings. Knowing about bearings will make you a better judge when you go to buy a tool.

First, what is a bearing? Well, the dictionary says a bearing is: *"A device that supports, guides, and reduces the friction of motion between fixed and moving machine parts."* So we can say that a bearing is used to reduce wear and makes operation between moving and fixed parts *smoother*. Almost everything manufactured with moving parts uses bearings.

Power tool construction utilizes three different types of bearings: *sleeve, roller* and *ball*. A *sleeve bearing* is machined from a piece of tubular, oil-impregnated bronze stock. A sleeve bearing is relatively cheap to produce, yet effective and simple, which makes it ideal for inexpensive power tools. The problem with sleeve bearings is they don't hold up well when subjected to constant heavy use. *Roller*, or *needle bearings* surround a part with several small rollers and protect if from another fixed part. They have less friction and are longer lasting than sleeve bearings. Roller bearings are also excellent for cushioning side loads. But they're a little more expensive and are therefore found in higher priced models. *Ball bearings* offer the best of all worlds. A ball has smaller surface contact than a roller, and that translates into less friction and longer life. Balls can be enclosed in steel and sealed with built-in lubrication, which makes additional oiling unnecessary. Ball bearings are the most expensive type of bearing. Only top-of-the-line quality tools will be "100% Ball Bearing." They will be the best you can buy.

Somewhere between the most inexpensive and top of the line will be the medium range tools. These models are usually made with a combination of the three types of bearings. As the quality improves, more ball bearings are used. You will sometimes see two tools side by side that appear the same, but one is priced higher and labeled "Pro." The use of ball bearings is one of the reasons for the higher price, and the label will tell you that the tool is designed for very heavy-duty work.

Whatever the tool, take the time to review the owner's manual *before* you operate it. Keep a shop file on product manuals so you can refer to them for parts, product warranty, or other useful information as the need arises.

Think Safety is an excellent motto—one too often taken for granted. *Think Safety* until it becomes automatic, second nature to your planning. Nothing you do with power tools is more important than safety. Whether you're just starting to explore the do-it-yourself field or you're a fairly advanced craftsman, form good safety habits as you proceed. Make safety a state of mind—a positive, unconscious approach to everything you do. All the rules and warnings in the world won't help if you don't take care when working with tools.

Here are a few basic rules with the reasons why they're mandatory. Rules, however, won't cover every situation. Only you know if a given action is safe. If it looks shaky, don't do it!

TAKE YOUR TIME

The first thing you should think about is patience. Don't be in a hurry. Work slowly and methodically. Speed will come with practice. After all, it's a hobby and you do have all the time in the world.

Developing patience can also improve the quality of the work you produce. So take it easy.

CONSIDER YOUR MOOD

If you've had a bad day at the office and everything you've touched has gone wrong, don't expect it to be any different in the shop. Watch TV or read a book instead of finishing a project. The right mental attitude is every bit as important when you pursue your hobby as it is at the office.

DON'T WORK
IF YOU'RE TOO TIRED

More accidents occur at the end of the day than at other times. Don't work when you're overly tired. That's when you get careless. If you find you're beginning to get sloppy or your feet are hurting, take a break. A ten-minute rest will not only improve your performance and attitude, it will also reduce the chances for an accident.

RESPECT YOUR TOOLS

A little fear is a healthy emotion when working with power tools.

Call it *respect* if you want. Your tools are all potential weapons, as is an automobile, in unthinking or contemptuous hands. Treat them with the respect they deserve. Never forget that they can bite through you just as easily as they can cut through wood *if* you become complacent and careless.

I said a little fear is good. By the same token, too much fear will cause your movements to become uncoordinated and lead to a possible accident. Tools exist to help you. And they will if you show them the respect they deserve. Practice enough to gain confidence in their use, and in yourself.

CONCENTRATE

If friends drop by, stop working. You can't talk and work at the same time. One or both will suffer. If I'm working in the shop and my best buddy comes by, I make it a point to stop, put on the coffee pot, and take a break. He thinks it's because I want to relax, which is partly true. But I can't concentrate on what I'm doing when someone else is around.

Incidently, I violated that rule this summer and cut a 3-foot piece of Burma teak 1 inch too short. At twelve dollars a board foot, it was an expensive reminder.

The same rule applies to small children. If they're active and into everything, you're going to be distracted. Show them the door! If they're quiet and just want to watch, that's another thing. Let them if you want to. Just don't compromise your own safety rules for the sake of courtesy.

Now it's time for a few *Do's & Don'ts*—simple rules to get you started and keep you out of trouble.

DO'S & DON'TS
DO take it easy.
DO know your tools.
DO show your tools respect.
DO keep tools clean and sharp.
DO wear safety goggles.
DO secure the work.
DO disconnect power *before* changing blades and bits.
DO remove adjusting wrenches *before* reconnecting power.
DO keep your work area clean.
DO ground all tools.
DO stop working when friends drop by.
DO keep children safe from harm.
DON'T drink and work.
DON'T wear loose clothes or jewelry.
DON'T force the tool.
DON'T lose your balance.
DON'T work in water.
DON'T stand in front of cutting edges.

DO'S

• **Do Know Your Power Tool.** Read the manufacturer's manual thoroughly *before* you operate the tool. Learn its specifications and limits. Study any tips or advice offered. Check out the warranty and what will *void* the warranty. Follow the recommended operating procedures.

• **Do Wear Safety Goggles.** A good pair of safety goggles costs around three dollars. When was the last time you priced an eye?

• **Do Keep Your Tools Clean and Sharp.** Clean, well-oiled tools *and* sharp edges work better with less chance of binding and failure.

• **Do Secure Your Work.** Always make sure the stock is securely clamped down before drilling or sawing. This leaves both hands free to operate the tool.

One of the most unmanageable things around a shop is a large, heavy, 4x8 sheet of uncut plywood. Making that first cut is almost always a cumbersome, unbalanced affair frought with much danger—both imagined and real. In the back of the book I've designed a workbench and a small table to rest the large sheet of plywood and the piece being sawn off. If you don't feel you want to build the tables, or you don't have the space, I highly recommend you buy or make four sawhorses. Two horses can be used to support the main sheet of plywood while the other two are used to catch the piece being cut off. You might even consider using C-clamps to hold the plywood to the sawhorses to insure against accidently dropping either section.

• **Do Disconnect Power Before Changing Blades & Bits.** Whenever you're changing blades, bits or abrasives, make it a habit to first pull the electrical cord from its power source. It's very easy to accidently brush the trigger and start the motor when your fingers are near the cutting edges.

• **Do Remove All Adjusting Wrenches.** Chuck keys, hex wrenches and screwdrivers should always be removed *before reconnecting* the power tool to an electrical outlet.

• **Do Keep the Shop Area Clean.** A messy workshop invites accidents. Keep the place neat and orderly.

• **Do Ground All Tools.** Use either a three-pronged plug or buy double-insulated tools.

DON'TS

• **Don't Drink and Work.** It requires far more concentration to operate a saw than to drive a car. A few beers can give you problems in either case.

• **Don't Wear Loose Clothes or Jewlery.** Take off those dangling medallions. Wear short-sleeve shirts or button your shirt cuffs. If your hair is long, wear a hat or bandana. Anything loose can get caught in a whirling drill or spinning saw. Don't let it happen to you.

• **Don't Force the Tool.** Guide it. Otherwise, the machine will protest by kicking back or bucking—sometimes on you.

• **Don't Lose Your Balance.** Always try to keep both feet properly planted. Use your free hand for balance. Working off balance is inviting disaster.

• **Don't Work in Water.** Standing in puddles, running electrical cords through water or working in the rain are all excellent ways to make your wife a widow. Even with double-insulated tools, avoid situations where you can get an electrical shock. Seldom is there a second chance on this one.

• **Don't Stand in Front of Tools.** Try to position yourself to one side of the cutting edge of all saws—and behind drills and routers. Even with safety goggles, power tools will throw chips that can nick you.

USE COMMON SENSE

I could go on and fill this chapter with an endless list of the Do's & Don'ts of safety. But I think it is far more important you understand safety is really just *common sense.* Whether operating power tools, driving a car, flying a plane or taking a walk, safety is doing the right thing. You can't regulate safety with a set of rules, just as you can't regulate common sense.

Some say a person has to be born with common sense. But I think it's an acquired attitude, usually developed early in life. We all have the talent for safety, it's a matter of recognizing our own common sense.

Notice how many of the safety rules are also good thoughts when applied to craftsmanship:

Patience certainly will lead to higher quality work, as will working when you're rested.

Knowing your machine is fundamental to being able to operate it effectively and to its fullest capabilities.

Secure your work. How can you saw a straight line if the wood is wobbling? Clamp it down to do a better job.

Keep the cutters sharp. They'll do a better job, make a cleaner hole or saw a neater edge.

A clean shop shows pride in your area and workmanship. Again, you'll be doing a better job when you look better. And you can find your tools, too.

EXTENSION CORD LENGTH CHART

Ampere rating on tool nameplate	0 to 2.0	2.1 to 3.4	3.5 to 5.0	5.1 to 7.0	7.1 to 12.0	12.1 to 16.0
Extension Cord Length in feet	Cord Wire Sizes					
25	18	18	18	18	16	16
50	18	18	18	16	14	12
75	18	18	16	14	12	10
100	18	16	14	12	10	8*
150	16	14	12	12	8*	8*
200	16	14	12	10	8*	6*

*Not normally available as flexible extension cord.

EXTENSION CORDS

An area many How-To books neglect is the importance of the proper *minimum* size extension cord when operating any power tool. Using a light-duty cord like the type used for lamps is not just poor economics. Because of the restriction and loss of power to the tool, it can be downright dangerous. The excess heat the undersize wire may generate as a result of the power demand of the tool can melt the plugs and even start a fire.

HOW THEY WORK

Electricity passes through wire much like water flows through a hose. Volts and amps are sometimes confusing to the average reader, but water, flow and pressure are easily understood. It's easy to substitute the words "extension cord" for "hose" and "electricity" for "water." Think of voltage as pressure and amperes as flow. Now, let's say we have a faucet with a 3/4-inch opening. We connect a hose with an inside diameter of 1/4-inch. It's easy to visualize how long it would take you to water your lawn using this arrangement. The pressure would be there, but the narrow hose wouldn't give enough flow to get the work done. If the 1/4-inch hose was replaced with a 3/4-inch hose, you'd get all the pressure *and flow* the faucet was capable of delivering.

The same thing applies to electricity. Pressure equals volts and flow is the same as amps. You have the identical situation of the small diameter hose when you use too small a wire in an extension cord. The pressure (volts) is the same, but when you pull the trigger of your power tool and demand flow (amps) to do work, the small cord can't give you the amperes the tool needs to operate properly. The motor doesn't deliver peak efficiency and the tool suffers a loss of power. Also, by demanding more flow than the small cord can deliver, you create molecular friction through the wires. This is indicated by a heating of the cord. In a gross misuse of an extension cord this friction can produce enough heat to melt the insulation around the wires and cause a short or even a fire. So you see how important it is to use the correct *minimum* size cord. An oversize cord presents no threat. It is prepared to deliver all the volts (pressure) and amperes (flow) your tool is capable of using.

CHOOSING A CORD

In order to figure the proper cord for your needs, find the *ampere rating* on the nameplate of the heaviest power tool you own. Then estimate the longest extension cord you expect to be needing. With these two numbers, it is easy to select the proper size extension cord with the chart on this page.

Let's say you've got a circular saw that draws 10 amps. Because you're getting ready to build a house, you want to buy a 100-foot cord. How large should the wire be to operate that tool safely? Find where your tool fits on the ampere rating line. Your 10-amp tool fits on the 7.1 to 12.0 column. Read down to the 100-foot line and you'll see that you need a cord with a wire gauge of at least #10 for safety and optimum performance.

If you plan on working outside or if you are going to use tools that are not double-insulated, be sure to buy an extension cord that has a third wire for grounding. This will prevent a possible shock.

CONNECTING CORDS

To keep the plug of your tool safely connected to the cord while working, tie the cords together with a simple knot before plugging them together. This is safer and you can drag the cord around behind you as you work without the minor frustration of the power tool becoming disconnected. Of course you may also buy a fancy plastic gadget at the hardware store that does the same thing, but why spend your money when the knot works just as well and it won't get lost?

SAFETY & CRAFTSMANSHIP

Good safety—Good craftsmanship. The two go hand in hand. By adhering to a safe philosophy, you are also creating an environment conducive to quality craftsmanship. So safety is not something that should be looked upon as a necessary nuisance. Instead, it should be thought of as something that is actually going to improve your skill and craftsmanship.

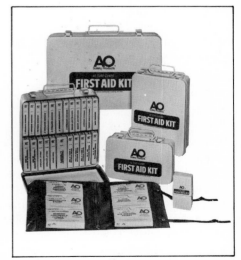

Having a first aid kit nearby is highly recommended whether your are doing a small repair job around the house or a large project in the shop.

3
Drills

I remember the first electric drill I ever saw in 1947. My grandfather bought it for his home workshop. When he opened the box and took out the shiny 1/4-inch electric drill, my eyes almost popped out of my head. It was big, as big as 1/2-inch drills are today. And it was heavy. I had to use both hands to hold this magical delight. Of course, I was a bit younger then.

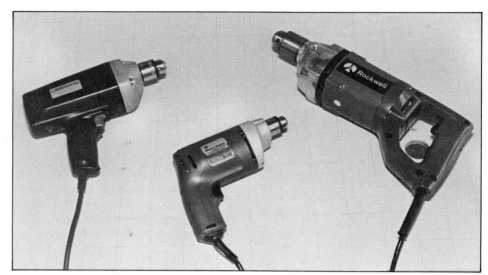

The 3/8, 1/4, and 1/2-inch drills. Small, medium, and large, they all have a place when you have the need, although I consider the 3/8-inch model to be the best all-around drill for the average craftsperson.

Today, the low initial cost of an electric drill and the wide variety of accessories available make it the first power tool every beginning home craftsman should purchase.

Besides drilling holes in wood, metal, and nearly everything else, the electric drill can also drive screws, stir paint, polish cars, sharpen scissors, sand surfaces, change the oil in your car, pump out an aquarium and cut shrubbery.

In addition, it can be converted to a circular saw, saber saw or router.

This simple, small, easy-to-use tool is indeed versatile.

THE BASIC DRILL

Now that you know what it will do, let me describe a typical drill. A small electric motor drives a two- or three-stage gear train that turns a device called the *chuck*. The chuck holds the *drill bit*, the business end of the drill. A spring-loaded trigger switch on the handle is used to turn the drill on and off. The whole thing is packaged in a housing to give it a pistol-like appearance, which makes it very convenient to use.

Electric drills come in three common sizes: 1/4-inch, 3/8-inch and 1/2-inch. This designates the maximum size of the bit shaft the chuck will accept. Chuck size does not necessarily indicate the drill-bit size: a spade bit with a 1-1/2-inch diameter has a 1/4-inch shaft. But chuck size does give some idea about the power and speed of the drill motor. A 1/4-inch drill may have a speed of 2250 revolutions per minute (RPM), yet develop only 1/6 horsepower (hp) at 2.0 amps (A), while a 3/8-inch drill may only turn 1200 RPM, but deliver 3/8hp at 3.0A. A 1/2-inch drill operating at 575 RPM has almost a 1hp motor. As a general rule, the bigger the chuck size, the slower the speed, but the more *torque* or twisting force the drill develops for the job.

It also follows that the bigger and more powerful the drill, the more it weighs. A 1/2-inch drill may weigh over ten pounds. This is certainly something to consider if you plan to stand on a scaffold and bore holes in the ceiling all day long. Obviously you want the lightest drill that can do the job in a reasonable amount of time.

SELECTING YOUR DRILL

Before buying a drill, think about the kind of work you will be doing with it. If all you have in mind is light-duty home repairs, and maybe a few shop projects, a 1/4-inch drill will probably be fine. If you plan to use the drill more constantly with a broad range of materials, the 3/8-inch drill will stand up better. A 1/2-inch drill is likely to be more of an accessory tool for the average home craftsman, something you'd buy after you already own a 1/4-inch or 3/8-inch drill. It is mainly for heavy-duty work such as drilling through thick steel or cement foundations.

Another thing to test when selecting a drill motor is how it feels. Does it fit well in your hand? Do you like the balance? Is it too heavy or too light? After checking chuck size and power, buy something you are comfortable with. It will make a big difference in the quality of work you produce if you are happy with your tools. A proper fit can also cut down on fatigue.

Expensive, but a super tool. Not only will it bore holes with variable speed and reversing capabilities, the unit can also be used as a rotary hammer for masonry drilling. Or, by twisting a cam it can be used as a power chisel for removing large amounts of stock.

Three-prong plugs indicate the drill is double-insulated. If you don't have a three-hole outlet, use an adapter to fit your plug.

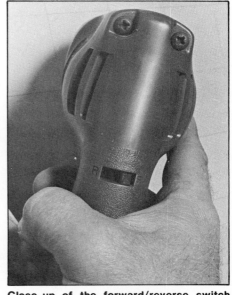

Close-up of the forward/reverse switch used on Black & Decker's drills.

INSULATION

Many of today's drills are *double-insulated*. You are protected from an accidental electric shock by an outer plastic housing which insulates you from the inner steel frame of the drill motor. Cracking the case is a minor concern because the plastic is extremely tough.

If the drill is not double-insulated, it will have three prongs instead of two protruding from the end of the electrical plug. The cylindrical center prong is a *ground connection* which connects the metal housing to a ground wire on the 110-volt outlet. If your outlets do not have three-prong receptacles, you can buy an adapter plug for less than a dollar and make the outlet safe, provided you ground the "tail" of the adapter to an electrical ground. All hand power tools should be either three-prong grounded or two-prong double-insulated. If you're buying an electric tool with a two-prong plug, look at the instruction sheet to be sure it's double-insulated. If it isn't, don't buy the unit! Don't take anyone's word for this. Check it yourself.

VARIABLE SPEED

Another feature found on many drills is variable speed. Some drills have a Hi-Lo switch to give a mid-range and a high RPM. Other models have a squeeze trigger, offering anything from zero to maximum RPM. Black & Decker has a model with a switch on the trigger enabling you to preset the RPM before you start drilling. The variable-speed option allows you to use your drill with a wide variety of materials and jobs.

REVERSE

One more feature I find useful is the forward/reverse selector found on many drills. Just flick the switch and your drill will turn either clockwise or counter-clockwise. If the bit gets stuck in the hole as you're drilling, which frequently happens when boring holes in metal, switch to reverse and the bit backs right out without damaging the material. The combination of variable speed and forward/reverse makes driving or removing screws a snap.

COST

Price is almost always a factor in buying. The price range in electric drills is wide, depending upon size, features and quality. Price runs anywhere from under ten dollars to well over a hundred. Like everything else, you get what you pay for. The ten-dollar drill is just that. It's good for very light-duty jobs around the house, but don't expect it to build a house for you. Twenty-five to thirty-five dollars should buy a good 3/8-inch drill capable of a broad range of uses. And, if you watch for the hardware sales in the local paper, that money can buy an outstanding tool.

Kits are another way to pick up extra value when buying a drill. Many manufacturers offer the drill with accessories, such as an assortment of bits and a sander/buffer, or a screwdriver set, together with a convenient carrying case, for little more than the price of the drill alone. This is an excellent way to get started with some of the accessories you'd probably buy later.

I use a 3/8-inch drill as my all-around shop drill and have never regretted my choice. I bought a model with variable-speed and reversing capability, and I don't know how I ever got along without those features before. The drill has given me years of service over a wide range of situations and materials. I even built a sailboat with it. It's light enough so that I don't tire when using it, yet it packs enough power to get the job done.

IMPACT OR "HAMMER" FEATURE

This last item is the most exciting to me. Think of it: a power wood chisel! Whether you use it to make mortise joints or carve a tree it can be a great time saver. Skil even says it can be used as a paint scraper or to remove wall paper. Naturally, a complete line of accessories are offered including drill bits, masonry bits, mortar chisels, scrapers and a set of wood chisels.

I think hammer drills will enjoy more and more sales when the public understands their full potential. Right now only two companies manufacture a hammer drill: Black & Decker and Skil.

Black & Decker's model is a two-speed rotary hammer. It can be operated as a conventional 3/8-inch drill with speeds of either 1200 or 2800 RPM. By moving a lever on the drill body, you convert the unit to a hammer drill capable of delivering the same RPM and a pulsating 18,000 to 42,000 blows per minute (BPM)! This means boring holes in masonry or brick suddenly becomes a lot easier.

Not one to caught napping, Skil offers a hammer drill with a 3/8 or 1/2-inch chuck. The big difference with Skil is they've managed to separate the hammering from the drilling operation to give you three distinct types of performance; a conventional variable-speed drill (0 to 800 RPM) with reverse; a hammer drill that spins up to 800 RPM while delivering up to 36,000 BPM for masonry or brick work; and a power chisel with only the hammering action.

Our craftsperson has properly removed all her loose jewelry and is wearing safety goggles; good safety habits to keep in mind. Using the left hand as a guide is another good idea.

USING YOUR DRILL

Operating a drill is simple:
● Wear safety glasses.
● If you have long hair or dangling jewelry, secure them out of harm's way.
● Select a bit and put it in the chuck. Even something as simple as putting a bit in the chuck can be done the wrong way. Make sure the shank is always placed as deeply in the chuck as it will go. Never have less than 3/4 inch of the the shank of the drill locked in the jaws of the chuck. Anything less than that can cause the drill bit to slip or fail to turn straight. This can also lead to the bit breaking or even flying out of the chuck and damaging the material or taking a nick out of you. Make sure very small bits are locked in by all three jaws of the chuck. It is possible to have only two jaws holding the bit. If this is the case, it will become readily apparent the first time you pull the trigger and observe the bit wobbling like it's bent. Merely rechuck the bit to straighten it out. Also with small bits, inserting the shank into the chuck up to the flute is sufficient to insure a tight grip on the drill bit. One exception to the rule of placing the bit as far into the chuck as it will go is when you need all the bit length you can get to

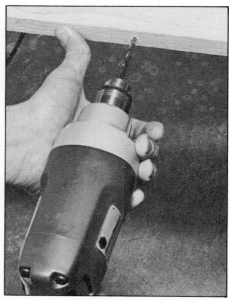

Use your free hand to guide and control the depth of the hole. Once you've mastered the technique, it will let you command the drill with more accuracy and reduce the chances of damaging the stock with the spinning chuck.

bore through thick stock or to drill an otherwise inaccessible spot.
● Tighten the chuck with the key.
● Plug the drill into a 110-volt outlet.
● Pick up your drill and pull the trigger.

A couple of hints on holding the drill will improve your accuracy when boring holes. The accompanying photos show you how. Study them and practice on a piece of scrap before you start making a fancy teak bookshelf.

WOOD

When drilling a hole through wood, clamp a backing board to the piece you want to drill. Use any piece of scrap that's handy. This reduces splintering when the drill bit breaks through the opposite side. If you are using a spade drill, bore until the point just sticks out the backside, then turn the drill around and finish boring the hole from the other side. This makes a clean, smooth cut with no ragged edges.

Nail Pilot Holes—Drilling a small pilot hole before nailing a board will prevent the wood from splitting. It takes a little more time, but it makes a much better finish.

Without the 1x4 backing, the drill bit will split the plywood when it breaks through on the back side.

second bit should be the same diameter as the screw shank. The countersink bit is used to make an angled area called a *countersink* so the head of the screw can be driven in flush with the surface.

First use the small bit to drill the *lead* or *pilot* hole. Bore only deep enough to match the screw length. You can mark this depth by placing a piece of tape on the bit. The second bit is driven only to the depth of the unthreaded shank. Use the countersink bit last to make the countersink for the screwhead. The

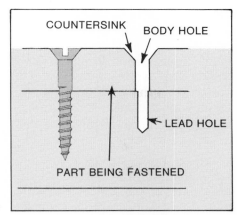

Depth of the body hole may be the full thickness of the part being fastened. Depth of lead hole should be about 1/2 the length of the threaded portion of the screw.

To prevent splintering when using a spade bit, back the stock with a piece of scrap or drill through the stock until the pilot is just poking out the back side. Reverse the stock and drill through the started hole, using the pilot hole as a guide to assure accuracy. This will give a clean cut every time.

SCREW JOINTS

Bookshelves, cabinets or any project involving joining two pieces of wood will be stronger and better if glue and screws are used instead of nails. Of course, cost and use are considerations. I heard of a man who built an entire house by gluing and screwing every joint! Undoubtedly this is a very strong form of construction, but also very expensive and unnecessary. However, where practical, the glue-and-screw method is best.

Drilling for Screws—There are two ways you can use your drill to bore holes for wood screws. The first method is to use two drill bits and a countersink bit. The smaller bit should match the diameter of the inside of the screw threads. The

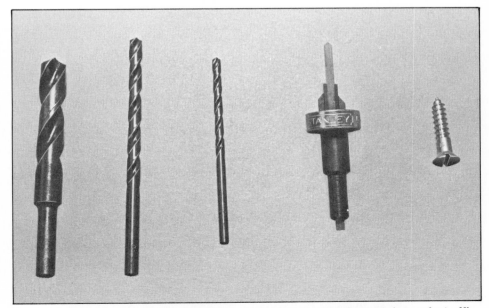

Stanley Adjustable Screwmate replaces the three bits on the left to produce a fast efficient hole for the screw. Timesavers like these more than justify their cost.

countersink should not be made too big or the head of the screw will be below the surface of the wood. If the countersink is left a little shallow, tightening the screw will usually draw the head in. This procedure is slow and time-consuming—particularly if you have a number of screws to place.

Method number two is far simpler. Buy a Stanley Adjustable Screwmate at your local hardware store. The Adjustable Screwmate performs all three of the functions described above—in one drilling. Decide what size screws you're going to use and purchase the Screwmate to match. Remember, the un-threaded-shank diameter is the screw diameter. Adjust the Screwmate lead and shank bits to the desired lengths and you're all set. The Screwmate will give you a perfect hole every time.

PLUGS

A nice finishing touch with wood screws is to sink the screwhead deep in a hole called a *counterbore,* and fill the hole with a wooden plug. First drill the counterbore, then the lead hole and finally the body hole. Combination cutters for this kind of hole are also available. The Stanley Adjustable Screwsink performs this operation perfectly.

Lumberyards sell ready-made wooden plugs of teak and mahogany. They can be hard to find and a little expensive, but worth every penny if your project is teak or mahongany. However, when the store-bought plugs don't match the wood you're using, Stanley's plug-cutting attachment comes to your rescue. It is inexpensive and simple to operate. By cutting the plugs out of the scrap wood from whatever it is you're building, you can match

the grain and color almost exactly.

Installing the plug is easy: Dab a little white glue around its edges and gently tap it into the hole with a mallet or hammer. Make sure the plug grain runs parallel to the wood being plugged. After the glue dries, use the biggest and sharpest wood chisel you own to trim the plug. Start at the top and work down. If the chisel seems to want to cut on an angle, reverse the chisel and cut from the other side of the plug. Once you have trimmed the plug close to the surface, finish with a sanding block and the plug will be almost invisible. Or you may want a plug of contrasting wood so the plug color accentuates the plug as a design feature.

METAL

It's a good idea to use a center-punch to dimple any hard-to-drill material when using a single-speed

Stanley Plug Cutter and its product. Another simple yet invaluable accessory when working with wood.

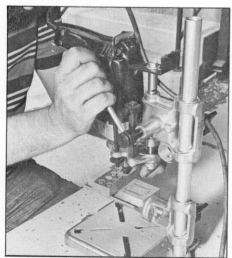
A drill press assures a clean sharp plug every time. It also lets you produce more plugs with less waste from a given piece of wood.

Install the plugs with the grain of the wood surface. Tap the plug very lightly until it bottoms against the hidden screwhead. Be sure to wipe off all the excess glue with a damp rag before it sets up, to prevent staining.

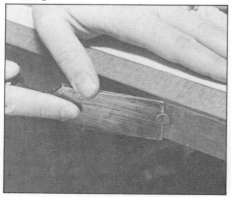
Trim as close to the surface as you can with a chisel. Finish with fine sandpaper wrapped around a block of wood.

Start at the top of the plug and work down when trimming. Always trim from the low side of the plug.

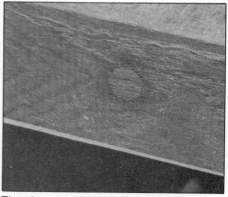
The plug should be almost invisible.

drill. This reduces the chance of the drill *walking,* or traveling all over the surface and scratching it in the process. I centerpunch all metals because it assures an accurate hole regardless of the type of drill I'm using—assuming I position the centerpunch accurately, of course.

A piece of scrap plywood placed behind thin metal helps make a clean, neat hole and reduces the chance of the metal warping out of shape as you drill.

Be very careful when drilling thin sheet metal. Don't under any circumstances, hold the metal with your hand. Sometimes the drill bit will catch as the hole is being bored. The material will spin out of your hand and the edge becomes a whirling knifeblade which can give you a very nasty cut. Therefore, CLAMP METAL DOWN WHEN DRILLING IT!

If your plans call for drilling a 1/2-inch hole in metal, drill a smaller pilot hole first and work up to the final size in steps. This makes a neater hole and puts less strain on the drill motor. It also helps to prevent the bit from grabbing the metal.

If you have a variable-speed drill, here's a good rule of thumb: Use high speed for light work and small holes—low speed for tough material and big holes. For really tough metal, light machine oil on the drill bit can also help. It acts as a lubricant and coolant, thereby making a smoother cut and extending the life of the bit. If the bit or work starts to smoke or turns blue, you are pushing too hard or running the drill too fast—or both.

PLASTICS AND MASONRY

Plastics are generally soft and should be drilled at high speed. Countersinking is not required and may be detrimental because of the brittleness of the material. If you plan to do a lot of work with plastics, I recommend you purchase a set of drill bits specially designed for that material. Their main feature is a very sharp point at the tip, which makes it easy to start

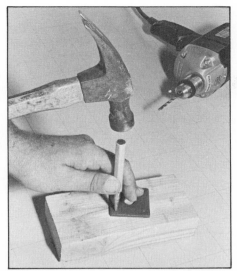

Metal should always be centerpunched before drilling to ensure an accurate hole and prevent the drill bit from walking across the metal surface.

A little light machine oil will help the drill bit cut when boring through metal. Notice the wooden backing block to protect the point of the bit and the vise.

an accurate hole on a slick surface. They are available at stores specializing in plastics.

Masonry, concrete and ceramics can all be drilled using a tungsten-carbide-tipped bit of special design. The bits are readily available at most hardware stores and come in a variety of sizes. Bits with 1/4-inch shank have a cutting diameter from 1/4 to 1/2 inch. Average lengths are 4 to 6 inches. Extra-long bits for drilling through foundations are also available.

For drilling concrete I recommend a 3/8-inch or larger drill motor. Tungsten-carbide bits are extremely tough, but so is the material to be drilled. Use a slow speed, 500 to 600 RPM, steady pressure, and plenty of water on the bit as a lubricant and coolant. Take your time; it'll be hard going for both you and the drill.

If your drill has the impact feature, select the impact/rotary mode of operation. Insert a tungsten-carbide-tipped drill and proceed with your hole making. Just push against the work with the drill and the impact/rotary motion will do the rest. Once you've used a drill with this feature you'll wonder how you ever managed to drill concrete before.

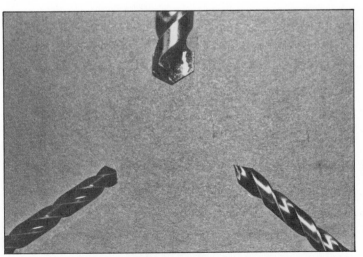

All bits are not the same. Here we have a welded tungsten-carbide masonry bit at the top, a sharp pointed plastic bit on the right, and a normal 118-degree utility bit on the left.

DRILL SPEEDS		
Material	**Thickness**	**Speed**
Wood	up to 1 inch	Fast
Wood	over 1 inch	Medium
Wood	with expansion bit	Medium
Wood	with plug cutter	Fast
Wood	routing	Fast
Wood/Metal	sanding/grinding	Fast
Metal	thin/soft	Fast
Metal	thick/hard	Slow
Plastics		Fast
Cement		Slow

value to tell you to operate your drill at a particular speed for the best cutting results. Instead, I've prepared this chart listing the speeds as *slow, medium* and *fast. Slow* is about a quarter pull of the trigger and equals 300 to 500 RPM. *Medium* is a half pull or about 600 to 900 RPM. *Fast* is squeezing the trigger all the way which should give you between 1000 and 2000 RPM, depending upon whether you're using a 1/4- or 3/8-inch drill motor.

MAINTENANCE

Under normal use, your drill will give you many years of trouble-free service with just an occasional application of a few drops of oil. Apply where indicated on the drill case. Make sure the cooling vents are kept clean and free from dirt. This extends the life of the motor.

Should an overhaul become necessary, rebuild kits that fit the model drill you own may be available from your local dealer. Before tearing into the drill motor, read the kit instructions. If you've kept the original specification sheet that came with the drill, review it before starting. Chapter 10, on Repairs gives more detailed information.

Because variable-speed drills do not have RPM gauges, it's of little

DRILLS, 1/4 INCH

MAKE/MODEL	HP	AMP	RPM	USE	FEATURES
Black & Decker					
7004	.20	2.0	2500	Light	Single-speed; 10-inch cord
7030	.33	3.0	2500	Light	Single-speed; Detachable cord
7080	.33	3.0	0-2500	Medium	Variable-speed; Detachable cord
7056	.40	3.5	0-1900	Heavy	Variable-speed, reversing; Detachable cord
7060	.33	3.2	0-2500	Industrial	Variable-speed, reversing; 10-foot cord
9033			1500	Light	Single-speed, reversing; Cordless
9001			750	Very Light	Cordless; Powerpack can be used with other tools
Millers Falls					
SP220		3.0	1900	Industrial	Single-speed
SP221R		3.0	0-1900	Heavy	Variable-speed, reversing; AC only
SP6015		2.7	0-2200	Industrial	Variable-speed; AC only
SP6014		2.7	2200	Industrial	Single-speed
SP6004		2.5	2250	Industrial	Single-speed
Penney					
1908A	.20	2.5	1300	Very light	Single-speed
Rockwell					
4076	.38	3.25	0-2300	Heavy	Variable-speed, reversing
4011			1300	Very Light	Single-speed; Cordless
Sears					
9HT-1140	.17	2.0	2000	Medium	Single-speed
9HT-1111			300	Very Light	Single-speed; Cordless
Shopmate					
T2000-11	.18	2.2	2400	Medium	Single-speed
Skil					
503	.20	2.1	2100	Light	Single-speed
501	.20	2.5	0-2100	Medium	Variable-speed
456	.25	2.7	0-2100	Medium	Variable-speed, reversing
596	.25	2.7	0-2000	Heavy	Variable-speed, reversing
2001			300	Very Light	Cordless; 110v or 12v charger
Stanley					
91-145		2.5	2250	Medium	
90-053		3.7	1700	Industrial	120v AC or DC
90-052		3.7	1700	Heavy	115v AC or DC circuit breaker
Ward					
82005		2.8	2500	Very light	Single-speed
Wen					
700	.50	2.6		Light	Single-speed

DRILLS, 3/8 INCH

MAKE/MODEL	HP	AMP	RPM	USE	FEATURES
Black & Decker					
7104	.22	2.0	1200	Light	Single-speed; 10-inch cord
7114	.25	2.3	0-1200	Light	Variable-speed
7130	.34	3.0	1200	Medium	Single-speed; Detachable cord
7180	.34	3.0	0-1200	Medium	Variable-speed; Detachable cord
7190	.34	3.0	0-1200	Medium	Variable-speed, reversing; Detachable cord
7156	.40	3.5	0-1200	Heavy	Variable-speed, reversing; Detachable cord
7159	.34	3.2	0-1200	Industrial	Variable-speed, reversing; 10-foot cord
9092				Light	Single-speed, reversing; Cordless, Powerpack can be used with other tools
9082			500	Light	Single-speed, reversing; Cordless
9085			750	Light	Single-speed, reversing; Cordless
Millers Falls					
SP240		3.0	1000	Industrial	Single-speed
SP240-1		3.0	600	Industrial	Single-speed
SP241R		3.0	0-1000	Heavy	Variable-speed, reversing; AC only
SP3139		2.5	0-1000	Heavy	Variable-speed, reversing; AC only
SP6005		2.5	1000	Heavy	Single-speed
SP6038		2.7	1000	Industrial	Single-speed
SP6039		2.7	0-1000	Industrial	Variable-speed, reversing; AC only
SP341-2		5.0	750	Industrial	Single-speed; Detachable handle
SP8802		5.0	3200	Industrial	Single-speed; AC only
Penney					
3045A	.25	2.8	1300	Light	Single-speed; Removable side handle
3052A	.25	2.8	0-1300	Light	Variable-speed; Removable side handle
2926A		2.7	0-1300	Light	Variable-speed, reversing
0785A	.25	3.0	0-1300	Medium	Variable-speed, reversing; Removable side handle; Speed lock control
1092A	.38	3.2	0-900	Heavy	Variable-speed, reversing, Ball bearing drive; Speed lock control
1316A			300	Medium	Cordless; Recharges in one hour
Rockwell					
4101	.25	2.7	1400	Light	Single-speed
4130	.34	2.7	0-1400	Light	Variable-speed
4177		4.0	0-1000	Medium	Variable-speed, reversing
4176	.38	3.2	0-1000	Heavy	Variable-speed, reversing
1181		4.0	1000	Industrial	Single-speed
1183		4.0	0-1000	Industrial	Variable-speed, reversing
Sears					
1142	.20	2.2	1200	Light	Single-speed
1143	.20	2.2	0-1200	Light	Variable-speed
1144	.20	2.2	0-1200	Light	Variable-speed, reversing
1050	.34	2.5	0-1200	Medium	Variable-speed
1136	.34	2.5	0-1200	Medium	Variable-speed, reversing
1145	.34	3.0	0-1100	Heavy	Variable-speed, reversing
1148	.38	3.0	0-1200	Industrial	Variable-speed, reversing; Ball bearing drive
Shopmate					
T2100	.20	2.4	1000	Medium	Single-speed
T2130	.20	2.4	0-1000	Medium	Variable-speed
T2151	.34	2.6	0-1000	Medium	Variable-speed, reversing
Skil					
560	.20	2.5	1300	Medium	Single-speed
569	.20	2.8	0-1300	Medium	Variable-speed
584	.20	2.8	0-1300	Medium	Variable-speed, reversing
597	.25	3.2	0-750	Heavy	Variable-speed, reversing
457	.25	3.0	0-1300	Heavy	Variable-speed, reversing
2002			100/200	Light	Two-speed; Cordless; 110v or 12v charger
2006			300	Medium	Single-speed, reversing; Cordless; 110v or 12v charger; Recharges in one hour

DRILLS, 3/8 INCH — cont.

MAKE/MODEL	HP	AMP	RPM	USE	FEATURES
Stanley					
91-048		2.8	1000	Medium	Single-speed
90-065		3.3	650	Heavy	Single-speed; 110v AC/DC, circuit breaker
91-064		3.7	0-1000	Industrial	Variable-speed, reversing, Built-in circuit breaker
Ward					
82006		2.8	1200	Light	Single-speed; 10-inch cord
82008	.33	3.2	0-2500	Medium	Variable-speed, reversing
82009	.40	3.3	0-1200	Heavy	Variable-speed, reversing
Wen					
800	.50	2.6	1200	Medium	Single-speed
801	.50	2.6	0-1200	Medium	Variable-speed
802	.50	2.6	0-1200	Medium	Variable-speed, reversing
2200			320	Medium	Single-speed, reversing

DRILLS, 1/2 INCH

MAKE/MODEL	HP	AMP	RPM	USE	FEATURES
Black & Decker					
7204	.25	3.0	550	Light	Single-speed; 10-inch cord
7230	.34	3.0	550	Light	Single-speed, reversing; Detachable cord
7224	.38	3.0	550	Light	Single-speed, reversing; Detachable cord
7254	.40	3.0	0-550	Medium	Variable-speed, reversing; Detachable cord
7264	.50	4.5	600	Heavy	Single-speed, reversing; Detachable cord, Detachable handle
7274	.88	5.0	0-650	Industrial	Variable-speed, reversing; 10-foot cord
7290		5.2	600	Industrial	Single-speed, reversing; 10-foot cord, D-shaped handle
Millers Falls					
SP6212		3.0	0-500	Heavy	Variable-speed, reversing; AC only
SP261R		3.0	0-600	Heavy	Variable-speed, reversing; AC only
SP2112		3.6	550	Heavy	Single-speed, reversing; AC only
SP351R		5.0	450	Industrial	Single-speed, reversing; Detachable handle
SP352R		5.0	450	Industrial	Single-speed, reversing; Detachable handle
Penney					
1159A	.38	3.2	0-500	Heavy	Variable-speed, reversing; Ball bearing construction; Speed lock control; D-shaped handle
2207A	.38	6.0	445	Industrial	Single-speed, reversing; Ball bearing construction; Not double insulated
Rockwell					
4201	.34	2.8	700	Light	Single-speed
4250	.34	2.8	0-700	Light	Variable-speed, reversing
4276	.38	3.25	0-700	Medium	Variable-speed, reversing
4277	.45	4.0	0-600	Medium	Variable-speed, reversing
4288	.60	5.0	600	Heavy	Single-speed, reversing; D-shaped handle
1191		6.0	600	Industrial	Single-speed, reversing, Detachable handle
1197		6.0	600	Industrial	Single-speed, reversing, D-shaped handle
Sears					
11191	.34	3.0	525	Medium	Single-speed, reversing
1129	.38	3.0	0-600	Heavy	Variable-speed, reversing; Detachable handle
1139	.75	4.8	575	Heavy	Single-speed, reversing; Detachable handle
1149	.88	5.0	575	Industrial	Single-speed, reversing; Detachable handle
Shopmate					
T2200	.34	2.6	750	Light	Single-speed
T2240	.34	2.6	750	Light	Single-speed, reversing
T2250	.34	2.6	0-750	Light	Variable-speed, reversing
T2243	.88	6.0	500	Industrial	Single-speed, reversing; Detachable handle

DRILLS, 1/2 INCH — cont.

MAKE/MODEL	HP	AMP	RPM	USE	FEATURES
Skil					
541	.25	3.0	750	Light	Single-speed
510	.25	3.2	500	Medium	Single-speed, reversing; D-shaped handle
598	.25	3.2	0-500	Heavy	Variable-speed, reversing
542	.50	4.0	500	Industrial	Single-speed, reversing; D-shaped handle
425	.80	5.0	0-650	Industrial	Single-speed, reversing; D-shaped handle
Stanley					
90-123		4.7	550	Heavy	Single-speed; D-shaped handle
91-066		3.3	0-650	Heavy	Variable-speed, reversing
91-721		4.5	425	Industrial	Single-speed, reversing; Right-angle drive
91-722		4.3	425	Industrial	Single-speed
Ward					
82513	.34	3.0	550	Medium	Single-speed, reversing
82515	.40	3.3	0-550	Heavy	Variable-speed, reversing
Wen					
953	.67	4.0	0-600	Medium	Variable-speed, reversing
955		4.0	0-600	Heavy	Variable-speed, reversing; D-shaped handle

HAMMER DRILLS

MAKE/MODEL	CHUCK SIZE IN INCHES	HP	AMP	RPM	BLOWS PER MINUTE	USE	FEATURES
Black & Decker							
7928	3/8	.34	3.0	2900	34,800	Medium	Single-speed
7932	3/8	.42	3.3	900/2400	13,500/36,000	Heavy	Two-speed
7935	1/2	.47	3.6	1250/2800	18,750/42,00	Industrial	Two-speed
Millers Falls							
2076	3/8		3.8	850/1900	17,000/38,000	Heavy	Two-speed
2078	1/2		4.4	540/1200	10,000/24,000	Industrial	Two-speed
2077	1/2		4.4	480/670/ 1500/2100	9600/13,400 30,000/42,000	Industrial	Four-speed
Penney							
0017A	3/8	.38	3.2	0-800	36,000	Heavy	Variable-speed, reversing
0025A	1/2	.38	3.4	0-800	36,000	Heavy	Variable-speed, reversing
Rockwell							
4190	1/2		4.0	2500	40,000	Heavy	Single-speed
Sears							
1810	3/8	.38	3.2	0-1200	24,000	Medium	Variable-speed
Skil							
599	3/8	.34	3.2	0-800	36,000	Heavy	Variable-speed, reversing; May be used as chisel
600	1/2	.34	3.4	0-800	36,000	Heavy	Variable-speed, reversing
Ward							
82011	3/8	.34	3.0	2900	34,800	Medium	Single-speed
4508	3/8	.34	3.2	0-800	36,000	Heavy	Variable-speed, reversing
82500	1/2	.34	3.4	0-800	36,000	Heavy	Variable-speed, reversing

4
Accessories

Let's look at the accessories and attachments you can buy to increase the capabilities of your electric drill. I say *some* because there are so many on the market that I may have overlooked a few.

The more popular accessories are produced by *all* of the major tool manufacturers. Selection becomes a matter of wherever your particular loyalties lie. Some people swear by Sears Craftsman, and some wouldn't own anything other than Black & Decker. All the *major* manufacturers take great pride in turning out quality products and back them with excellent warranties. Unless I specifically mention a brand, it's because the item is available from most, if not all, of the large companies.

DRILL BITS

Let's start with the various bits available. Earlier I discussed the basic parts of the drill bit. Now I want to review them again and go into more detail to give you a fuller understanding of what they do and what's available.

Points—Drill bits are offered in several point styles. The most common is a 118° point. However, to prevent *walking* when starting to drill metal, the spot to be drilled should be dimpled with a center punch. Special bits with a 135° point are available. They will bore their own hole without the help of a centerpunch. This is because of the chisel edge formed at the point by the wider angle. The 135° point

Behind this 1/4-inch drill are a few of the many accessories available that expand your capabilities with this basic power tool.

is recommended for drilling sheet metal and other hard materials. For drilling plexiglass or plastic you should use bits with an extra sharp 60° point which prevents grabbing the material.

Shanks—In addition to different types of points, there are several types of shanks available. For the most part you'll be using either a *straight* or *reduced* shank. A straight shank limits your bit to the size of your chunk—usually 1/4 or 3/8 inch. However, by buying a bit with a reduced shank, you get bit sizes up to 1/2 inch for metal and as big as 1-1/2 inches for wood. The diameter of the body of the bit is larger, but the shank is reduced to fit a 1/4- or a 3/8-inch chuck. It is possible to even exceed these bit sizes, but you will put a tremendous strain on your drill motor and risk burning it out from the overload. I don't recommend using a bit larger

than 1-1/2 inches in a 1/4- or 3/8-inch-chuck drill.

Length—Most drill bits come in a standard length, called *jobber lengths.* These will work for 99 percent of your projects, but once in a while you will face a situation in which your bit is just not long enough. Longer bits are available—called *aircraft extension drills* because they are used in the aircraft industry. They come in 6- and 12-inch lengths. Diameters range from 1/16 to 1/2 inch and they have 135° points.

If you're working with wood and using a spade bit larger than 5/8 inch, a *power-bit extension* can be used. These extension rods will accept any bit with a 1/4-inch shank. So, you only need one extension instead of a whole set of bits to do the job. Extensions are only good for wood bits; they do not work well with metal drills.

DRILL BIT SIZES

Drill bit sizes are divided into four categories.

Fractional Sizes run from 1/64 to 4 inches or larger. Sizes increase by 64ths of an inch in the smaller bits and by 32nds and 16ths in the larger bits.

Wire Gauge Numbers are numbered 1 through 80, with 80 being the smallest size. All numbered bits are less than 1/4 inch in diameter. They range from 0.2280 of an inch, #1, to 0.0135 of an inch, #80. These numbers are the same as standard wire sizes and the bits are used where exactness is required, such as for tapping threads.

Letter Size bits are sizes larger than #1, 0.2280 inch, and are designated by letters. They run from A, 0.2340 inch to Z, 0.4062 inch, which is just smaller than 7/16 inch. They are also used where exactness is critical.

Metric Sizes are measured in millimeters. One millimeter, mm, equals 0.394 inch. One inch equals 25.40mm. A conversion chart, found on page 156 relates metric sizes to inches.

FLEXIBLE SHAFTS

Flexible shafts increase the versatility of your drill and its attachments. Of course, the first benefit is being able to reach a spot where the drill motor won't fit. Because of the unusual control you have when working with a flexible shaft, delicate drilling, precision grinding, stripping and sanding are much easier and more accurate.

A drill motor requires that you use your arm and shoulder muscles to do the pushing. A flex shaft works with your finger tips—much like a pencil. The extra control is the key advantage to using this tool. You can easily overload and break a 1/16-inch drill bit when guiding it with a drill motor, but not when you're using a flex shaft. You are more aware and have more control over the pressure being exerted on the bit.

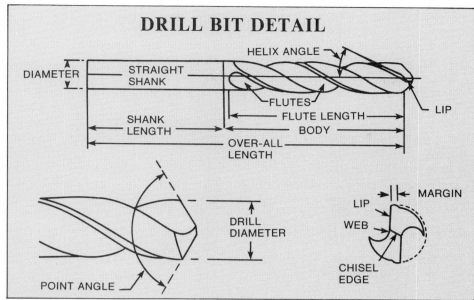

DRILL BIT DETAIL

In drilling, the shank is locked in the drill chuck. The cutting edges of the point, or lips, do the actual cutting. The flutes remove the waste.

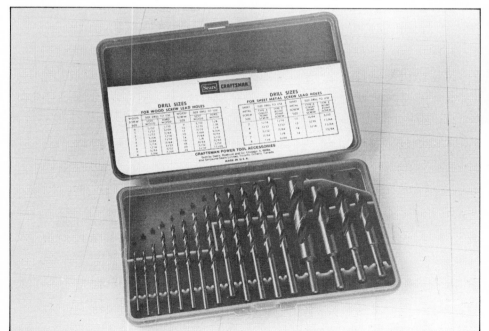

Drill bits will probably be your first accessory purchase. Buy a top quality set with a broad selection. A 17-piece kit will give you the latitude you'll need without bankrupting your budget.

Several companies make drill bit extensions. They're inexpensive and useful when you need a long reach. Irwin Tool Co. manufactures the model you see here.

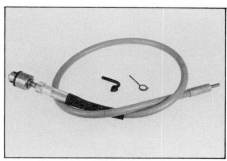

A flexible shaft gives you very close control.

Touching up router bits or sharpening chain saw blades is much easier because of the close control. Even freehand engraving in wood can be performed with the proper bits.

Flex shafts come in a variety of lengths and sizes. A 40-inch, 1/4-inch core is most common. It lets you work with small drill bits, grinding wheels and sanding discs.

A word of caution: Always run the flex shaft in the direction indicated by an arrow marked on the shaft. Reversing will unwind the inner core and destroy the shaft.

MASONRY BITS

Masonry drill points are tipped with tungsten carbide, an ultra-hard metal necessary for the tough job of cutting concrete or masonry. The point is angled 118° and the flutes are wider than on other bits for better dust removal. Masonry bits commonly range from 1/8 inch to 1-1/2 inches in diameter, and 1-7/8 inches to 6 inches in length. However, lengths of up to 18 inches may be purchased for special jobs.

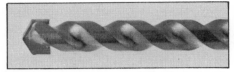

The welded tungsten carbide tip and wide flukes identify this as a masonry bit. Good for cement, brick or stone, the bit doesn't possess the fine machining necessary for use on wood or metal.

BROKEN BOLTS

Sooner or later you're going to have to deal with a broken bolt. There is nothing more frustrating than finishing a job and snapping off the head of a bolt as you apply the final tightening. Or, as so often happens, you're taking something apart and a corroded bolt snaps off before you can break the threads loose. We've all had it happen.

While you're regaining your composure, put a few drops of penetrating oil around the base of the bolt and let it soak in. If there's enough of the shank of the bolt sticking out, try getting a grip on it with Vise-Grips and slowly unscrew. If you can't get a good grip with the wrench, the only way that bolt is going to come out is by drilling and using a *Screw Extractor*.

If the top of the bolt snapped off at an angle or it was a jagged break, use a file or a drill with a grinding wheel and flatten the break.

Next, centerpunch right in the middle of the bolt. Dimple it with enough force so there'll be no problem getting a drill bit started. If the bolt is large enough, you might consider drilling a pilot hole first and then move up to the final size as indicated on the chart. Be very careful when you bore the hole. Drill straight down the center of the bolt. Bore just deep enough to allow the screw extractor to be inserted, plus about a 1/16 to 1/8 inch. The deeper you drill, the more chance you have of angling into the threads unless you use a drill press. If the hole is too shallow, the extractor won't get a good bite on the wall of the bolt. Avoid both extremes.

Once you have bored the hole, select a screw extractor of the right size from the chart and insert it with a tap wrench into the hole. Apply firm pressure from the top of the wrench and slowly twist it in a counterclockwise direction. The flutes on the extractor are left-handed, so the more you twist, the harder the extractor wedges itself in the bolt. If all goes well, the bolt will loosen as you turn the extractor.

Follow the same procedure if you break off a threaded pipe. Only instead of a screw extractor with left-hand threads, you'll need to use a straight tapered flute model because straight flutes work best with soft metals, such as tubing or pipe, and with thin-walled pipe and tapered threads. You could distort the casing by using a speral flute extractor.

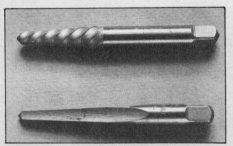

Extractors are available in two types: spiral fluted, top, and straight fluted, below. Each type is available in a wide range of sizes.

SELECTING EXTRACTORS

To Remove Bolts or Screws (in inches)	To Remove Pipe (in inches)	Use Drill Bit size (in inches)	Use Extractor Size No.
3/32 to 5/32	—	5/64	1-Spiral Flute
5/32 to 7/32	—	7/64	2-Spiral Flute
3/16 to 5/16	—	9/64	1-Straight Flute
7/32 to 9/32	—	5/32	3-Spiral Flute
3/8	—	3/16	2-Straight Flute
7/16	1/8	15/64	3-Straight Flute
9/32 to 3/8	—	1/4	4-Spiral Flute
3/8 to 5/8	—	19/64	5-Spiral Flute
1/2 to 9/16	1/4	5/16	4-Straight Flute
5/8	3/8	3/8	5-Straight Flute
5/8 to 7/8	—	13/32	6-Spiral Flute
3/4	1/2	15/32	6-Straight Flute
7/8 to 1-1/8	—	17/32	7-Spiral Flute
7/8	—	9/16	7-Straight Flute
1-1/8 to 1-3/8	3/4	13/16	8-Straight Flute
1-3/8 to 2	1	1-1/16	9-Straight Flute

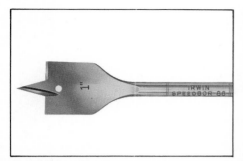

The Irwin Tool Company's Speedbor 88 spade wood bit. A first-rate product. They are sold singularly or in a 5-piece set with sizes from 3/8 to 1 inch. Buy the set. You'll eventually have a use for all of them and you'll save money over single unit purchase.

Cupped hole saws are sold singly or in sets.

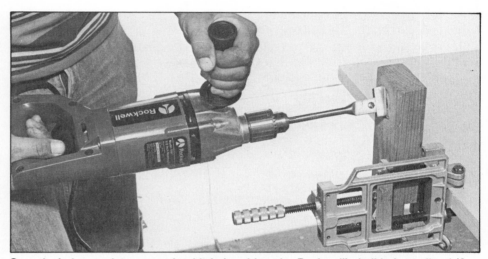

Convalco's heavy-duty expansion bit being driven by Rockwell's builder's quality 1/2-inch drill. The vise is sold by Coastal and is one of the most versatile I've ever used.

SPADE BITS

Spade bits are excellent for boring large holes in wood. Made of tool steel and heat-treated for strength, the hollow-ground point bores a clean hole fast. The length of the spade shank causes the bit to run true without any tendency to wobble or drift. The rear of the shank tapers to 1/4 inch and is *flattened* on six sides to allow the chuck a positive grip and prevent any unwanted slipping due to torque. Spade bits are available in sizes from 1/4 inch to 1-1/2 inches. The most popular sizes range from 3/8 to 1 inch and are sold in sets. Several manufacturers offer these drill bits—I prefer Irwin's Speedbor 88. I believe they were the first with this design, and their quality is excellent.

MAKING LARGE HOLES

Hole Saws—Holes larger than 1 inch can be drilled using a *cupped hole saw*. They are available in diameters ranging from 3/4 inch to 2-1/2 inches and require a separate mandrel attachment. They are heavy-duty pieces of equipment and make a neat, clean hole. While they may not tear on the opposite side after breaking through, it's good practice to drill part way through the hole and then finish the hole from the opposite side so the cut is actually finished inside the hole. Because of the cup design, these saws are limited in the depth they will handle: usually less than 1 inch. They are excellent when used on plywood. And I've even used this

type of hole cutter to drill through fiberglass, though it dulls the teeth.

Expansion Bits—If you ever have the need to bore a large hole in stock 2 inches thick or larger, the Connecticut Valley Manufacturing Co. sells an excellent expansion wood bit under the name *Convalco Expansion Bit*. It's unusual for an expansion bit to be adapted for electric drills because of the high power and low RPM required for the best performance. I recommend you use these bits with a 1/2-inch drill. Convalco markets two sizes, one will bore a 1/2- to 1-1/2-inch hole, while the large model can be adjusted to drill from 7/8- to 3-inch diameters. Either bit will drill to a depth of 6 inches. This can be a real

advantage if you ever need to drill a hole in thick timber. All you need is a screwdriver to adjust the cutting edges to bore whatever size you require within the tool's range.

Very Large Holes—Convalco makes another attachment for cutting still larger holes—up to a whopping 18-inch diameter. Called an *industrial compass cutter*, it will cut 2-inch thick wood planking, fiberglass and even 1/4-inch aluminum plate. You may not have a need for holes this big, but what about wheels? This is an ideal tool for making wheels for lawn furniture or toys. True, a saber saw will do the same job. While this accessory fits on a drill motor, I'd recommend you use it only in a drill press so you can select an

I like the Compass Cutter because of its varied uses and reasonable price. You don't have to use it every day to justify the price.

appropriate slow speed and do the cutting on pieces clamped to the work table. I've tried it on several projects and it works well. But you have to go slowly because the hardened cutting bit is brittle and will break if too much pressure is applied to it. Considering the wide range of material it will cut, the ease of use, and the exactness of the results, it is a bargain.

MORE DRILLING ACCESSORIES

Screw Holes—I mentioned the Stanley Adjustable Screwmate in Chapter 3. They're a *must* for anyone planning to work with wood. The Screwmates are offered in four screw sizes: #6, #8, #10 and #12. In one operation you can drill the lead hole, body hole, and the countersink or counterbore. Plus, each Screwmate can be adjusted for screw length. There's no need to worry about not having the right length tool with the Adjustable Screwmate. Other companies have similar tools, but I prefer Stanley's.

Plugs—A companion to the Screwmate is Stanley's Plug Cutter, sold in sizes #6 through #12. I consider them required tools for finishing cabinets or furniture making. While you can buy pre-cut plugs, the grain and color will seldom match the wood you're using. By using a plug cutter and scraps of the same wood you're working with, you can get a much closer match. Plugs can be cut freehand, but for best results a drill press or Portalign tool is recommended. They provide a steady platform, which ensures a straight plug.

REMOVING PLUGS

After you've plugged a project, there's always the problem of a plug snapping off below the surface during trimming. Or maybe the grain is not aligned and you want to remove that particular plug.

If you go in with a knife or chisel you're probably going to damage the hole which will make the new plug fit poorly.

Like most everything, the answer is easy—if you know how.

Take a 1-inch or 1-1/2-inch number 8 or 10 wood screw and chuck the body in your drill. Clamp the drill to the work bench and turn it on. With a file, grind off the head of the screw until it's the same diameter as the body. You've just made a plug removal tool.

To use this gadget, first drill a small pilot hole in the bad plug. Place the headless screw in the chuck and drill into the pilot hole. The plug will pop out of the wood as soon as the point of the headless screw comes in contact with the head of the screw buried beneath the plug.

Make several of these plug removal tools of different sizes and you'll be ready the next time you've got to pull a plug.

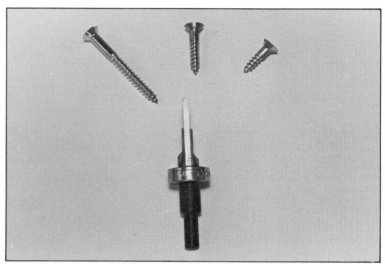

The Stanley Adjustable Screwmate with only three of many lengths of screws it will make holes for. This is an indispensable addition to your tool chest.

Wooden plugs dress up any job. Plug cutters let you match the plugs to the wood by using scrap from the project. Both Stanley and Convalco make excellent plug cutters.

Reversible Speed Reducer and Screwdriver—If you don't have a variable-speed drill with forward and reverse capabilities, you may want this unit. It not only provides forward and reverse operation, it also reduces the output speed at the chuck through internal gearing to give you better control when driving screws. In the forward mode the reduction is a ratio of 11:1 which supplies enough torque to drive even large #14 screws. The reverse is geared to a 4:1 ratio for fast removal of screws. Not only screws, but nuts and bolts can be handled using a special socket set.

A reversable speed reducer gives your drill better control and higher torque at low speeds or very high-speed operation.

Dowel Joint Kits—Dowel joints are an excellent means of butting one piece of wood to another where no secondary support is practical. They are used extensively in boat building and furniture and cabinet making. What makes dowel joints difficult is that everything must fit perfectly. If you buy a dowel kit consisting of dowel centers, a specially designed bit and a drill stop, the job becomes much easier. A drill press or Portalign is also needed to ensure perfectly perpendicular holes.

Drill Stops—Several companies sell little gadgets called *drill stops*. They look like plastic chucks and are positioned on the drill bit to allow you to drill holes to a predetermined depth. They're inexpensive and do a fair job. I think a piece of masking tape wrapped around the bit at the depth you want does the same thing without the fear of slipping. The tape also makes a little fan which blows away sawdust so you can see what you are doing.

Dowel joint kits insure perfect fit every time, but you should use them with a drill press or Portalign.

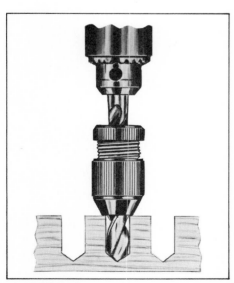

Arco's Adjustable Drill-Stop and a piece of tape wrapped around the bit. They both perform the same function. The tape is cheaper and faster.

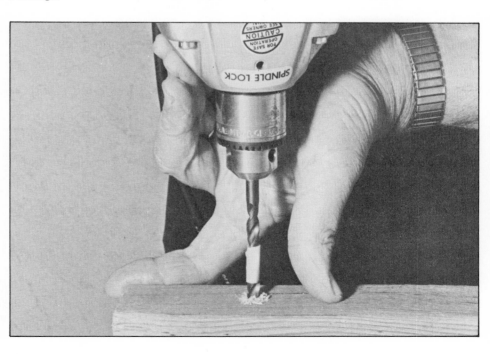

MAKING DOWEL JOINTS

Briefly, here's how to make a dowel joint:

Drill two holes into one board to a predetermined depth using a drill press or Portalign to ensure a 90° angle. Dowel centers are then put in the holes and pressed against the second board. This marks or *dimples* the second board with the dowel centers to provide exact positions for the dowel holes. The depth stop is adjusted to the correct depth for the drill bit and the holes are drilled on the second board with either a drill press or Portalign. If more than two dowels are required, drill all the holes you need in the first board. Use dowels and dowel centers to maintain proper alignment for the additional holes by plugging and dimpling the holes two at a time.

Dowel centers come in sets and make accurate dowel joints a snap.

Drill your first set of holes exactly where you want them. Then put a dowel center in each hole with the point out.

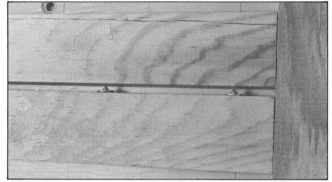
Press the piece to be joined against the centers hard enough so they leave a mark.

Use the marks to center your drill. Be sure your drill is perpendicular to the surface of the wood.

The holes will match exactly. Glue the dowels in one side and let dry.

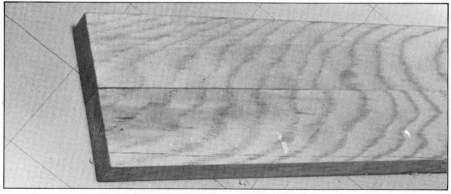
Glue the second side in place and the joint is complete.

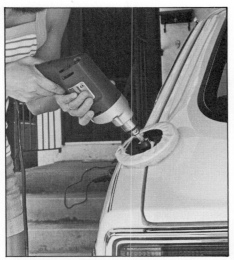

Buffers are often sold with drill motors as part of a kit. You won't use them continuously, but they are nice to have around. The hard part is talking your wife into polishing the car.

Angle drive lets you hold a polisher more comfortably. It's also perfect for use in tight places where your drill won't fit.

SANDING, CUTTING, STRIPPING AND GRINDING ATTACHMENTS

The electric drill motor can be readily adapted for use as a disc sander, polisher or bench grinder with a few accessories. Whether you attach a sanding disc directly to the chuck or use a two-speed angle drive, you've increased the capacity of your drill. You can polish your car or your silverware. Sand a floor or a fence. Cut brick or sharpen drill bits. All of these tasks are possible with drill-motor attachments.

Sanders—Many manufacturers offer a two-speed, right-angle *buffer/ sander kit* as an accessory. The advantage of the two-speed gear box is that you can slow down the RPM for buffing and polishing, and prevent *burning* the finish. By reversing the attachment, you double the speed of your drill motor, giving you the RPM for a smooth, clean sanding job. Buying these accessories in kit form offers the added advantage of getting a rubber pad, a lamb's wool buffer and a supply of sanding discs. It's cheaper than purchasing everything separately, and you know all the parts work together.

Drum sanders are perfect for smoothing the edges of large holes and scroll work in plywood. Benchmounting the drill and using a drum

Drum sanders are mounted on the drill or at the end of a flex shaft. They can be used freehand, on a drill stand, or mounted upside down on your workbench, as shown.

Rockwell's Tungsten Carbide Rotary Disc, a long-lasting workhorse when it comes to removing heavy stock.

sander lets you sand small pieces in minutes that would otherwise be a tedious and time-consuming process. And, they are convenient to use with a *flexible shaft* when doing precision work, such as model making.

Any time you have a lot of stock to remove, of if you ever need to grind fiberglass, the *Tungsten Carbide Rotary Disc* by Rockwell is the perfect solution. Non-clogging, open-grit chips of carbide are impregnated onto this tool-steel disc, giving you a super-tough grinding wheel that you use like a sanding wheel. It will outlast conventional sanding discs by ten to one, and at the price of sandpaper today, that's a bargain. Let's face it—*all* grinding is messy, hard work. Any way you can cut down on this chore is a plus. Whether it's saving time changing discs or avoiding the frustration of clogged sandpaper, the Rockwell Tungsten Carbide Disc makes the best of a tough job.

Another excellent sanding disc is the *Zippidi Do*, made by Coastal. It can be used as both a disc sander *and* a cutting tool. This all-purpose disc is made of silicon-carbide grains imbedded in a nylon mesh screen. There are no teeth and no backing pad is required. Because of the open-weave nylon, the disc is non-clogging when sanding wood, metal, tile, rust or plaster.

As a cutting tool, it's handy for plastic, ceramic tile, fiberglass, steel, aluminum, copper and galvanized pipe. The Zippidi Do may also be used to sharpen knives. It can be mounted as a stationary tool, or operated safely by hand-holding the drill motor. The 7-inch disc is sold in a kit complete with the necessary 1/4-inch arbor and flange.

Zippidi Do will smooth or cut almost any material without clogging.

The Roto Stripper will remove lots of material very quickly, but treat it with respect. Keep your fingers and loose clothing out of the way.

Surface Stripping—If you've got a big job around the house that requires the removal of a lot of paint or rust, the *Roto Stripper* is the tool for the job. Stripping siding or cleaning up decorative steel, such as on staircases or front porch scroll-work, are but two of the many jobs this accessory handles with ease. Boat owners can use the Roto Stripper for cleaning the under-water portion of their hulls after a season in the water. And the stripper will also remove paint from sidewalks. If you do body and fender work, it's easy to clean up a rusted dent prior to repair. The Roto Stripper is sold in three degrees of roughness; fine, medium and coarse. One should be right for any heavy stripping job.

The unit is impossible to clog, even when removing paint. The tempered wires that actually do the cutting may be re-sharpened on a grinder when they become dull. Operate it with a light touch and let the tool do the work. **CAUTION: Safety goggles are a MUST when using the Roto Stripper. Use a respirator when removing paint.**

Grinding—An accessory by Arco actually converts your drill motor into a mini-bench grinder. A 3-inch aluminum-oxide grinding wheel is mounted on a 1/4-inch arbor. A guard wraps around the grinding wheel to help prevent sparks from flying into your face. The twist drill sharpener handles bits up to 1/2-inch diameter. Included in the kit is an adjustable tool rest suitable for sharpening chisels, knives, scissors and plane blades. The stand for the drilling motor is a separate accessory.

Sharpening—If you're only interested in keeping an edge on the kitchen knives and making sure scissors are sharp, the Coastal *Knife Sharpener* is all you need. Two angled grinding wheels attached by a 1/4-inch arbor provide the correct angle to put a sharp edge on almost any blade. Coastal also makes a similar attachment for sharpening lawnmower blades.

Even though a drill bit is made of tool steel, the point wears. A dull bit is practically useless and must be resharpened. The simplest way to resharpen drill bits is with a Black & Decker *Drill Bit Sharpener.* Operation is straightforward because the unit works a lot like a pencil sharpener. Attach the drill to the protruding shaft of the sharpener and then insert the drill bit in the hole that is closest to its

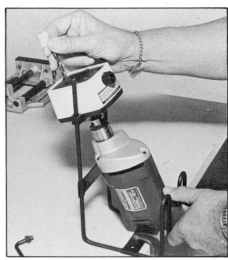

Black & Decker's Drill Bit Sharpener is more useful than it seems. Once you pick up the knack of using it, you'll like it.

You need a bench stand to use this drill bit and tool sharpener kit. It supplies the adjustable tool rest and grinding wheel to convert your drill to a small bench grinder.

diameter. When you turn on the motor, a rotary grinding wheel sharpens one side of the bit at the correct angle. There's an adjustment knob to ensure a proper angle on the cutting lip of the bit.

Stop the machine and twist the drill 180° to sharpen the other side. Use care to sharpen both sides equally by counting off three seconds for each side. The unit accepts 11 of the most common bits between 1/8 and 3/8 inch. With bits smaller than 1/8 inch or larger than 3/8 inch you'll have to find another method. Page 83, shows how to sharpen drills by hand.

An inexpensive yet very handy accessory for your drill motor is a *bench stand*. With it your drill motor becomes a mini grinder, polisher and even a crude lathe for special projects.

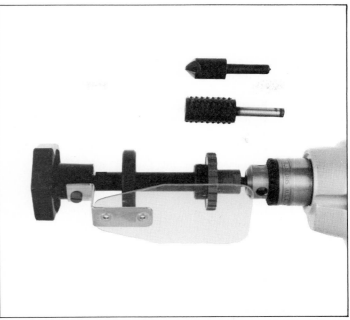

Coastal's Router Rasp is a good way to introduce you to the delights a router can perform, only you use the drill motor as a power base.

SHAPERS

You can buy accessories for your drill that convert it to a passable router and shaper. Naturally, it won't do as fine a job as a router, but it's a good interim measure until you can afford a real one. The rotary rasps are fastened to a handle and disc guides, giving you the capability of cutting rabbet joints, concave or convex moulding. You can also make both single and double slots. A bevel rasp is also available. As long as you're working with soft woods, pine or fir for example, these tools give satisfactory results. Go slowly when cutting because the drill doesn't have the speed and power of a regular router. But it doesn't have the cost either! Shaper attachments are made by Black & Decker, Coastal and Arco.

DRILL PRESS

A drill press is another very helpful accessory for your drill motor. It lets you do more precise work than you can with a hand-held drill. Anytime you have to make a series of similar parts, you can do it quicker and easier with a drill press because both the bit and the parts are held firmly in place to give you exact and repeatable control.

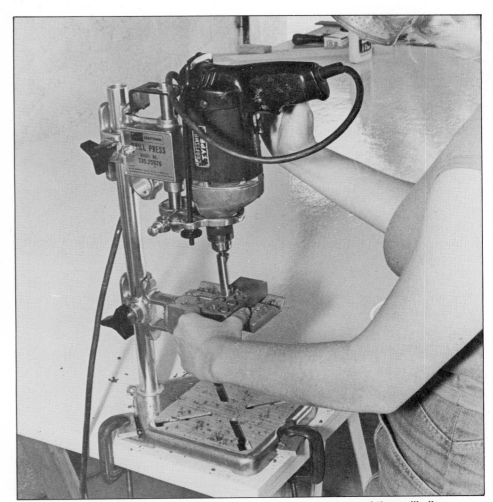

You'll need a drill press around a shop. They're not too expensive and they will allow you a precision you couldn't possibly duplicate freehand. By the way, that's Convalco's 3/8-inch plug cutter chucked in the drill.

By making a few simple jigs out of wood, such as a guide fence, the drill press becomes even more useful. Anytime you have a project that involves a drill press, stop and consider whether a jig or attachment would help you do the job better. If you need one, take the time to make the accessory out of whatever scrap you have handy. Before long, you'll have a whole drawer full of *helpers* to make future jobs that much easier.

If you decide to buy a drill press, it is wise to look at many different models. Because of their poor construction, some presses are just toys that are frustrating to use. Check each unit for close tolerances and precise construction. After all, you can't produce quality work if your tools aren't quality-made, so buy a good one.

PORTALIGN

If you can't afford a drill press or if you need a *portable* drill press, I recommend the *Portalign*. I've owned mine for years and wouldn't be without one in my shop. The Portalign converts your drill to a portable drill press, allowing you to take the precision you need to the job, instead of vice-versa. It accurately drills bar stock right through the middle. By adjusting the two sliding rods as stops, you can make precisely centered holes in any wood up to a 2x4. The baseplate assures a 90° entry whether you're using the drill vertically, horizontally or even upside-down. The tool can be adjusted to bore holes of the same angle and depth over and over again. You can mount the Portalign upside-down under your work bench and convert your drill to a stationary drum sander or router and shaper. The Portalign won't replace a drill press, but it will do 85 percent of it's duties, *and* it's portable. Nor can a drill press replace a Portalign because the Portalign can also convert your drill to a router for soft woods.

Jigs or guides don't have to be elaborate, sophisticated pieces of equipment. They just need to be solid enough to hold the work. The two scraps of wood you see here worked fine during the building of the hutch in Chapter 11.

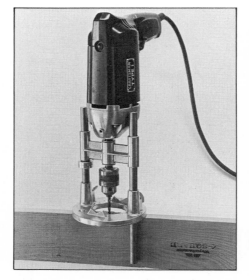

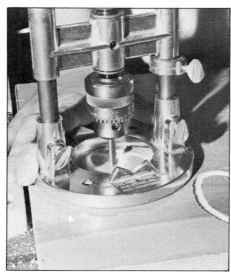

Portalign—one of my favorite tools. As shown here, it will accurately centerbore wood planks or round pipe, make repetitive angle holes, serve as a router, or even perform limited use as a bench-mounted shaper. Inexpensive, versatile, convenient—what more can I say?

PUMPS

Rotary pumps have become increasingly popular in the last few years. They are almost indispensible any time you have to transfer liquids. This occurs very often in the average household. For example, changing oil in your car or boat is normally a messy, time-consuming job. But with a rotary pump, you can just stick the suction end down the *fill* spout or dipstick hole, put the discharge line in a bucket or jug, and squeeze the trigger on your drill. A clogged sink is also one messy job, but with a pump you can at least empty the water before diving in to clean out the obstruction.

I've also used the pump to change water in a fish aquarium.

CAUTION: Flammable liquids can catch fire or explode from sparks created inside your drill motor, so I can't recommend using a rotary pump for gasoline, paint thinners or other flammable liquids.

The average pump moves about 200 gallons per hour when connected to a 1/4-inch drill turning 2,250 RPM. They're self-priming and will lift fluid 8 to 10 feet. Several companies sell this type of unit. The only major difference between them is the hose connectors. Some are set up for garden hoses and others have a 1/2-inch nipple for plastic or rubber hose.

The rotary pump is a simple effective means to transfer fluid using your drill motor. It sure beats using a bucket.

SNAKE

After emptying the clogged sink with the rotary pump, you may want to unclog the drain with another handy tool—a power snake. Arco makes this unit with a safety clutch to fit any electric drill. The snake can be fed down drains, traps or toilets easily and quickly without damaging the plumbing. Snakes are available in lengths from 6 to 25 feet.

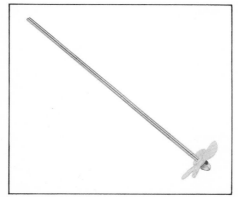

For quick, even mixing, nothing beats this stirrer. Be careful not to lift it out of the liquid while it is spinning.

PAINT STIRRER

Have you ever tried stirring a can of paint after the pigment has settled to the bottom? It's a hard job. Your arm muscles get tired, the paint slops over the top and the pigment takes forever to dissolve. A paint stirrer eliminates all that. It

takes a few effortless minutes to do the mixing job. There's only one thing to remember: If you are stirring a full can of paint, pour about a quarter of the paint into a separate container before you start mixing. Otherwise, the paint will overflow when you turn on the drill. After the pigment is mixed, use a wooden spatula to blend in the part you poured off. CAUTION: Stir paint in a well-ventilated area. Some paints and varnishes are flammable and their vapors can ignite from sparks created inside your drill motor.

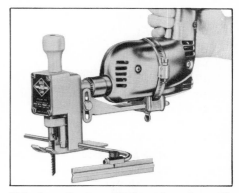

This Arco jigsaw attachment works well, but it cannot replace a good saber saw.

JIGSAW

If you can't yet afford a saber saw, you may find a jigsaw attachment by Arco suits your needs. This unit comes complete with a circle cutter and rip gauge. It will fit any 1/4-inch drill and you can cut perfect circles up to 20 inches in diameter or accurately rip a board to 10 inches wide. You can even do scroll work in wood, plastic or light metals with the proper blades. Plunge cuts are also possible. The jigsaw attachment has self-lubricating bearings which last the lifetime of the saw.

HEDGE TRIMMER

A hedge trimmer attachment for your drill is light enough to be used with one hand. It has a 14-inch blade made of hardened tool steel. An adjustable handle is included with the accessory to allow holding the trimmer either by the side or on top. The handle can also be locked at ten different angles to best suit your needs.

5
Saber Saws

After you've chosen a drill, the next power tool you should consider for your shop is the saber saw. With the right blade, you can produce straight or curved cuts in different woods, leather, plastic, fiberglass, Formica, aluminum, light steel and ceramic tiles. Accessories are available to allow you to make scroll designs, cut circles or use the saw as a jigsaw.

FEATURES

The saber saw is a lightweight, hand-held power saw. An electric motor drives a series of gears and levers that give the blade an up-and-down cutting action. Saw motors range from 1/6 to 1/2hp and, depending on the size of the motor, the up-and-down blade stroke ranges from 1/2 to 1 inch. Naturally a more powerful motor is able to do heavier cutting jobs. Smaller saws are fine for light woodworking tasks and cutting smooth curves.

Because the blade teeth point upward, the blade cuts on the up

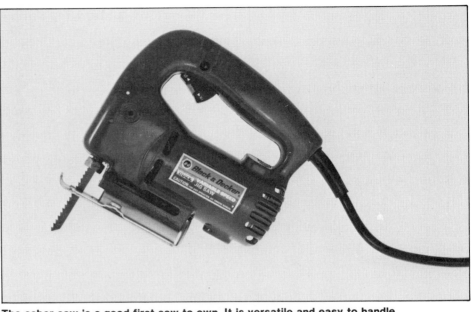

The saber saw is a good first saw to own. It is versatile and easy to handle.

stroke. If the blade travels straight up and down and is in constant contact with the material, it can overheat and wear out the teeth. Better saws avoid this problem with an *orbital stroke*. The blade cuts straight up, then backs away from the material on the down stroke and comes down in the kerf. This

produces better cutting and less blade wear.

Saber saw speed is measured in *strokes per minute* (SPM). Saws are available with single speed, dual speeds, and variable speeds. The cutting speed for single and dual-speed saws range from 1000 to 4000 SPM. Variable-speed saws give

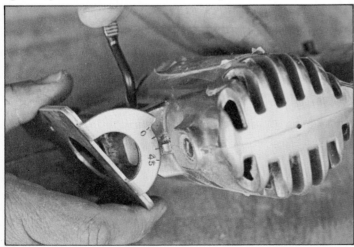

Setting the baseplate at an angle to make a bevel cut is a snap with this Black & Decker model. Pull back on the lever at the left, adjust the baseplate, then push the lever forward to lock it at the angle you've selected.

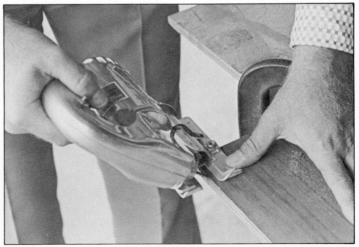

A tilting baseplate allows you to make perfect bevel cuts. Use your free hand to guide the saw for accuracy, but keep clear of the blade.

you a choice of speeds from zero to the maximum, about 3500 SPM. Dual- or variable-speed saws are a good investment because different materials require different cutting speeds. Using the optimal speed for a cut will do a better job and extend blade life.

The switch is on the saw handle. With many saws, once the switch is turned ON, it stays on even if you take your hand off the switch. Variable-speed saws have a sliding switch so you can adjust the speed of the saw during the cut if necessary.

Sometimes, the front of the saw's baseplate prevents you from sawing as far as you want to because it hits a vertical surface. A flush-cutting blade, designed to eliminate this problem, is discussed on pages 40 and 41.

All but the most inexpensive saws have a tilting base, making it easy to make accurate bevel and compound cuts.

Safety Features— Most models have a double-insulated housing and a cord extending straight out the back of the saw. Generally, the saber saw is safer than a circular saw because the blade is smaller. This is why many people choose this saw, but it can still be dangerous if wrongly used.

Always wear eye protection when sawing. Keep fingers away from the blade and never force the saw. You'll only strain the saw and blade, and possibly damage the material and yourself. Never set the saw down while it is running.

BASIC OPERATION

Operating a saber saw is deceptively easy because it is so light and versatile. But for maximum utility with this and any other tool, I urge you to read the manufacturer's instructions and to practice with the saw each 'time you plan to make a cut you've never made before.

Practice— Clamp a piece of scrap plywood to your bench or sawhorse and draw a straight or curved line on it. Put on your safety goggles, plug in the saw and place the front of the base plate on the sur-

For accurate cuts, lean over the saw so you can see where the blade is cutting. Use an edge guide for long straight cuts.

face of the wood. Turn on the saw, and with one hand on the handle and the other on the side or back of the saw, guide it into the wood along the line. Don't start the saw with the teeth touching the wood. The saw could lurch into the wood and stall the motor.

Let the saw do the cutting; don't force it. The saw tends to pull the baseplate to the surface of the material because the teeth cut up. If the material is not properly clamped, or you don't hold the saw firmly, or you feed too fast, the saw can chatter and make a rough, crooked cut.

If you want to remove the saw from the wood before cutting through, turn the saw OFF and lift it out of the kerf *after* the blade has stopped. Otherwise, the moving blade could hit the surface when the saw is lifted out and mark the material or break the blade.

Cutting Characteristics—Because the blade cuts on the up stroke, the bottom of the cut is smoother and less frayed than the top. Make the layout on the backside of the material and the facing side of the project will stay clean and have a sharper edge.

Because the blade has thickness, it will create a kerf thicker than the drawn line. For this reason, always place one side of the blade along the drawn line so the kerf is on the scrap side of the material, giving you an accurately cut piece.

Depth of Cut—Saber saws do not come with a built-in depth adjustment, but you can control depth of cut. One way is to make a *shim* out of wood and attach it to the bottom of the saw's baseplate with screws or bolts. This makes the saw ride higher above the material and prevents the blade from reaching its full depth.

Another way is to use a short blade. Cut and grind a broken blade so the tip resembles the original blade. This customized blade will give you shallower cuts.

These depth adjusters must never be so short that the blade comes completely out of the kerf on the up stroke. The tip could hit the material on the down stroke and break the blade. You should not make plunge cuts with these arrangements, either. Always start the cut through a guide hole or from the edge of the material.

Guides—Because the saber saw is light and easy to handle, you can make freehand cuts with ease. But for some cuts, a guide should be used. A *rip fence*, sometimes called

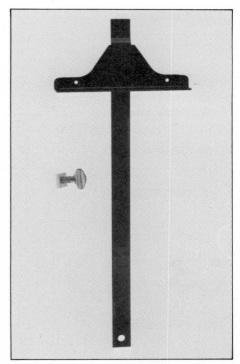

A T-guide or rip fence can be purchased separately or with your saw. Be sure your saw will accept a guide if you plan to buy one later.

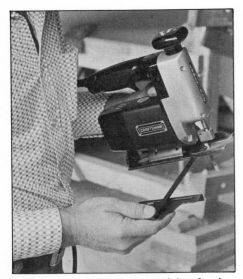

This is one of the many models of saber saws sold by Sears, Roebuck and Co. Notice the edge cutting attachment held in my right hand. This particular saber saw has the ability to do scroll work by just turning the knob at the top—which is directly connected to the blade.

a *T-guide*, comes with many saws and is handy for long rip cuts and crosscuts. The long arm of the metal guide slides into a slot on the saw's base plate where it is held with a screw. The arm is usually graduated in inches, so it acts as an adjustable, built-in scale. The end of the guide, called the *fence*, is a flat piece of metal perpendicular to the scale arm. It rides along the edge of the material and keeps the cut line parallel to the edge.

If the edge of the material is not parallel to the cut you want to make, or if the guide is too small, you can clamp a straight edge to the material and let the side of the saw's base plate ride against it during the cut.

For crosscuts and miters, a tri-square or protractor guide is help-ful. Hold these guides against the front surface of the wood and move the saw against the guide edge which is parallel to the cut.

Adjustable circle-cutting guides are available which help you make large circular cuts accurately. They attach to the saw like the rip fence and let you revolve the saw around a center point determined by the end of the guide.

BLADES

Saber saws are so versatile because they accept a wide array of blades. Each blade is designed for a specific cutting job. They come with different tooth designs and lengths, are made of different kinds of metal, and have different coatings. When you change blades and cutting speeds, you have actually changed saws.

SABER SAW BLADE GUIDE

	Blade Type	Description of Blade and Use	Type of Cut	Speed of Cut	Length in Inches	Teeth per Inch
	Flush Cutting	Hard or soft wood over 1/4" thick. High carbon steel. Set teeth for fast cutting.	Rough	Fast	3	7
	Plaster Cutting	Special V-Tooth design provides constant abrading action most effective in cutting plaster, masonry and high density plastics. High carbon steel.	Rough	Fast	3-5/8	9
	Double Cutting	Most wood and fiber materials. Tooth design allows for cutting in both directions with equal speed. High carbon steel.	Rough	Fast	3	7
	Double Cutting	Cuts most wood and fiber materials. Tooth design allows cutting in both directions with equal speed and quality. High carbon steel.	Medium	Medium	3	10
	Skip Tooth	Special tooth design with extra large gullets provide extra chip clearance necessary for cutting plywood and plastic. High carbon steel.	Rough	Fast	3	5
	Wood Cutting Coarse	Cuts soft woods 3/4" and thicker. Canted shank provides built-in blade relief helping to clear the sawdust and cool the blade. High carbon steel.	Rough	Fastest	3	7
	Wood Cutting Fine	Cuts soft woods less than 3/4" thick. Canted shank provides built-in blade relief helping to clear the sawdust and cool the blade. High carbon steel. More teeth per inch allow for finer quality of cut.	Medium	Medium	3	10
	Wood Cutting Hollow Ground	Hard woods less than 3/4" thick. Hollow grinding provides no tooth protection beyond body of blade, thus imparting an absolutely smooth finish. Canted shank for blade clearance. Heat-treated high carbon steel.	Smooth	Medium	3	7
	Metal Cutting	For cutting ferrous (iron) metals 1/4" to 3/8" thick and nonferrous (aluminum, copper, etc.) 1/8" to 1/4" thick. M-2 high speed steel heat treated to spring temper hardness. Straight shank.	Medium	Medium	3	14
	Metal Cutting	For cutting ferrous (iron) metals 1/8" to 1/4" thick and nonferrous metals 1/16" to 1/8" thick. M-2 high speed steel heat treated to spring temper hardness. Straight shank.	Smooth	Medium	3	18
	Metal Cutting	For cutting hard ferrous (iron) metals 1/16" to 3/16" thick. M-2 high speed steel heat treated to full hardness spring temper. Straight shank.	Fine	Slow	3	24
	Metal Cutting	For cutting hard ferrous (iron) metals 1/64" to 3/32" thick. M-2 high speed steel heat treated to full hardness spring temper. Straight shank.	Very Fine	Slow	3	32

The *shank* or *tang* of blades varies according to the brand of saw it fits, but some blade manufacturers make their blades compatible with many different makes and models. The packaging for the blade usually lists the different brands the blade fits.

Tooth Design—The number of teeth per inch (TPI) of a blade determines the type of cutting the blade will do. A coarse blade, such as a 7 TPI blade, cuts soft material quickly and leaves a rough surface. Coarse blades are best for rough cutting where smoothness isn't necessary. There are coarse blades designed to cut hard and soft woods, plywood and plastics.

Blades with more TPI cut slower and leave smoother surfaces. Fine blades, such as a 32 TPI blade, are designed to cut metal. They cut much like a hacksaw blade, slowly and finely.

Another factor in tooth design is the *set* of the teeth. Teeth are set by bending alternate teeth in opposite directions from the body of the blade. This lets the blade make a cut wider than the blade thickness, reducing blade drag and giving a fast, but rough, cut. The wider the set, the faster and rougher the cut.

Blades without set teeth are used for jobs requiring very smooth finish cuts. Some of these blades have *hollow-ground* teeth, while others have *hollow-ground* or *tapered sides* to reduce drag in the kerf. Blades without set teeth are usually made of heat-treated high-carbon steel for strength and durability.

Special Blades—Most blades are 3 to 5 inches long. This range allows you to cut material as thin as sheet metal or as thick as a 2-1/2-inch piece of wood. Blades 6 inches long are also available for making coarse cuts in thicker wood.

Offset Blades are used when you have to make a cut in wall panelling flush to floor level and the front of your saw's base plate blocks you from cutting the last inch or so. With an offset blade you can make cut fast because there is less friction on the blade on the down stroke.

Offset or Flush-Cutting Blades are used when you have to make a cut in wall paneling flush to floor level and the front of your saw's baseplate blocks you from cutting the last inch or so. With an offset blade you can make cuts flush to the perpendicular barrier because the blade's cutting edge is in front of the baseplate.

SABER SAW BLADE GUIDE

	Blade Type	Description of Blade and Use	Type of Cut	Speed of Cut	Length in Inches	Teeth per Inch
	Hollow Ground	For cutting plywood 1/2" to 3/4" thick. For absolutely smooth finish on all wood products. High carbon steel. Straight shank.	Extremely Fine	Medium	4	10
	Hollow Ground	For cutting plywood and finish materials 3/4" and thicker. Hollow ground for very smooth finish on all wood products. High carbon steel. Straight shank.	Smooth	Medium	4	6
	Hollow Ground	For cutting soft woods up to 2" thick and where fine finish is desirable. Thicker blade provides less flexing when cutting 1" to 2" stock. Not recommended for scroll-type cutting. Hollow ground for smooth finish. High carbon steel. Straight shank.	Smooth	Medium	4	6
	Hollow Ground	For cutting plywood up to 1" thick. Hollow ground for very smooth finish. Heat-treated high carbon steel. Straight shank.	Fine	Medium	3	10
	Hollow Ground	For cutting plywood 3/4" thick and less. Hollow ground for very smooth finish. Heat-treated high carbon steel. Straight shank.	Smooth	Medium Fast	3	7
	Hollow Ground	For plywood 1/4" to 1" thick. Hollow ground for smooth cuts. Heat-treated high carbon steel. Straight shank.	Medium	Fast	3	5
	Knife Blade	For cutting leather, rubber, composition tile, cardboard. High carbon steel. Straight shank.	Smooth	Fast	3	—
	Fleam Ground	For green or wet woods 1/4" to 1-1/2" thick. Fleam-ground teeth provide shredding action most effective in sawing hard, green or wet materials. High carbon steel. Straight shank.	Smooth	Medium	4	10
	Fleam Ground	For green or wet woods 3/8" to 2-1/2" thick. Fleam ground provides shredding action most effective in sawing hard, green or wet materials. High carbon steel. Straight shank.	Coarse	Fast	4	6
	Scroll Cut	For cutting wood, plastic and plywood 1/4" to 1" thick. Set teeth and thin construction allow this blade to make intricate cuts and circles with radii as small as 1/8". High carbon steel. Straight shank.	Smooth	Medium	2-1/2	10
	Wood Cutting Coarse	Cuts most plastics and wood up to 4" thick. Tooth design with extra large gullets provides extra chip clearance for fast cutting in thicker materials. High carbon steel.	Rough	Fast	6	3
	Wood Cutting Medium	Makes fairly smooth cuts in wood up to 4" thick. Extra thick back provides greater resistance to breaking during intricate scroll-type cutting. High carbon steel.	Medium	Medium	6	7

Scroll Blades are flexible, narrow blades used to make intricate curves and circles like a jigsaw. Regular blades are too wide to make small-radius cuts and they may bind and break in the kerf during tight curve cuts.

Knife Blades have no teeth and are useful for fast, smooth cuts in cardboard, leather or rubber. Another toothless blade made by Remington consists of tungsten-carbide grit attached to the leading edge of a metal blade. This incredibly tough coating is available in three grits: *fine, medium* and *coarse*. These blades are strong enough to cut fiberglass, ceramic or Formica. They cut wood so smoothly you don't need to sand it. They cut slower and cost more than regular blades, but last much longer.

CUTS AND JOINTS

A saber saw is not the ideal tool for making long, straight cuts or for cutting stock thicker than 2 inches. A circular saw has the power and precision for such jobs. But the saber saw is ideal for making straight and curved cuts in thinner stock or materials such as plywood, sheet metal and soft woods. It is an agile tool able to make many cuts much faster and better than you could do with a handsaw or portable circular saw.

Ripping and Crosscutting—If you don't have a circular saw, it is best to use a guide with your saber saw on long rip and crosscuts. The narrowness of the saber saw blade is a disadvantage for long, straight cuts done freehand and you are likely to make a crooked cut.

Choose a blade that will leave the finish you want. If a rough finish is acceptable, use a coarse blade for a fast cut. If you need a smooth finish on a crosscut piece, use a finer-toothed blade. It will cut slower, but won't leave the rough surface characteristic of a coarse blade.

Another way to get a smoother edge on a crosscut is to score the line with a razor knife before sawing. This breaks some of the surface

PLUNGE CUTS

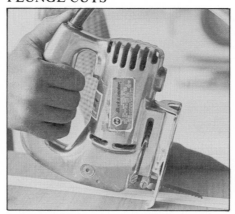

This is what the start of a plunge cut looks like. The left hand—not shown—should be holding the baseplate firmly against the wood.

...until the baseplate is resting flat on the surface to be cut.

After the saw has been started, slowly lower the running blade into the plywood...

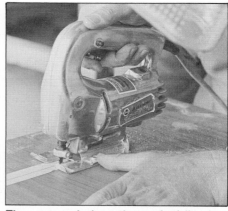

Then proceed along the marked line in a normal fashion. The material is a veneered plywood so I used masking tape to keep it from chipping.

fibers of the wood and helps to minimize frayed edges.

Miter, Bevel and Compound Cuts—These cuts can all be made with the saber saw because it is so easy to guide. It is even easier with saber saws that have tilting bases. Depending on the size of the cut, you can either saw freehand or use a guide. Freehand cutting with a saber saw is not difficult for small jobs, but you'll get best results if you clamp the stock. This will prevent the stock from chattering and shaking during the cut.

Plunge Cuts—The plunge cut requires a bit of skill and practice to master, but it is worth the extra effort because it minimizes waste. If you are making a plywood cabinet with doors, it is nice to have the grain of the doors match the grain

of the cabinet. But you can't drill pilot holes for the blade to enter because they would mar the door. The saw must make its own pilot hole and enter the wood from the top surface. This requires making a plunge cut.

The saber saw is ideal for the plunge cut. Draw the outline of the piece you want on the *back side* of the material, which will be the *top surface* during the cut. Place the front of the baseplate on the plywood and tilt the saw so the blade is parallel to the material and aligned with cut line. Start the saw while firmly holding the front of the baseplate against the wood. *Slowly* lower the pulsating blade into the wood along the cut line. You must hold the baseplate firmly against the wood or the tip of the

One way to make accurate circle cuts using a saber saw is to drill a hole in the end of your edge guide and screw it to the center of the intended circle. The saw will track on whatever radius you select. Here I am rounding plywood corners.

saw blade will hit the groove you're starting and cause the saw to jackhammer and gouge the wood. Practice on a piece of scrap before you do it on a project.

When the blade is at full depth and the baseplate is resting flat on the wood, continue cutting to the corner. When you reach the corner, stop the saw and remove it from the wood. Turn the saw around and cut to the opposite corner along the line you've just cut. Repeat the plunge cut on all sides of the cutout. When you're finished, the cutout will make a perfect door.

Circular Cuts—Cutting circles freehand is the quickest and easiest method, but if accuracy is important, a guide designed to revolve around the center point will help you make the smoothest circle.

You can buy this guide or make your own out of a piece of metal that fits into the slot on the baseplate of the saw. Hammer one end into a right angle and drill a small hole into the extended piece. This hole will be the center of the circular cut. For the saw to track accurately, the hole must be located a distance equal from the front edge of the guide bar to the distance from the blade teeth to the same edge. Different saw blades may require different center holes.

Draw the circle you want on the material. Adjust the guide to the desired radius and tack or nail the center hole of the guide to the center mark of the circle. The easiest way to start a circular cut is by entering the blade through a pilot hole drilled into the waste side of

the wood. You can make a plunge cut into the circle, but you cannot attach the guide until after the saw has entered the wood.

Use a narrow blade with set teeth for clearance in the kerf. A regular blade may bind and break in the kerf if the angle is too sharp. You can make the saw blade even narrower by removing some of the back edge of the blade by grinding.

Here is one way to check the minimum radius a blade can cut. Make a straight cut in a piece of scrap wood. Turn off your saw and remove the blade. Place it in the kerf and twist it until the back of the blade rests against the kerf. The angle between the blade and the cut indicates the sharpness of curve it can make.

Cutting Thin Materials—Sometimes you can't cut material with the good side down. When this happens with veneer or thin plywood, you can still get a relatively smooth cut on top by laying masking tape where you intend to saw and drawing the cutline on the masking tape. The tape will help prevent the wood from splintering. Use a sharp, fine-toothed blade so at least two teeth are in contact with the material at all times. Anything less and the saw may vibrate and chatter, making a poor cut. Scoring the line with a sharp knife will also help you ensure a smooth cut.

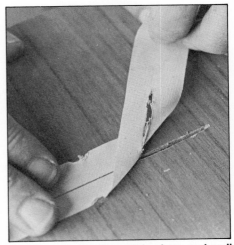

As you can see, the cut is sharp and well defined under the tape. It is a good idea to use this procedure on all veneers to avoid chipping and splintering.

Sheet metal is often so thin that the saw will chatter even when the metal is clamped. One way to avoid this is to clamp the metal to a piece of scrap plywood and cut both pieces at the same time. You can also clamp the sheet metal between two pieces of plywood before making the cut.

Cutting Round Stock—Masking tape is also useful for cutting round stock such as a dowels, plastic tubing or metal pipe. Make two marks on the stock so one edge of the tape aligns with both marks. Be sure the tape is straight, not spiralled. A block of wood with a V-shaped notch cut in it will help hold round stock. Clamp the stock in the notch, in a vise or to a table, and cut along the edge of the tape. You'll get a perfect cut every time.

Making Joints—Rabbet, dado, lap and dovetail joints have straight-line cuts, and the saber saw can be used for some of them. But generally, the saber saw is impractical because of the extra hand work required to finish the joints. A circular saw and router are the best tools to use to make these joints.

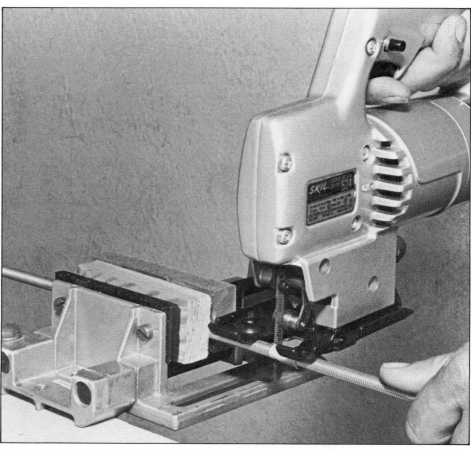

The masking tape guiding the saw's baseplate against the wooden block ensures a square cut on round stock.

SABER SAWS

MAKE/MODEL	HP	AMP	STROKES PER MINUTE	TILTING BASE-PLATE	USE	FEATURES
Black & Decker						
7504	.20	2.1	3200	Yes	Light	Single-speed; 10-inch cord
7530	.33	3.0	2500/3200	Yes	Medium	Two-speed; Detachable cord
7580	.33	3.0	0-3200	Yes	Medium	Variable-speed; Detachable cord
7575		2.5	0-3000	Yes	Heavy	Variable-speed; 10-foot cord
Millers Falls						
SP6060		2.1	3000	No	Heavy	Single-speed; 1/2-inch stroke
SP6262		2.1	2300/3000	No	Heavy	Two-speed; 1/2-inch stroke
SP561		2.5	3000	No	Industrial	Single-speed; 1/2-inch stroke
SP9060		4.5	0-2600	No	Industrial	Variable-speed
Penney						
1825A	.20	2.5	3500	No	Light	Single-speed; 1/2-inch stroke
3821A	.25	2.5	2800/ 3500	Yes	Medium	Two-speed
6352A	.34	3.2	0-3500	Yes	Heavy	Variable-speed; 5/8-inch stroke
1163A		4.0	0-2800	Yes	Heavy	Variable-speed; 1-inch stroke

SABER SAWS — cont.

MAKE/MODEL	HP	AMP	STROKES PER MINUTE	TILTING BASE-PLATE	USE	FEATURES
Rockwell						
4301		2.5	3300	Yes	Light	Single-speed
4310		2.6	2400/3300	Yes	Light	Two-speed
4320		2.7	0-3300	Yes	Medium	Variable-speed
4370		2.8	0-2900	Yes	Medium	Variable-speed
4380		3.0	3200	Yes	Heavy	Single-speed
Sears						
1717	.16	2.0	3200	Yes	Light	Single-speed; 1/2-inch stroke
1718	.16	2.1	2600/3200	Yes	Light	Two-speed; 1/2-inch stroke
17215	.20	2.2	0-3200	Yes	Medium	Variable-speed; 1/2-inch stroke; Edge guide
1070	.25	2.5	0-3600	Yes	Medium	Variable-speed; 5/8-inch stroke; Edge guide
1072	.25	2.5	0-3600	Yes	Heavy	Variable-speed; 5/8-inch stroke; Edge guide; Scroll head
17251	.38	2.8	0-3200	Yes	Heavy	Variable-speed; 3/4-inch stroke; Edge guide; Scroll head
1726	.38	3.0	0-2700	Yes	Industrial	Variable-speed; 1-inch stroke; Edge guide; Scroll head
1728	.50	3.5	1300/2700	Yes	Industrial	Multi-speed; 1-inch stroke; Edge guide; Scroll head
Shopmate						
T2300	.34	2.5	2800	Yes	Medium	Single-speed
T2302	.34	2.5	2300/2800	Yes	Medium	Two-speed
T2305	.34	2.5	0-2800	Yes	Medium	Variable-speed
Skil						
482	.20	2.5	3500	No	Very light	Single-speed
487	.25		2800/3500	Yes	Medium	Two-speed
497	.34		0-3500	Yes	Medium	Variable-speed
499	.34	3.2	0-3500	Yes	Heavy	Variable-speed
524	.25	2.5	3000/4000	Yes	Heavy	Two-speed; Orbital action
Stanley						
90-456		2.7	2400/3000	Yes	Medium	Two-speed; 5/8-inch stroke
90-455		2.7	1100/3100	Yes	Heavy	Variable-speed; 5/8-inch stroke; Ball bearing drive
90-076		3.0	3600	No	Heavy	Single-speed; 5/8-inch stroke; Ball bearing drive; AC/DC
90-454		2.7	3100	Yes	Heavy	Single-speed; 5/8-inch stroke; Ball bearing drive
Ward						
81004		2.8	3200	Yes	Light	Single-speed
81005	.34	3.0	2500/3299	Yes	Medium	Two-speed
81006	.34	3.0	0-3200	Yes	Medium	Variable-speed
81007	.40	3.3	0-3200	Yes	Heavy	Variable-speed
8919	.67	4.0	0-2800	Yes	Heavy	Variable-speed; 1-inch stroke
Wen						
PR50				Yes	Light	Single-speed; 3/4-inch stroke; Rip guide
PR51			2400/3000	Yes	Medium	Two-speed; 3/4-inch stroke; Rip guide
531			0-2800	Yes	Medium	Variable-speed; 1-inch stroke; Edge guide; Scroll head

6
Circular Saws

Circular saws were invented by the Skil Corporation just after World War II. They were designed to serve the booming home-construction industry. This saw enables a carpenter to slice through a 2x4 stud in seconds when previously he took minutes with a handsaw. Converting minutes to seconds makes good economic sense, and the circular saw was soon being used for a multitude of jobs. Not only is a circular saw faster than a handsaw, it is also easier. And it's portable, which is a great advantage because you can take the power saw to the job, instead of vice-versa. This speed, ease and portability has saved millions of dollars in the housing industry.

Naturally, anything this good couldn't be kept out of the hands of do-it-yourselfers. Today, home craftsmen buy 5 circular saws for every 1 bought by a professional builder. For any large-scale building project, it is the first choice of the home craftsman because it saves time and effort.

In addition to standard ripping and crosscutting, the circular saw makes miter and bevel cuts, rabbet and dado joints, and slices through a 4x8-foot sheet of plywood with much more ease than a table saw. With the right blade, it can even cut metal, fiberglass, brick and tile. Although a circular saw can't completely replace a good stationary table saw, it can do many of the same jobs at a much lower purchase price.

A circular saw is the tool to call on for heavy-duty cutting.

A circular saw also has several advantages over a saber saw. The saber saw with all its versatility is still a light- to medium-duty tool. Extended use on heavy projects will cause the tool to fail prematurely. The reciprocating saw—a bigger version of the saber saw—will do heavy work, but it doesn't come close to matching the circular saw for speed. Therefore, if you have a lot of medium to heavy work the circular saw is the unit you'll want to buy.

CHOOSING A SIZE

Circular saws are measured by the maximum blade diameter they can accept. The deepest cut a circular saw can make is slightly less than half the diameter of the blade. For instance, a 7-inch saw will take a blade with a diameter of 7 inches. The deepest cut it can make is about 3-1/4 inches.

Circular saws come in sizes from 4 to 10 inches, with power ratings from 1/2 to over 2 hp. A good, all-around size for average home use is 7-1/4 inches.

It is important to remember that the larger the saw, the heavier it is, and the faster you will become fatigued while using it. But a saw that is too small may force you to make two passes to complete a cut. This can be very annoying and multiplies your chances for making mistakes. Small 4- and 5-inch models are ideal for cutting plywood and 2x4s in projects that do not require deep bevel cuts. They are lightweight for easy handling, and durable enough to give years of trouble-free use, so don't discount them. Consider the type of work you'll be doing and check the buyer's guide at the end of this chapter. Then buy the saw best suited to your needs.

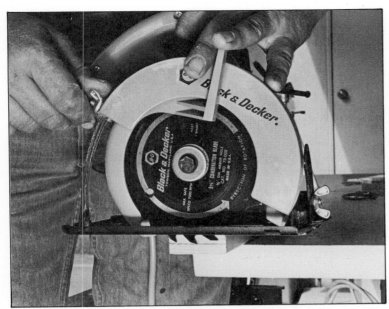

Depth of cut is controlled by adjusting the baseplate, as shown here. The retractable guard is manually raised when precision cuts are required.

BASEPLATES

Most saws have baseplates that are adjustable and allow you to control the depth of cut. Most baseplates can also be tilted up to 45 degrees, allowing you to make bevel or compound-bevel cuts. A 7-1/4-inch blade allows you to cut through a 2x4 stud on a 45 degree bevel with one pass, and this range should cover about 95 percent of your workload.

SAFETY FEATURES

An interesting feature on all circular saws is a trigger switch with *no* locking button. The manufacturer wants the motor to shut off anytime you release the trigger. Another safety feature on some saws is a *lockout button.* It is located next to the trigger switch and prevents accidentally starting the saw until the button is pushed *and* the trigger is squeezed.

Even though the blade is still spinning after you turn the saw off, you can set the saw down after a cut because you are protected from the upper half of the blade by the housing and the lower half of the blade is covered by the spring-loaded, retracting guard. Some deluxe saws have an electric brake, which stops the blade almost instantly when the trigger is released, rather than letting it spin to a stop.

Most saws, including those with plastic and metal housings, have double-insulated housings, something I especially like for outdoor work. Do not be dismayed by saws with plastic housings. This strong, lightweight plastic makes the saw lighter and easier to handle. The plastic is almost indestructible.

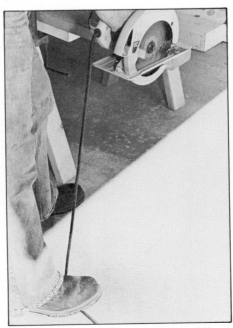

Trouble underfoot. Keep off the cord!!

CORDS

Ideally, the cord should extend out the rear of the saw in line with the blade. This way, if the cord becomes restricted somehow, it will only stop the forward movement of the saw and not cause it to twist to one side and bind.

Some saws have only a short cord so you have to use an extension cord with the saw. I prefer a longer cord on the saw so the plug won't get in my way as I work.

BASIC OPERATION

Because so much of the blade rides in the kerf, a circular saw cuts very straight and is easy to guide. This, plus its speed, portability and the variety of blades, combine to make an extremely versatile tool. But it does its job fast and accurately only in skilled hands.

Practice—Before tackling a project with your new circular saw, practice with it. Clamp a piece of scrap 2x4 to your table or sawhorse and draw a straight line across the wood. Put on your safety glasses and plug the saw into the nearest electrical outlet.

On the saw's baseplate in front of the blade is a notch indicating where the saw will cut. Line up this notch with the drawn line by resting the front of the baseplate on the wood. The motor of the saw should be on the clamped side of the stock and you should stand behind the saw, slightly to that side. This way the saw is well sup-

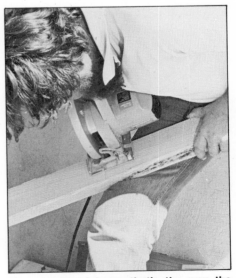

More trouble. I know that's the way the *pros* do it on construction sites. But don't *you* do it—unless you want to find out how well your insurance policy pays.

ported during the cut and you can see exactly where your cut is going.

Make sure the blade is not touching the wood, then start the saw. If the blade is against the wood, the saw may stall. Slowly guide the saw into the line and notice how the lower blade guard retracts automatically. Right away you can feel the power and see the cutting speed this tool is capable of producing. You must *never force the saw:* Guide it along the drawn line, holding the saw down so the blade doesn't climb out of the work.

As you are cutting, the wood should support the tool, but at the end of the cut you must start to carry the weight of the saw so it doesn't fall or swing dangerously. All it takes is a little practice and concentration to do it right. You'll quickly master controlling the tool *if* you practice first.

Cutting Characteristics—As you are cutting, notice that the saw makes a kerf about 1/8 inch wide. For accurate cuts, align the blade so one edge of the kerf just touches the pencil line and the rest of the blade is on the waste side of the stock. Actual blade alignment may vary with different blades and you should check before you cut. The best way to do this is to mark the baseplate each time you change blades. With the new blade installed, retract the safety guard and lay a straight edge along the blade so it touches the front of the baseplate. Mark that spot and repeat on the other side of the blade. The two marks show exactly where the blade cuts.

As with the saber saw, the blade of the circular saw cuts upward. Therefore, the cleaner cut is on the bottom side. So, place the face of the material on the bottom before you cut and you'll end up with a better looking project.

AVOIDING BINDING

The average circular-saw blade spins about 5500 RPM when it is unloaded. Its cutting RPM is slower. The saw becomes very dangerous when the blade RPM slows so much that is almost stops cutting while the motor is still ON. This is called *binding.* The blade may be stuck in a pinched kerf or not able to cut the material with the feed you are giving it. When the saw binds, it can buck out of the material and cut you, or it can damage the motor. *Whenever* the saw begins to bind, *immediately* shut it off. Find the problem and correct it. If you were pushing the saw too fast, either slow down or change to a blade better designed for the work—or to a sharp blade if the one you've been using is dull.

If the kerf is pinching shut because you are making a long or curved cut, install a *riving knife* on the saw or put a wedge in the kerf just behind the saw. A riving knife is a metal tab that protrudes below the baseplate just behind the blade. It rides in the kerf and prevents the kerf from closing around the blade. The riving knife is removable for those operations in which it is unnecessary. A wedge placed in the kerf will also keep the saw from binding. A thin piece of scrap wood works well. This separates the cut sections of wood so they won't pinch the blade.

Some saws have a *slip clutch* that automatically releases the motor from driving the blade if the saw binds.

After you have corrected the cause of the binding, back the saw until the blade is in the kerf but not cutting. Then start it. Never start the saw when the blade is against the material and never back up a saw that is still on. It can kick out of the work and hurt you and the work.

DEPTH OF CUT

Controlling cut depth is another important factor to take care of before you begin sawing. To help keep the blade from overheating

The smooth kerf on the left is the underside of the cut, while the rough slice on the right is what you see. That's why it's best to cut plywood and panelling with the good side down.

One blade tooth protruding below the stock is all you need.

and to ensure the most power in the cut, adjust blade depth so one blade tooth protrudes below the stock being cut. Depth is controlled with the adjustable baseplate which is tightened and loosened by a wing nut or threaded knob on the saw housing. The safety guard covering the bottom half of the blade will retract automatically when it contacts the work, unless you are cutting extremely thin material. In this case, set the saw for minimum depth. Just as you start the saw into the work, use your left hand to raise the safety guard manually with the small knob or lever.

If you are cutting very thin material such as veneer or sheet metal, clamp it to a larger piece of wood to make the cut easier and to lessen the chances of splintering or shattering. Clamp the wood under the cut line and adjust the depth of the blade to cut past the thin material and through the bottom piece.

GUIDES

Unless you can follow a pencil line exactly, use some kind of guide. The type of guide depends on what is being cut. Some cut pieces must

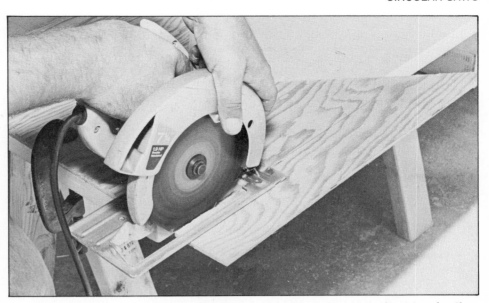

On thin plywood with the baseplate adjusted to a minimum cut, you may have to raise the automatic retractable guard manually. It's a safe operation if you don't get careless. Use your thumb or forefinger to lift the guard and steady the rest of your hand on the saw's main body.

fit together more accurately than others and a good guide attachment for your saw is a worthwhile investment.

Homemade Guides—For many jobs, a straight piece of wood clamped to the material works well. You must place it parallel to the cut so one side of the base plate rides along the straight edge of the guide. Whether it is on the waste or good side of the material depends on where it will be most out of your way. Remember to allow for the motor housing if it extends beyond the base plate.

Buying a Guide—Rip fences similar to those for saber saws are available for circular saws. They are used for long cuts. A tri-square or protracter guide are also handy guides for crosscutting and mitering.

An edge guide to help you make precision rips is a must. Always cut with the blade on the waste side of the stock.

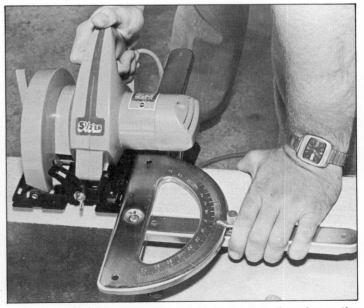

A protractor is a good investment. Note the pencil marks on the baseplate just forward of the blade. One mark will always line up with the pencil line I've drawn on the stock. Which one depends on which is the waste side.

CIRCULAR SAW BLADES

Cut off—flat ground: Used in squaring and trimming to size. Long lasting, smooth cutting. Available with Teflon coating.

Combination—flat ground: Popular with building contractors. Coarse tooth spacing for easy feeding. Ideal for trimming, roofing and all-purpose construction work. Cross cuts, rips, miters. Available with Teflon coating.

Fine tooth cut off: Extra fine teeth for very smooth finish cut. Ideal for plywood.

Combination—flat ground: Similar to style above but with finer tooth spacing for smoother cuts. Available with Teflon coating.

Plywood—hollow ground: Special design for smooth, splinter-free plywood cuts. Available with Teflon coating.

Combination—flat ground: Ideal home workshop saw for all-purpose combination jobs. Gives a smooth, fine finish for rip, diagonal or crosscutting. Available with Teflon coating.

Fine tooth plywood: A fine tooth blade for extra smooth finish cuts in plywood.

Flooring—flat ground: Durable, special steel and temper for rough work. Ideal for old, used lumber where nails may be encountered. Cuts in any direction.

Planer—hollow ground: Designed for finishing work. Allows cutting in any direction and produces extremely smooth cuts requiring no sanding. Available with Teflon coating.

Abrasive blade—metal: Ideal for cutting ferrous and non-ferrous metal tubing, sheets and round stock.

Rip—flat ground: For cutting with the grain only.

Abrasive blade—masonry: Used for cutting tile, patio block, slate and concrete block.

BLADES

Most circular saws are sold with a *combination blade*. It does an adequate job on crosscuts and rip cuts, but for best results, use a blade designed for the job you are doing. Many different blade types are available for different cuts and materials. The chart on this page will help you select the right one for the job.

Tooth Design—Teeth on a *cross-cut blade*, sometimes called a *cut-off blade*, must cut across the grain of the wood. It must *shear* the wood fibers. Therefore, the teeth are small, closely spaced and set. Teeth on a *ripsaw blade* are spaced farther apart and are larger because cutting with the grain, *ripping*, is easier than cutting across the grain.

The combination blade is a compromise between these two designs. It usually has more teeth than a ripsaw blade and the *gullet*, or space between the teeth, is not as deep. There are many variations of this design. Some combination blades have more teeth for a smoother cut. Some are *hollow-ground* which means the teeth are thicker than the rest of the blade. This eliminates the need to set the teeth and creates an extremely smooth cut which is ideal for general finishing.

A *plywood blade* is the best choice for cutting veneer products and plywood cleanly. It has many small, closely spaced teeth that prevent the frayed edges other blades produce in plywood.

Long-Lasting Blades—It is very tempting to buy the least-expensive blade available. But the actual cost of a cheaper blade can be more than the cost of a long-lasting blade because cheap blades dull faster and make rougher and slower cuts. I find two kinds of specially made blades most useful.

Teflon-Coated Blades have the same advantages as Teflon-coated cookware—less sticking. The blade cuts cleaner, faster and longer than conventional blades. A coated blade costs only a little more than an uncoated blade and is available in a

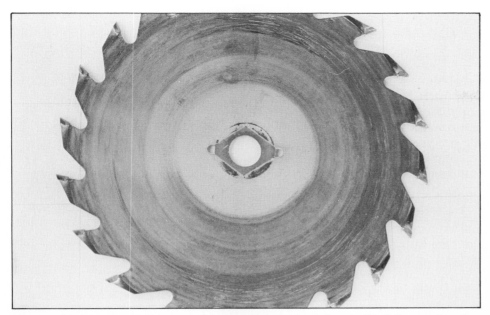

Most sawblades are manufactured with universal knockout rings to fit all the popular circular saws. If the hardware store where you shop doesn't carry this type of blade, you must know the diameter of your saw's arbor to buy the right blade.

inch deep, in hard materials than try to cut it all at once.

BLADE CARE

A sharp, clean blade does the best and fastest job. Use a rag and kerosene or turpentine to clean the blade after each use. Sharpening should be done by a professional. It doesn't cost much and is an absolute must. A dull blade is dangerous because the saw can burn the material or bind and buck out of the stock, possibly injuring you in the process.

Before a blade can be sharpened it must be set at a precise angle. That's one of the reasons I recommend using a professional to keep your blades in top condition.

variety of tooth designs, including crosscut, rip, combination and plywood types.

Tungsten-Carbide-Tipped Blades are also a good investment. They cost two or three times as much as regular blades, but they hold a sharp cutting edge up to *20 times longer*. The tungsten-carbide-tipped blade is available in a variety of tooth designs. For all-around work, a combination blade with these special teeth is tough to beat. They are ideal for cutting hard woods and composition wood. I use one on my saw 90 percent of the time.

Cutting Non-Wood Materials—Abrasive blades or wheels are toothless and rely on a special material in a sandwich mesh to do the cutting. A *masonry blade* is designed to cut brick, cement block, masonry and fiberglass. Other abrasive blades are specially made to cut ferrous and non-ferrous metal sheets, tubes and bars.

There is nothing complicated about cutting these materials, but there are a few precautions you need to follow. First, make sure the RPM rating marked on the blade is appropriate for your saw. Never use one of these blades at a faster RPM than it was designed for be-cause they can fly apart. Second, always cut in a straight line because the blade is made of a fibrous compound and can shatter if twisted. Third, feed the saw *slowly*. These materials are tough and take time to cut. Fourth, do not make too deep a cut. It is better to make several shallow passes, say 3/16

This masonry blade turned those old bricks and mortise to butter.

Never use a cracked or split blade. The blade spins at about 5000 RPM. If the blade shatters, the potential danger to you and your work is far more expensive than the few dollars you'd spend for a replacement blade.

CHANGING BLADES

Because you'll be using a variety of blades, you need to know how to change them. As with all power tools, unplug the saw before starting to work around the cutting edges. Next, use the wrench supplied with the saw or select a wrench from your tool kit to fit the nut on the spindle, called an *arbor*. To keep the arbor from turning as you loosen the nut, jam a piece of scrap wood into the blade teeth and apply torque counterclockwise on the nut. Some blades have holes so you can place a nail between the blade and baseplate to keep the blade from turning.

Remove the nut and washer. Power saws with a slip-clutch assembly have a spring washer sandwiched between the nut and flat washer. Lay them out in the sequence of disassembly so you'll know how they go back together.

Retract the safety guide and remove the blade from the arbor. Before installing the other blade, make sure its hole fits the arbor. Most blades are made with *universal knockout rings,* which make them adaptable to any power saw. The common arbors are 1/2-inch, 5/8-inch and a diamond pattern. If your saw has a 5/8-inch arbor, punch out the 1/2-inch ring before mounting the blade. If for some reason the diamond filler dropped out of the blade, don't worry. Seat it back in place and install the blade as you normally would. It won't affect the saw's operation.

The blade of a circular saw turns counterclockwise and the teeth bite upward. An arrow printed on the blade indicates the direction of rotation, so make sure you mount the blade correctly.

Next, reinstall the washer and nut and tighten it with your fingers.

Use the same piece of scrap or the nail you used before to hold the blade in place while you tighten the arbor nut with your wrench. If your saw has a slip clutch, consult the instructions that came with your saw before making the final adjustment on the nut. Tightening the nut too much can eliminate the slipping action. If it is too loose the blade will stop turning when sawing.

CUTS AND JOINTS

The circular saw is designed to make fast, straight cuts. It does an excellent job of sawing most of the straight cuts required in building construction. The saw can do slight curves, but because of the hazard of binding, I don't recommend cutting curves with this saw. Use a saber saw instead.

Crosscutting—For straight crosscut work, any of the guides mentioned previously work well. However, if you have to make many cuts of the same size, the rip fence helps you do the job faster than other guides. For crosscutting pieces longer than the rip fence, you'll have to use one of the other guides.

One of the characteristics of a crosscut is the roughness of the cut face. To avoid having to sand this surface before gluing, use a crosscut blade designed to create smooth-finish cuts.

Ripping—Any time a long rip cut is required, as when sawing a length of plywood, clamp on a straight piece of wood to act as a guide. This is the best and fastest way to make a long, true cut every time. But don't forget to figure in the measurement from the blade to the side of the baseplate before making the cut.

A rip fence is useful for ripping, but it has the tendency to wobble if extended too far because the fence doesn't make enough contact with the edge of the material. One way to counteract this is to attach a 12-inch 1x1 to the fence. The 1x1 then rides along the material and gives you better control.

Plunge Cutting—To make perfect-fitting cutouts in wood panels you

PLUNGE CUTS

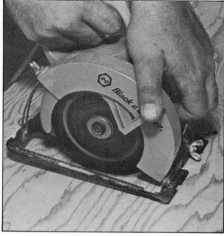

Plunge cuts are easy to make. Lower the baseplate so the sawblade does not touch the wood and set the saw so it will cut exactly where you want.

Turn on the motor and lower the blade into the wood.

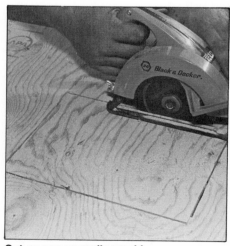

Cut as you normally would.

must use a *plunge cut,* which is also called a *pocket cut.*

Lay out the cutout shape on the *backside* of the material. Remember, the shape must be made of straight lines if the circular saw is going to work efficiently. Adjust the saw's baseplate on the sheet and the blade above the sheet. To ensure a straight entry of the blade, attach a piece of wood alongside the cut to help you hold the saw perpendicular to the material.

Start the saw and lower the blade into the wood. Make sure you keep the front of the baseplate in contact with the wood at all times. When the baseplate is resting flat on the sheet, advance the saw along the line to the corner. Because a circular saw does not cut straight up and down as a saber saw does, stop the saw when the top of the blade reaches the corner. A handsaw or saber saw can be used to finish the corners after all the sides are cut.

Follow the same procedure for each side of the cutout. Be sure to turn off the saw and let the blade come to a stop before you remove it from the cut. Never back the saw or remove it while the blade is still spinning. This can damage the material and you too. Don't try to cut the line behind the plunge by backing the saw, either. Finish the forward cut, remove the saw and turn

it around to finish the cut. Put the saw in the kerf with the baseplate resting flat on the material. Then start the saw and finish that side.

Miter, Bevel and Compound Cuts— A *miter* is a crosscut at an angle of less than 90 degrees to the wood. For best results, use a protractor or straight edge as a guide and always keep the motor side of the saw on the clamped side of the stock. Use a crosscut blade for best results.

A *bevel* or *chamfer cut* is made by adjusting the angle of the saw relative to the top surface of the material. Many saws have a built-in adjustable protractor on the baseplate to show angles as you tilt the saw from 45 to 90 degrees. A wing-nut or knob tightens and loosens the base plate.

A *compound cut* is a combined miter and bevel cut. First adjust the saw for the bevel cut and then layout a line on the material at the appropriate angle for the miter cut. A fine-toothed combination blade makes the smoothest cut.

For all of these cuts, the *T-bevel square* is a handy tool to use. The actual sawing is simple once you've made the proper adjustments and markings. Measure the proper angle with the T-bevel either from a protractor or from the work you want to match. Use the T-bevel to transfer the angle to the saw or the material.

A T-Bevel Square is an indispensible tool in any shop. A must when it comes to transferring angles. The angled miter cut of the board on the right is easily drawn on the left plank using the bevel square.

To make bevel cuts with a circular saw, first measure the angle with a bevel square and transfer it to the saw by tilting the baseplate. Always unplug the saw from any electrical outlet when performing this operation.

Miter cuts are neater if the saw is angled with the grain of the wood.

A compound miter cut being made using a protractor as a guide. As you can see, two steps are performed at the same time with ease and efficiency.

Rabbets—A rabbet cut can be tricky with a large circular saw because you may have to cut along a narrow edge of wood. If you are careful and clamp the wood well, you should be able to do a good job.

Lay out the rabbet on both faces of the wood you want to join. The first cut should be on the narrow end of the wood. To support the wood and get a straight cut, you may have to clamp a piece of scrap to the side of wood parallel to the line to be cut. Make sure the ends are all flush so the baseplate can ride over them smoothly during the cut.

Adjust the depth of cut so the bottom of the blade barely touches the bottom of the rabbet. Set the edge guide and make the first cut with the kerf *inside* the rabbet.

To rip a rabbet on long stock, first layout the rabbet and mark the waste area with an X. Clamp another board flush with the top of the first board to make a surface wide enough for the saw's baseplate to ride on.

Use an edge guide to assure accuracy. Here I've cut a notch in the board because I only want the rabbet on part of it.

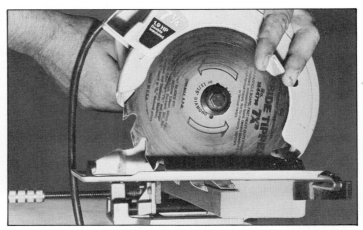

Turn the stock on its side and adjust the blade to the proper depth for the second cut.

Set the edge guide and make your cut.

You should have a perfect rabbet.

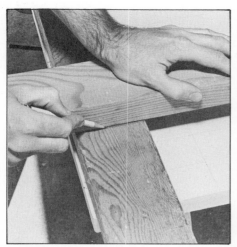

An easy way to connect two crossed 2x4s is to cut dadoes in each to form a lap joint. First, mark the outline of each board on the other.

Clamp the two together and carefully set the cutting depth to half the board width.

Make a series of parallel cuts between the outlines and remove the waste with a chisel if necessary.

For the second cut, which is at right angles to the first, remove the extra wood and clamp the material flat. Align an edge guide parallel to the end of the wood with the cutline *inside* the rabbet. Adjust the depth of the blade so it just meets the kerf of the first cut. If you adjust the angles and depth carefully, you'll get a perfect rabbet every time.

Dado Cuts—A circular saw can make dado cuts and grooves with ease, and saves time by eliminating hand chiseling the inside of the slot. The critical steps are adjusting the depth of cut and placing the kerf properly.

Clamp the material and draw two parallel lines defining the edges of the dado. Adjust the blade so it cuts as deep a groove as you need. Use an edge guide and carefully make the first cut along one line so the kerf is between the two drawn lines. Do the same cut on the other line. After the two side cuts, you can make several cuts between them to clean out the groove. You don't need an edge guide, but you should take care not to hit the side of the dado. Once you've cut out most of the stock, you can either move the saw sideways to clean up the groove or remove the waste with a hand chisel. Either way the pieces should match and make a perfect dado.

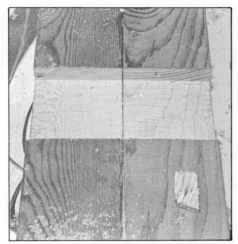

The finished dadoes should match.

The fit should produce a perfect joint.

Lap Cuts—Variations or combinations of dado and rabbet cuts are used to make a lap joint. Sometimes both pieces in a lap joint are cut and careful matching of width and depth of cut is essential. One trick is to cut both pieces at the same time to get a perfect match.

Suppose you want to cross two 2x4s at a 90 degree angle, and you want them flush when joined. This requires a *half-lap* joint. Cross the pieces and mark where they intersect by drawing a pencil across the corners they make. Separate the boards and clamp them side by side so the scribed pencil lines make two straight lines across both boards.

Measure the thickness of the wood, for a 2x4 this is 1-5/8 inches, and set the depth of the blade to *half* that thickness. Use the same cutting method described for the dado cut and cut both pieces of wood. When all the stock is cleared out, the pieces should match exactly.

Other Joints—The circular saw can be used for most joints, but for certain cuts it is impractical. You can make various tenons, but the mortise must be made with other tools such as a combination of drill and chisel, or a router and chisel. Any joint or cut that does not have to be cut through, such as in a blind dado or dovetails, requires extra handwork to complete the corners of the cuts. When planning a job, choose joints you can do easily with the tools at hand. If the job demands others, use the tool that does it best.

ACCESSORIES

You can convert a circular saw into a stationary table saw by turning it upside down and fastening it under a table. This feature is a real plus because some jobs are easier to do with a mounted saw. On long cuts, using your circular saw as a table saw leaves your hands free to guide the lumber.

You can make a special table for the saw or add it to the workbench project shown in Chapter 11. Ready-made tables are also available. If you buy a table, select carefully and buy one which is well built and heavy enough to give steady support.

MAINTENANCE

An important safety feature of the circular saw, the retractable blade guard, must be scrupulously checked each time you use the saw. Sawdust can build up in it and make the retracted guard stick in place. The guard must work well every time to avoid an accident when you set the still-spinning saw-blade down after making a cut. Before you even plug in the saw, make sure the guard swings freely. Occasional lubrication is also a help. Follow the manufacturer's suggestions.

It's really very simple to convert your portable saw to a very creditable table model. The table and mount you see here were built using the plans in the Projects Chapters.

Or, if you don't feel that confident about building your own table, here's one you can buy in a kit. The assembly time takes about an hour. When you're finished you've got a first-rate table saw. Sears sells this particular model.

CIRCULAR SAWS

MAKE/MODEL	HP	AMP	RPM	MAXIMUM BLADE DIAMETER IN INCHES	DEPTH OF CUT IN INCHES 90°	45°	USE
Black & Decker							
7300	.50	5	4000	5-1/2	1-3/4	1-1/8	Light
7308	1.33	9	5300	7-1/4	2-7/8	1-7/8	Medium
7390	1.50	9	5300	7-1/4	2-7/16	1-7/8	Medium
7394	1.62	10	5300	7-1/4	2-7/16	1-7/8	Heavy
7356	2.00	10	5300	7-1/4	2-7/17	1-7/8	Heavy
7396	2.00	10	5500	6-1/2	2-1/16	1-3/4	Industrial
7397	2.25	11.5	5500	7-1/4	2-7/17	2	Industrial
7398	2.50	12	5500	8	2-13/16	2-1/4	Industrial
Millers Falls							
SP6075		10	5000	7-1/4	2-3/8	1-15/16	Heavy
SP826		10	5500	6-1/2	2	1-11/16	Industrial
SP827		12	5500	7-1/4	2-3/8	2	Industrial
SP828		13	5500	8-1/4	2-7/8	2-9/32	Industrial
SP877		12	5500	7-1/4	2-3/8	2	Industrial

CIRCULAR SAWS — cont.

MAKE/MODEL	HP	AMP	RPM	MAXIMUM BLADE DIAMETER IN INCHES	DEPTH OF CUT IN INCHES 90°	45°	USE
Penney							
1650A	1.25	9	4200	7-1/4	2-3/8	1-7/8	Light
0348A	1.75	10	4600	7-1/4	2-3/8	1-7/8	Medium
3664A	2.00	10	5500	7-1/4	2-3/8	1-7/8	Heavy
9133A	2.25	10	5500	7-1/4	2-3/8	1-7/8	Industrial
Rockwell							
4511	1.25	9	5800	7-1/4	2-3/8	1-7/8	Medium
4525	1.50	9	5800	7-1/4	2-3/8	1-7/8	Medium
4572	2.00	10	5800	7-1/4	2-3/8	1-7/8	Heavy
4577	2.00	10	5800	7-1/4	2-3/8	1-7/8	Heavy
4586		11	5800	6-1/2	2-1/16	1-5/8	Industrial
4587		12	5800	7-1/4	2-7/16	1-29/32	Industrial
4588		13	5800	8-1/4	2-15/16	2-1/4	Industrial
4596		11	5800	6-1/2	2-1/16	1-5/8	Industrial
4597		12	5800	7-1/4	2-7/16	1-29/32	Industrial
4598		13	5800	8-1/4	2-15/16	2-1/4	Industrial
Sears							
1180	1.25	8.5	5000	7	2-3/16	1-13/16	Light
1181	1.50	9	5100	7	2-3/16	1-13/16	Light
1082	1.60	9.5	5200	7	2-3/16	1-13/16	Medium
1085	1.75	10	5200	7-1/4	2-3/8	1-15/16	Medium
1086	2.00	11	5400	7-1/4	2-1/4	1-15/16	Heavy
1188	2.13	12	5500	7-1/2	2-9/16	2-3/16	Industrial
1189	.37	3	7000	4	7/8		Heavy
Shopmate							
T2400	1.00	8	4500	7-1/4	2-7/16	2-1/8	Light
T2402	1.33	9	5500	7-1/4	2-7/16	2-1/16	Medium
T2403	1.50	10	5000	7-1/4	2-7/16	2-1/16	Heavy
Skil							
538	1.40	9	4500	7-1/4	2-3/8	1-7/8	Light
534	1.50	9	5000	6-1/2	2-3/16	1-3/4	Medium
574	1.75	10	4600	7-1/4	2-3/8	1-7/8	Medium
537	1.87	10	5100	7-1/4	2-3/8	1-7/8	Heavy
552	2.25	10	5800	6-1/2	2-1/8	1-3/4	Industrial
553	2.30	12	5200	7-1/4	2-3/8	1-7/8	Industrial
554	2.50	13	5200	8-1/4	2-7/8	2-1/8	Industrial
Stanley							
80-278	2.00	12	5500	7-1/4	2-1/4	2-1/8	Industrial
90-288	2.50	13	5500	8-1/4	2-13/16	2-3/8	Industrial
90-612	2.50	12	5500	6-1/2	2-1/8	1-3/4	Heavy
90-714	2.75	13	5000	7-1/4	2-1/2	2	Heavy
Ward							
80001	.80	5	4000	5-1/2	1-3/4	1-1/8	Light
80005	1.33	9	5300	7-1/4	2-7/16	1-7/8	Medium
80006	1.5	9.5	5300	7-1/4	2-7/16	1-7/8	Medium
80007	1.75	10	5300	7-1/4	2-7/16	1-7/8	Medium
Wen							
961	2.00	11	5100	7-1/4	2-3/8	1-7/8	Medium
963	2.00	11	5100	7-1/4	2-3/8	1-7/8	Medium
962	2.00	12	5100	7-1/4	2-3/8	1-7/8	Heavy

7
Sanders

Almost every building project requires some sanding, either to shape a piece for a perfect fit, or to give your project a professional finish. Sanding works by using an abrasive to make smaller and smaller cuts in the surface of the material until it looks and feels smooth. Often a single job will require several separate types of sanding. You *can* do it by hand, but it's much easier and faster with power tools.

TYPES AVAILABLE

There are three basic types of sanders: *disc, belt,* and *vibrator* or *finish.* To some extent, each can perform the job of the others. However, each sander has certain functions unique to that particular tool, making ownership of all three very desirable. I'll discuss all three types, pointing out their advantages and various uses, and give a few hints so you can get the most from each tool.

First let's talk about the heart of all the sanders, regardless of the type, the abrasives.

ABRASIVES

There are basically six different types of abrasives, each designed for a different use. And, as is often the case, the more expensive abrasive may prove to be the cheapest in the long run.

Flint, which is actually quartz, is a natural abrasive. Sandpaper made with flint has the lowest cost per sheet of any sandpaper. It is made with a paper backing and is not waterproof. Although it is not recommended for power sanders because the backing wears out in a

These are the three types of portable sanders to be discussed in this chapter. From left to right they are the belt, the disc, and the vibrator or finish sander.

short time, flint paper can be used by cutting a standard sheet with scissors to fit a vibrator sander. Sanding softwood is the only real use I can think of for this low-grade material.

Garnet is also a natural abrasive. Garnet paper is recommended for sanding wood and is used dry because it is not waterproof. It has a reddish-brown color and has a paper backing. It comes pre-cut to fit most power sanders. Garnet is a bit more costly than flint, but it's also much harder and will last longer.

Emery is available with either a cloth or paper backing. It is good for removing rust. Or you can use it as a metal polisher. Emery works best with a little water as a lubricant.

Aluminum-Oxide is a man-made grit noted for its hardness and long life. It is available with either cloth or paper backing. The initial cost per sheet is higher than garnet paper, but because of the durability

of aluminum-oxide paper, it's much cheaper in the long run, particularly if you plan on doing a lot of sanding. It can be used for wet or dry sanding. For belt sanders it is identified by its brown grit. If you purchase aluminum oxide in sheets, the color is white. This is probably the most popular all-around sandpaper used by the home craftsman today.

Silicon-Carbide is a man-made abrasive that is harder than emery. It is black and bonded to a waterproof backing, making it perfect for wet or dry sanding. In fact it is sometimes called *wet or dry* paper. Use it wet for removing paint, but be sure to wipe off the sanded surface occasionally to remove the paste-like mixture of paint and water that builds up. You can also wash out the paper to prevent clogging and to ensure peak performance. Automobile finishes are sanded with silicon-carbide to achieve their mirror-like gloss. This abrasive is ideal for sanding undercoats and primers, or any fine work.

Tungsten-Carbide is the toughest, most durable and fastest-cutting abrasive. It is sold in thin discs or strips to fit most machine sanders. This man-made grit resists clogging, is almost indestructible and is definitely best for any project requiring removing a lot of stock by sanding. Tungsten-carbide is also the highest-priced abrasive, but it will outlast anything else by 10 to 1, making it cheaper in the long run. Paint removal is a "piece of cake" with a tungsten-carbide disc. Shaping or grinding fiberglass is almost a joy with this wonder abrasive.

ABRASIVE USE CHART

Abrasive	Use
Tungsten-Carbide	Remove paint and varnish. Shape and sand fiberglass. Grind cement. Shape and sand all woods.
Silicon-Carbide	Sand and polish hard metals. Sand paint and varnish. Sand glass. Sand and smooth fiberglass.
Aluminum-Oxide	Sanding and shaping all wood, plastic, fiberglass, paint and varnish. Sanding soft metals.
Emery	Polishing and sanding metal. Removing rust and scale.
Garnet	Sanding all woods, spackle wall fillers, and plastic.
Flint	Removing paint and varnish, old finishes. Sanding soft woods.

GRIT SIZE

Grit size determines abrasive coarseness. Abrasive is sifted at the factory before it is glued to the backing. The smaller the grit, the finer the abrasive. Grit-size designa-

tions can be confusing, however. Some sandpapers are numbered from a large coarse grit of 12, to a super-fine, almost jeweler's polishing rouge, of 600. Some manufacturers simplify the grading system by identifying their produce as *Coarse, Medium, Fine* or *Extra Fine*. Other manufacturers use an older system that ranges from 4-1/2, for very coarse grit, to 10/10, for extra-fine grit. The charts on this page will help you familiarize yourself with the various grits and grading systems. All sanding jobs should begin with a coarse or medium grit and progress to a fine abrasive.

ABRASIVE GRADING CHART

English Grade	Grit Number	Number
Very Coarse	12	4-½
	16	4
	20	3-½
	24	3
	30	2-½
Coarse	36	2
	40	1-½
	50	1
Medium	60	½
	80	1/0
	100	2/0
Fine	120	3/0
	150	4/0
	180	5/0
Extra-Fine	220	6/0
	240	7/0
	280	8/0
	320	9/0
	360	—
	400	10/0
	500	—
	600	—

COATING

Most abrasive coatings are *closed-coat*. That means the grit particles are packed closely together to form a high-density surface. Closed-coat abrasives are fast-cutting and durable, and are used for most types of sanding. However, for removing paint or working with resin-filled woods, *open-coat* sandpaper is

more advisable. With open-coat types only about 50 to 70 percent of the backing is impregnated with grit, making the paper far less likely to clog. You will have to slow down when using an open-coat abrasive because there is less grit on the surface, but the money you save in sandpaper will more than compensate for the little extra time to get the job done.

CARING FOR ABRASIVES

All abrasives will give better life if you give them a little care. Whenever a coating becomes clogged, slapping it with the flat of your hand or scrubbing it with a stiff-bristle brush will remove most of the built-up dust. Of course, never do this with the machine running.

Sanding belts may even be washed with a mild laundry soap and luke-warm water. Scrub vigorously with a stiff brush to loosen up the saw-dust. Pat the belt dry with a cloth or paper towel and remount on the sander to dry. This will prevent shrinking.

Even when the sandpaper appears all used up, you can still get more mileage out of it by treating it as a finer grade paper A throwaway *medium* can become a perfectly usable *fine.*

GENERAL TECHNIQUES

The whole idea of sanding is to get a smooth finish. A rough piece of wood, rusty metal or even a coat of primer paint must be sanded to get a smooth professional gloss. Start with a coarse or medium grit and work by stages to a fine sandpaper for the final finish. For example, you might want to give your plywood box a really beautiful finish. After an initial sanding with 80-grit medium paper, apply two coats of sealer. After the sealer dries, sand it with 100-grit medium paper and coat it with varnish. Sand that surface with 150-grit fine paper and add another coat of varnish. Sand once more with 220-grit extra-fine paper and give it a final coat of varnish. Finally, rub the surface with pumice to remove any specs of dust. This will produce a mirror-like finish on plywood. However, with a rough piece of fir, you might have to start with a 40- or 50-grit coarse paper and work to the 80-grit medium paper to get the necessary smoothness before applying sealer.

If you find a rough spot, you may have to sand again with a coarser grit. Then you must work the material back through the various stages of coarseness until the spot matches the rest of the finish in smoothness. If you go from 50-grit coarse paper to 220-grit extra-fine, the 220 will not be able to remove enough material to rub out the scratch marks left by the 50-grit coarse paper. You will have to use a grade in between those two to finish the job.

The same rule applies to power sanders. A disc or belt sander is used first, moving from a coarse to a medium sandpaper. The finish sander is brought in last with the medium to fine abrasives. This will assure a smooth, even finish.

LUBRICATION

Another aid in sanding is to use water as a lubricant with waterproof papers. This makes the cutting easier and faster for the abrasive. Water also seems to give a surface a more uniform smoothness. Naturally, water will only work on a nonporous stock. A light machine oil works well with emery cloth on bare metal.

WORK WITH THE GRAIN

When working with wood, always try to sand *with* the grain, particularly in the final stages. Sanding in any other direction raises the wood fibers and makes an uneven surface, or leaves scratch marks from the abrasive itself. The only time cross-grain sanding is acceptable is when you must remove a lot of stock to create a basic shape or thickness. In that case, be sure to leave enough extra material so the final sanding stages will eliminate all the cross-grain marks left by the sandpaper.

A disc sander will cut cross-grain because of its circular motion.

That's why it is only used for rough sanding. Belt sanders can be used either across or with the grain. A vibrator sander makes a fine pattern, ideal for the final stages of your project. Remember—sand *with* the grain for the best finish.

SANDING SEVERAL PIECES

If you have several pieces all the same size and it's important they remain the same size after they're sanded, clamp them together in a stack and sand all at once. You can keep the sharp edges on the outside pieces by placing a piece of scrap wood on each end of the stack. Everything in between will be square when you remove the clamps. When a clamp won't work, you can drill a small hole through the pieces and hold them with a long bolt and nut.

OPERATING YOUR SANDER

Always start your power sander before allowing it to come into contact with the material to be sanded. After sanding, always make sure the sander has stopped before setting it down. A belt sander can walk right off the bench and crash on the floor if you fail to heed this little rule.

Let the sander do the work. The tool's weight is usually sufficient to provide the sandpaper with the friction necessary to cut the stock. This is less fatiguing to you and produces the best results. About the only things gained by excessive bearing down are gouge marks on

the wood and frustration for you.

Another safety point: Always clamp the stock to be sanded or secure the sander. It's very dangerous to try to work freehand with both part and power tool. It is also highly inaccurate and assures sloppy joints and surfaces. For safety and accuracy, one or the other must be anchored.

Each type of power sander can perform some of the work of the others. A disc sander can produce an acceptable surface for a finish sander to smooth, which eliminates the need for a belt sander. A belt sander can cut like a disc sander and in some cases you can get as smooth a surface as a finish sander. Although slower, a finish sander with a coarse grit can do small shaping chores and still do finishing work. You will have to decide which will work best for you. A good finish sander is certainly handy for final smoothing. A belt sander is a nice tool that lets you go beyond plywood and work with the more exotic hardwoods, such as Burma teak. All sanders have a place and function. Believe me, once you own all three types you'll appreciate their uses, and probably wonder how you ever managed without them.

DISC SANDERS

There are four basic types of disc sanders: *sanders, polishers, sander/polishers,* and *grinder/polishers.*

Disc sanders come in several sizes, anything from a small 1/4-inch drill to the angled drive industrial model shown in the background.

The difference between the various types is primarily a matter of power and speed. A simple sander will have a 6-inch disc, be fairly lightweight, and have a single-speed 3/4hp motor turning about 4500 RPM. A similar polisher will be identical to the sander, except the speed is slower, about 3500 RPM. The lower RPM is required for the best buffing results. Most units sold today are two-speed polisher/sanders. The largest models have a 1-1/2hp motor that spins a 9-inch wheel at either 3600 or 4600 RPM. These two-handed monsters weigh over 14 pounds. The sandpaper is usually held by a screw in the center of the disc.

Small polisher/sanders resemble an electric drill in appearance, except the handle is located farther forward. This gives the operator better balance and control. They are usually slightly heavier than an electric drill because a more powerful motor is required.

Grinder/polishers are even heavier and use a right-angle drive to turn the sander. One handle is located at the rear of the motor and another in the front, over the disc. This design may take a little getting used to before you gain proficiency.

Disc sanders are always used for initial rough sanding. They cannot

PAINTING

To me, painting is the most difficult shop chores. I can turn out a piece of furniture that's a cabinet maker's delight. But when it comes to painting, I always approach the task with dread. If you're like me, let me offer a few tips I've learned.

Preparation is almost the whole ballgame in painting. The surface has to be clean, smooth and free of any dust. A vacuum cleaner is a big help in removing dust from wood. So is a *tack cloth*. A tack cloth is cheesecloth impregnated with a mildly sticky mixture that lifts dust off the surface without leaving a chemical film. Tack cloths can be purchased at almost any paint or hardware store.

Always try to paint out of the wind. While you do need ventilation to carry the fumes away—you don't need a minor hurricane to bring in bugs and dirt on your about-to-be beautiful surface.

Use good quality brushes and keep them clean. A good brush will give fine service for years with proper care. I'll explain how to clean and store brushes at the end of this dissertation.

Fill all cracks, seams and holes with glazing putty or wood dough. Some places will take two or three applications before they are level with the surface. It's better to put on thin layers. They dry faster and smoother than thick gobs.

Sand the wood smooth—working the sandpaper from coarse (if required) up to at least 80 grit. Seal the wood with two coats of a good, clear sealer. Sand between coats with a 100 grit paper. Use a vacuum cleaner and tack cloth to wipe off all traces of dust.

Apply one or two coats of white undercoat, sand after each dries with 100 grit paper.

For the final color coats, I've had great success with a combination of foam roller and brush. I realize this will kill some of your purist friends, but it really works well. Here's how it's done: After the undercoat is smooth as glass, buy three cheap, throwaway 3-inch rollers and roll on a coat of the final color. Roll on a couple of square feet, put the roller down and pick up the dry brush. Very lightly brush the rolled-on paint. The brush will wipe out the pattern of the roller and leave you an even, hand-brushed finish. Roll on some more paint and follow it up with the brush until you've completed painting. For a really first-class job you should figure on two or three coats of color. Sand between coats with 200 grit paper.

When the final coat has dried, remove any dust or grit that may have settled on the paint with a very soft cloth and some pumice powder or a fine polishing compound.

If you follow these steps, your paint job will reflect the care and craftsmanship that went into the rest of the project.

CLEANUP

Throw the rollers away after each use. They're almost cheaper than the thinner you use to clean them with.

For the brush, get a clean coffee can and some paper towels. First squeeze all the excess paint out of the brush, using a paper towel. Pour about one inch of thinner in the can and soak the brush. Use your fingers to knead the bristles, loosening up all the paint stuck between the hairs. Pour the polluted thinner into a larger can or bottle. Shake and wipe the brush dry with another paper towel. Repeat this step three or four times until the thinner remains clear when the brush is resoaked.

If you're not going to use the brush for a while, wrap the bristles in a paper towel to protect them from damage. Either lay the brush flat in a drawer or hang it up by the handle with the paper wrapping still in place.

In a few days the thinner in the large container will clear up with all the paint pigment settling to the bottom. Carefully pour the clear thinner back into the original can to be used again and clean up the paint residue with still more paper towels. This will give you a little more mileage out of your thinner and save you a few bucks.

The proper angle to operate a disc sander is almost flat with the front portion doing the cutting. The sander will buck and spin all over your stock if laid perfectly flat on the surface.

give the smooth finish required for most projects, but for fast shaping of wood, fiberglass and body-putty, or removing paint and rust, they are hard to beat. Rough wood can be smoothed for final finishing with a finish sander by a disc sander. Exterior surfaces such as fences or siding may be painted after smoothing with the disc sander. Additional sanding is usually unnecessary.

When you use a disc sander, hold the sanding wheel at a slight angle to the surface of the work. Only 1/4 to 1/3 of the wheel should be in contact with the material at any one time. The opposite side of the disc should be 1/4 to 1/2 inch above the stock. Too steep an angle will cause bucking and the sander will walk all over the place.

As I said earlier, let the machine do the work. You just provide the guidance. On large areas, use long straight strokes overlapping each other by about half the diameter of the disc. With wood, stroke parallel to the grain. Even though the turning disc is cutting across the grain, stroking with the grain will produce a more even surface for the final sanding.

Wear safety glasses. The sander throws out a lot of fine particles. If you're working with fiberglass or metal, a nose and mouth mask is a good idea. Fiberglass is nasty to breathe and very hard on your lungs. Disposable dust masks are available. They're comfortable and only cost around a quarter.

To keep the sandpaper from tearing while you are working, I recommend you use a *disc adhesive*. It is similar to contact cement and keeps the sandpaper flat against the rubber backing pad. This will extend the life of the abrasive.

Removing paint and varnish requires an open-coat sandpaper and low speed. This will reduce paint build-up on the disc. Start with a coarse grit and work towards a medium. To remove paint from soft wood, use an open-coat, medium grit and progress to finer grits. This will help prevent possible damage to the wood.

Rockwell Corporation makes an open-coat Tungsten-Carbide metal disc that is excellent for heavy sanding or shaping. It's practically non-clogging. I've used it on uncured fiberglass and was amazed at the results.

I got my wife to polish the car again, only this time I let her use a bigger, two-speed 6-inch model. She said it worked faster than the drill attachment. You've got to be nice to your spouse; I may buy her a new table saw for Christmas.

ROTARY POLISHING

You can achieve deep lustre when you use your disc sander as a polisher. Not only on your car, but even wall panelling can benefit from this feature.

Use the lowest speed and hold the buffer almost flat on the surface. Work with broad strokes in a back and forth motion. Avoid

making circles because the sander will leave swirls that will have to be re-buffed again. Don't bear down on the polisher, let it do the work. Just guide it.

Make sure the wax or buffing compound you choose is suitable for machine use. Some waxes are buffed when dry, others while still wet. Follow the directions on the bottle or can. The waxes you apply by hand will mat and clog the lamb's wool disc. If this happens to you, a little mild soap and warm water, and some light scrubbing will clean the wool. Wring out the excess water and let it dry overnight. It should be as good as new.

BENCH-MOUNTING YOUR DISC SANDER

Many disc sanders can be converted to an excellent stationary grinder or polisher with a bench mounting bracket. The sander's speed and power make it superior to an ordinary drill motor used the same way. In addition to using the grinding wheel for sharpening and the lamb's wool pad for buffing, a rotary wire wheel can be attached to the sander motor for a multitude of jobs such as cleaning up auto parts, polishing rusty metal or stripping paint.

Stanley makes this swivel disc attachment to be used on a drill motor. I tried it and it worked well. An optimum amount of abrasive surface was always in contact with the wood.

USING YOUR DRILL

The disc sander has many uses, but if you only need one occasionally, consider using a 3/8-inch drill

Back to the drill and angled drive. Instead of a buffer we've attached a sanding disc. It works very well for occasional use.

with a sanding disc attachment. It will do many small jobs as well, but not as fast, as the disc sander. A right-angle drive with 2:1 gearing will double your drill's speed, further helping the sanding disc. The drill will not replace the disc sander for speed, power or endurance, but it can be used on *some* jobs without over-straining the drill motor. And it will save you the investment until you need a disc sander as part of your shop.

BELT SANDERS

This is the powerhouse of the sanding tools. Properly handled, it can do rough work like the disc sander and handle finishing jobs with equal ease. Removing varnish and resurfacing an old floor is no problem. Surfacing and smoothing rough wood or rounding a 4x4 can be accomplished quickly and easily with this sander. You can fit a door, sharpen tools or polish metal. Mounted on your bench, this sander is excellent for finishing edges and small parts.

A belt sander usually uses a 3x21-inch or 2x24-inch continuous sanding belt. A wide range of grits is available to suit various applications. The belt is driven by the rear roller. The forward roller acts as an idler and keeps tension on the belt. It is adjustable to ensure proper belt tracking. In addition, the belt passes over a 3x5-inch or 4x6-inch platen where the cutting takes place.

Sander speed is measured in surface feet per minute (SFPM). A typical 3-inch sander with a 1hp

motor will have a speed of 1300 SFPM. A 4-inch model with a 1-1/2hp motor will run at about 1500 SFPM. Variable-speed control is a useful feature available on some sanders.

Make sure the door is securely wedged open and you've a good grip on the sander. Use very light pressure until the area that is binding has been removed.

Here's a close-up of the business side of a belt sander evening up some random blocks of wood.

As you can see, the blocks are now flush with each other. A vibrator sander can be used to clean the marks left by the coarse belt.

A little arithmetic will tell you that the sanding area of the 3-inch model is about 15 square inches, compared to 24 square inches for a 4-inch sander. The large unit also has an extra 200 SFPM. This translates to about twice the sanding speed of the 3-inch machine. But

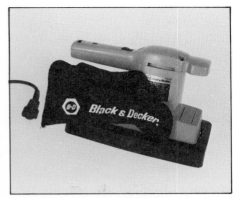

A dust collector can help you keep your shop area clean.

the bigger sander may weigh as much as 4 pounds more than the smaller model. This is an important consideration if you anticipate sanding the side of a wall or fence. The heavier sander will tire you out a lot sooner even though it will cover more area in a shorter period of time. A big advantage to the larger unit is it will sand flatter and have less tendency to gouge the wood or to produce a wavy surface.

Many models offer a *dust collector* as standard equipment or as an optional accessory. This is attractive because the belt sander throws out a lot of sawdust. A dust bag attachment can save in cleanup. If you're like me, a dust collector also cuts down on sneezing.

Some manufacturers offer a stand for their belt sanders, another handy extra, particularly for sanding small parts. In page 64 you'll find photos for a small stand that works well for me.

LOADING AND ADJUSTING

Installing a sanding belt is not complicated, but it has to be done right. Make sure the sander is unplugged before you change belts. Next, either squeeze the two rollers together or rest the sander vertically on a bench and press down on the front wheel until it locks in a retracted position. Then you can easily remove the old belt.

On the inside of the new sanding belt you'll see an arrow which shows the direction the belt should travel. Mount the belt with the arrow pointing toward the rear of the

To change a belt, first unplug the sander. Squeeze the rollers together to remove the belt.

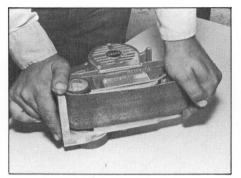

Put on a new belt. On this model the front roller is pressed sideways to return the roller to its normal extended position.

machine as it passes over the platen. Release the front roller so it springs back to its normal extended position. This is accomplished differently on different makes. Usually there is a lever on the side of the sander. Sometimes a sideways push on the roller will pop it out of the retracted position. Be very careful of the metal spring plate covering the platen. It becomes razor sharp from the continuous passing of the sanding belt. A careless move can give you a nasty cut.

Plug the sander in and start it up. Turn the sander upside down and check how the new belt is tracking. If you want to move the belt left or right, turn the knob on the side of the machine while the sander is running. The knob changes the idler-wheel angle. Some adjustment may be necessary until the new belt is broken in. However, if the belt won't stay in alignment and you continually have to make adjustments, take the sander to a repair shop. You may have a problem with the unit itself.

When the belt is removed, the platen will spring out. Watch for sharp edges.

Connect the sander to a power source, turn it upside down and start it up to check how well the new belt is tracking. Adjustments are made by turning the knurled screw on the side of the body while the machine is running.

Use both hands when sanding with this tool. It's got a lot of power and traction. It will walk away from you if handled carelessly.

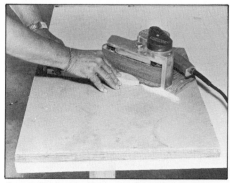

A small piece of scrap plywood and some particle board was all I needed to make this sanding table.

USING THE BELT SANDER

Let's assume that the belt is tracking true and you're ready to begin.

First, clamp down the stock to be sanded.

Next, put on your safety glasses.

Now, using both hands, turn on the sander and lower it to the material. Keep it moving steadily back and forth over the surface. Stopping will gouge or produce a wavy finish on your project. When you get to the edge of the material, lift the sander, but keep it level. Otherwise, the weight of the machine will tend to round off sharp corners and edges.

Move the sander with the grain for the smoothest results. Sanding across the grain will speed the cut if you've got a long way to go, but it will make a rougher surface. Always finish up by sanding with the grain.

You can clamp your belt sander upside down in a vise and use it as a grinder.

If this doesn't suit your needs, consider purchasing a ready-made stand. Several companies offer them as accessories.

REMOVING PAINT

First, use a little paint remover and a scraper on the old surface to get rid of most of the excess paint. You will save time, money and sandpaper. Then use the belt sander to remove the remaining paint and varnish. Select a coarse, open-coat abrasive belt for heavy paint build-up, or a medium, open-coat belt for the lighter varnishes. If the sanding belt starts to clog from old paint, stop sanding.

SANDING METAL

Techniques for sanding metal are basically the same as for sanding wood. The major difference is the choice of abrasive belt. Use silicon-carbide, emery or aluminum-oxide abrasive when working with metal. They're stronger and will stand up better than other types.

If your sander has a dust collector, make sure you empty the sawdust before sanding metal. The combination of sawdust and hot metal sparks could start a fire.

Special belts and polishing compounds are available for buffing. Stanley and Black & Decker are two of several manufacturers who sell both. Follow the directions provided with the product for trouble-free operation.

FINISH SANDERS

This lightweight tool is properly called a *finish sander,* although it is also called a *vibrator* or *pad sander.* A finish sander won't remove heavy stock or shape like a disc or belt sander. But it will give you a smooth surface that, combined with the paint or varnish of your choice, will highlight and enhance your project.

Finish sanders are probably the easiest and safest of all power tools to use: just turn them on, and go. And they do make a big difference in final finishing.

CHOOSING A FINISH SANDER

These sanders come in several shapes and sizes. Some large models use a 1/2 sheet of sandpaper and are great for big areas. A few models accept only 1/4 of the standard sandpaper sheet. However, the most

The smallest vibrator sander uses 1/4 sheet of standard size sandpaper, the largest takes a full 1/2 sheet. Another popular size handling 1/3 of a sheet is not shown. They all work well. Select whichever feels the most comfortable.

Many finish sanders utilizing either a 1/3 or a 1/2 sheet also feature dual action modes, giving you the option of selecting orbital or in-line sanding strokes by the flick of a switch or twist of a screw.

sheet. Sandpaper is held on the pad by clamps. Follow the manufacturers directions for changing paper.

Weight is again a factor to consider before purchasing. The bigger models are more powerful and heavier, but they cover more area faster. Many models are designed to be used with two hands. This is to give you better *control* over the sander, not so you can apply more force when sanding.

Finish sanders can be used on wood, metal, fiberglass or paint—wherever a good finish is desired. This tool is ideally suited for fine sanding between coats of paint, whether on wood or metal. Re-painting your car or refrigerator is easier to do with the help of a finish sander. The weight of a sander is usually all that's necessary for good sanding. Bearing down will mar the surface and those scratches will

have to be sanded out. No use creating more work for yourself.

This sander is excellent for sharpening chisels and knives. Use a rigid pad and a fine grit. A little lubricant—water or light machine oil—will make the blade edge that much sharper. Secure the sander to your bench before sharpening.

SANDING PATTERNS

Two different types of sanding patterns are used by finish sanders. The *orbital type* sands in very tiny circles. *Reciprocating* sands in a back-and-forth movement. The orbital will do a faster job, but the reciprocating model will produce a finer finish. Most finish sanders are available as either orbital or reciprocating types. A few offer both motions with a selector switch. You can start off in an orbital mode and finish by using the reciprocating pattern, moving with the grain for a satin-smooth finish. These dual-action models seem to offer the best of both worlds.

I personally like the heavy-duty, lightweight orbital sander from Rockwell. It is designed for one-hand operation, and uses a small 4x4-inch pad. Yet, the motor is powerful enough to drive the sander at 12,000 RPM. The sanding pattern is so fine, the swirls it makes can only be seen through a magnifying glass.

SELECTING AN ABRASIVE

As with the belt sander, the type of grit you use determines the finish you'll get. Start with a coarse or medium grit and work up to a very fine grit. You may even wet sand between coats if you want a mirror-like finish. Don't let water get in the motor or cooling vents of the sander when wet sanding. I also recommend you wear rubber gloves as added protection against possible electric shock.

Most sanders are designed to work right up to a vertical edge. The side of the sander that does not chatter as you sand to the obstruction is the side to use close to an edge.

ACCESSORIES

There are few accessories available or needed for most finish sanders. A dust collector is about the only major extra offered. A lamb's wool polishing pad is also sometimes available.

One nice, inexpensive addition is a pad with adhesive on the sanding side. This allows you to change sandpaper by peeling off the old paper and sticking on a new sheet. If you're doing a lot of sanding, changing papers can become tiring and time consuming. The 3M Corporation has come up with an adhesive *pad* that you install on your sander as you would a single sheet of sandpaper. You can quick-change papers by just pulling the old sheet off the pad and sticking the new one. You must use 3M's companion sandpaper to make it work. This paper is also available for disc sanders.

FINISH SANDERS (VIBRATOR)

MAKE/MODEL	HP	AMP	ORBITS PER MINUTE	PORTION OF STANDARD SHEET	USE	FEATURES
Black & Decker						
7404	.15	1.5	10,000	1/3	Light	Orbital only
7432	.15	1.5	10,000	1/3	Light	Orbital only; Polishing pad; Detachable cord
7480	.34	3.0	4000	1/2	Medium	Orbital only; Detachable cord
7490	.34	3.0	4000	1/2	Medium	Dual action; Detachable cord
7456	.34	3.0	4000	1/2	Medium	Dual action; Detachable cord
7465	.25	3.0	10,000	1/2	Heavy	
Millers Falls						
SP6080		1.7	10,000	1/3	Heavy	
SP9080		2.0	10,000	1/2	Industrial	Dual action
Penney						
2744A		1.2	8400	1/4	Light	
6675A		2.5	4000	1/3	Medium	Dual- action
0938A		2.0	10,000	1/3	Medium	Ball bearing construction
Rockwell						
4401	.10	1.3	10,000	1/3	Medium	Easy change paper clamps
4420	.10	1.3	12,000	1/3	Medium	Easy change paper clamps
4480		1.3	12,000	1/4	Medium	
4440	.15	1.5	12,000	1/3	Medium	Easy change paper clamps
4485		2.3	10,000	1/2	Heavy	Easy change paper clamps
Sears						
1062	.70	1.3	9200	1/3	Very light	
1163	.20	2.0	4000	1/3	Light	Dual action
1164	.20	2.5	4000	1/3	Medium	Dual action
1165	.25	2.8	4000	1/3	Heavy	Dual action; Built-in vacuum
1166	.50	4.0	4000	1/2	Industrial	Dual action; Ball-bearing drive
1168	.50	4.5	4000	1/2	Industrial	Dual action; Built-in vacuum; Ball-bearing drive
Shopmate						
T2502	.25	2.5	3000	1/3	Light	
T2503	.25	2.5	3000	1/3	Light	Dual action
Skil						
439		1.2	8400	1/4	Very light	
490	.20	2.5		1/3	Medium	Dual action
459		2.0	10,000	1/3	Medium	Easy change paper clamps
661		2.0	10,000	1/3	Heavy	Easy change paper clamps
Stanley						
91-036		1.5	4500	1/3	Medium	Not double-insulated
90-501		3.0	11,000	1/2	Heavy	Easy change paper clamps
90-502		3.0	10,500	1/2	Heavy	Easy change paper clamps; Built-in vacuum
Ward						
84003		1.6	10,000	1/3	Medium	
84004		1.6	10,000	1/3	Medium	Sure grip clamps
84005	.25	2.8	4200	1/3	Medium	Dual action
84006	.34	3.0	4000	1/2	Heavy	Dual action
Wen						
310		1.0	7200	1/3	Very light	Straight line only; Not double-insulated
PR30		2.6	4000	1/3	Medium	Dual action

DISC SANDERS & POLISHERS

MAKE/MODEL	HP	AMP	RPM	DISC SIZE IN INCHES	USE	FEATURES
Black & Decker						
7960	1.25	7.0	2400	7	Medium	Single-speed
7971	1.25	7.0	2400	7	Medium	Single-speed; Polisher only
7951	1.25	7.0	4500	7	Medium	Single-speed; Sander only
7965		10.0	4800	7	Heavy	Single-speed; Sander only
7955		6.5	2300	7	Heavy	Single-speed; Polisher only
Millers Falls						
GSP707		5.0	1500	7	Heavy	Single-speed; Polisher/sander
GSP712		7.0	2600	7	Industrial	Single-speed; Sander only
SP710		7.0	2600	7	Industrial	Single-speed; Polisher only; Angle drive
GSP715		7.0	5500	7	Industrial	Single-speed; Sander only; Angle drive
SP7115		6.5	1800	7	Industrial	Single-speed; Polisher only; Angle drive
Penney						
1167A	.67	4.0	1220/ 1550	7	Light	Two-speed
2371A		4.0	1550	9	Medium	Sander/polisher/scrubber
0995A	2.00	10.0	1660/ 2500	7	Industrial	Two-speed
1100A	2.00	10.0	5000	7	Industrial	Sander/grinder
Rockwell						
4710	.34	3.1	2000/2400	6	Medium	Two-speed; Sander/polisher
1084		10.0	4500	7	Industrial	Single-speed; Sander only
1087		10.0	2300	7	Industrial	Single-speed; Polisher only
4770		4.0	4000	7	Industrial	Single-speed; Sander only
4775		4.0	2000	7	Industrial	Single-speed; Polisher only
4790		4.0	4000	6	Industrial	Single-speed; Paint remover
Sears						
1152	.75	5.5	3500/4200	6	Industrial	Two-speed; Sander/polisher; Ball-bearing drive
1156	1.00	8.0	4600	7	Industrial	Single-speed; Sander only; Ball-bearing drive
1157	1.00	8.5	3600/4600	7	Industrial	Two-speed; Sander/polisher; Ball-bearing drive
1158	1.50	9.0	3600/4600	9	Industrial	Two-speed; Sander/polisher; Ball-bearing drive
Shopmate						
T2541	.34	2.8	2000/2500	6	Medium	Two-speed; Sander/polisher
Skil						
914		4.5	12,500	4-1/2	Industrial	Single-speed; Portable grinder
1140		6.5	4500	7	Industrial	Single-speed; Sander only
1145		6.5	2500	7	Industrial	Single-speed; Polisher only
Stanley						
90-368		10.0	6000	7	Industrial	Single-speed; Sander/grinder; Ball bearing drive
Ward						
84312	.34	3.0	2500	6	Light	Single-speed
84312	.34	3.0	2500	8	Light	Single-speed
8166	.67	4.0	1200/ 1550	7	Medium	Two-speed
84311	.67	4.0	5000	9	Medium	Oscillating orbital action
8576	1.75		1600/ 2500	7	Industrial	Two-speed
85271	1.75		5000	7	Industrial	Single-speed
84301	1.75	10.0	4500	7	Industrial	Single-speed; Ball bearing drive
84310	.50	3.7	11,500	4	Heavy	Grinder only
Wen						
942		2.6	1200	6	Very light	Single-speed; Sander/polisher
943	.67	4.0	1210/1500	7	Light	Two-speed; Sander/polisher
2100		2.6		8	Light	Single-speed; Sander/polisher/scrubber
2500		4.0	1550	9	Medium	Single-speed; Sander/polisher/scrubber
1500	2.00	10.0	1600/2500	7	Industrial	Two-speed; Sander/polisher
1503	2.00	10.0	1600/2500	7	Industrial	Two-speed; Sander/polisher
1501	2.00	10.0	5000	7	Industrial	Single-speed; Sander/grinder

BELT SANDERS

MAKE/MODEL	HP	AMP	SURFACE FEET PER MINUTE	BELT SIZE IN INCHES	USE	FEATURES
Black & Decker						
7451	.75	5.2	1200	3x24	Medium	Single-speed; Built-in vacuum
7461	.85	5.5	1050/1250	3x24	Medium	Two-speed; Built-in vacuum
Millers Falls						
830		6.0	1300	3x21	Industrial	Single-speed
840		7.5	1350	4x21	Industrial	Single-speed; Sands flush to baseboard
Penney						
2835A		4.0	1000	3x18	Light	
4555A		5.0	1150	3x21	Medium	Ball bearing construction
4795A		5.5	1000	3x21	Medium	Ball bearing construction; Dust pickup system
Rockwell						
4460	.75	6.5	900	3x21	Heavy	Single-speed
4461	.75	6.5	900	3x21	Heavy	Single-speed; Built-in vacuum
4470		7.0	1300	3x21	Industrial	Single-speed
4471		7.0	1300	3x21	Industrial	Single-speed; Built-in vacuum
Sears						
1172	1.00	7.0	1300	3x21	Heavy	Single-speed; Ball bearing drive
1175	1.00	7.5	1300	3x21	Heavy	Single-speed; Ball bearing drive; Built-in vacuum
1176	1.50	7.5	1500	4x24	Industrial	Single-speed; Ball bearing drive
1178	1.50	7.5	1500	4x24	Industrial	Single-speed; Ball bearing drive
Shopmate						
T2531	1.60	8.0	1375	4x24	Heavy	Single-speed
Skil						
400		7.0	1350	4x21-3/4	Heavy	Single-speed; Built-in vacuum
405		7.0	1350	2x21-3/4	Heavy	Single-speed
594		5.0	1000	3x21	Medium	Single-speed
595	.75	5.5	1000	3x21	Medium	Single-speed; Built-in vacuum
Stanley						
90-031		8.0	1600	3x24	Heavy	Single-speed
90-496		8.5	1100/1275	4x24	Heavy	Two-speed
90-497		9.0	1200	4x24	Heavy	Single-speed; Built-in vacuum
90-321		6.0	900	3x21	Industrial	Single-speed
Ward						
8543	.67	4.0	1000	3x18	Light	
Wen						
919	.67	4.0	1000	3x18	Light	Single-speed

8
Routers

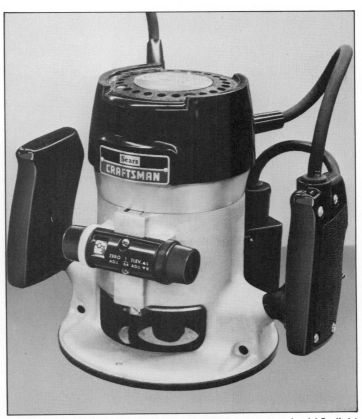

This quality router features micrometer adjustment and a 110v light that shines right on the cutting area.

A router is a fun tool. I say this for two reasons. First, minimum skill is required to see spectacular results. Your work suddenly takes on a professional appearance. Second, a router and your imagination make a very creative combination. It allows you to beautify and dress up otherwise ordinary projects to suit your individual tastes.

I shied away from buying a router for years, partly because of the cost, and partly because I didn't think of them as useful for my particular desires. I was wrong and regret not purchasing one much earlier.

It took a boatbuilding project before I could convince myself of the need and justify the cost. Once I started using the router, I couldn't put it down. Everything I did seemed to require the touch of the router.

Truly, the uses for the router are almost limitless. It will quickly and easily make all the common joints used in woodworking, and it offers a multitude of design possibilities. Dado joints, rabbet joints, even complicated dovetail joints can be quickly and successfully accomplished with a router. It even seems to turn brittle Formica to butter as it trims and melts away the excess overlap.

Scroll work, numbers and letters can be knocked out with the ease of an Old World craftsman—and in about one tenth of the time. Reversing the scrolling procedure will give you beautiful relief work. On

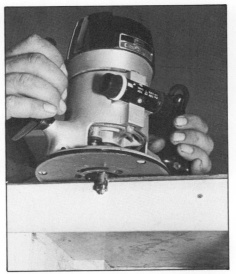

This close-up shows you a tungsten-carbide blade with a roller bearing pilot effortlessly trimming a Formica table top. Work can be done in seconds with a router that would take you hours by hand.

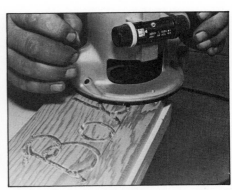

A little freehand styling for a nameplate. If it looks easy—it is.

the practical side, a router will make a mortise for a door hinge faster than most people can sharpen their chisels.

The router is simplicity itself. No gear trains, no fast/slow speeds, no forward/reverse switches, just one direct-drive electric motor that spins at very high speed, up to 35,000 RPM, depending on the model. This motor is controlled by a simple on/off switch and drives a fixed collet chuck that accepts a 1/4-inch shank. Models which take a 1/2-inch shank are usually used for heavy-duty work.

A bit is inserted into the chuck and locked down. The motor and chuck are enclosed in a housing ending in a flat base plate that rests on the material to be cut. Two strong handles are attached to the base plate so the operator can exercise close, firm control while guiding the router. An adjustment and locking device between the motor and the base plate allows you to set the cutting depth. The tolerance of this adjusting device is hundredths of an inch. This is one of the reasons the router is such a precision tool.

Routers come in a variety of sizes, anywhere from 1/3 to 1-1/2 horsepower, with speeds from 18,000 to 35,000 RPM. You probably won't need a large model unless you plan to do an enormous amount of work. A smaller model will not cut as fast as a larger one, and you may have to make several passes over the work instead of one to get the needed depth. But a small model will deliver the same precision as its big brother, and it will cost less.

One major difference between routers is in their bearings. Inexpensive models have *sleeve bearings.* Moderately priced units have *roller bearings.* Only top-quality routers have *ball bearings.* Sleeve bearings are perfectly fine if you plan to use your router only occasionally. For continual hard use, ball bearings are necessary to withstand the load. You decide your requirements and buy the router which seems best for you.

Size makes no difference as far as the quality of work is concerned. The larger model will do it faster and maybe last a little longer.

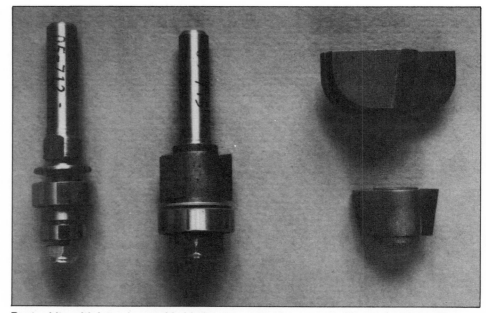

Router bits with interchangeable blades are a good investment. The pilot on the shank at the left unscrews so you can put on various blades. In the center is a bit ready to go. At the right are additional blades.

ROUTER BITS

The cutting bit is the secret of the router's versatility. Different shape and size bits are usually of one-piece design. There is a *shank* on one end and the *cutting blade* or *flutes,* on the other. Bits may also be purchased as a screw together unit. This bit has two or three components consisting of a *shank* with threads on one end, a *cutting blade* and, if needed, a small *pilot bearing.* These parts screw together to make a complete bit. A screw together bit can increase your options and save you a few dollars when buying additional cutting blades. Because you already own a shank and pilot, all you need to buy is additional cutters.

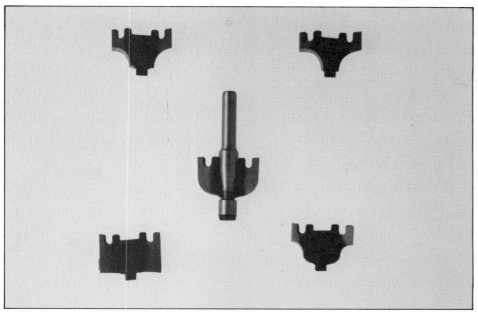

Router bits with interchangeable blades are sold in sets. You simply unscrew the shaft and replace the blade any time you want to change your cut.

The pilot bearing acts as a guide against the edge of the wood, preventing the cutters from removing too much stock.

There is a broad selection of bits to pick from. By careful choosing, many bits can do two or three different jobs. Straight bits can be used for dadoing and making rabbet joints. A 1/2-inch straight bit can cut as wide a groove as you want by just moving the router guide. This eliminates the need for a 3/4-inch or 1-inch bit. A *corner round* bit can be used for beading by changing the pilot to a smaller size. So, you probably won't need more than seven or eight carefully chosen bits to do most of your work.

Pilot—I've used the term *pilot* several times with reference to router bits. A pilot is a round bearing attached to the bottom of the cutting blades. It acts as a guide which allows you to do freehand edge work without any additional attachments. Pilots are a fixed part of the one-piece bits and an optional addition on the Screw Together type. They may be solid round steel, or a roller bearing. With a Screw Together bit, you have the advantage of being able to change to a larger or smaller pilot, or leaving it off altogether. This increases your design flexibility.

Veneer Bits—One cutter you may need is a *veneer bit*. It is always made of carbide to withstand the dulling effect of plastic laminates. A pilot set flush with the cutting blade allows you to trim a table top with surprisingly little effort and time. Veneer bits are sold in two

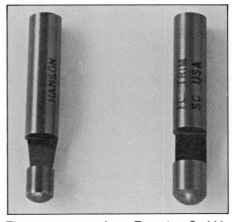

These are one piece Tungsten-Carbide laminate trimmers with fixed pilots.

SELECTING BITS

If you plan to work with soft woods, bits made of *high-speed steel* are adequate. Don't waste your hard-earned money on bits made of lower grade material. They won't hold up and will require frequent replacement.

High-speed steel bits may also be used on hardwoods, but *carbide-tipped bits* retain their sharpness far longer. Carbide-tipped bits cost two to three times more than conventional bits, so buy only what you need at the time. That way the cost is spread out over many months and before you realize it, you'll have built up quite a collection.

ROUTER BITS

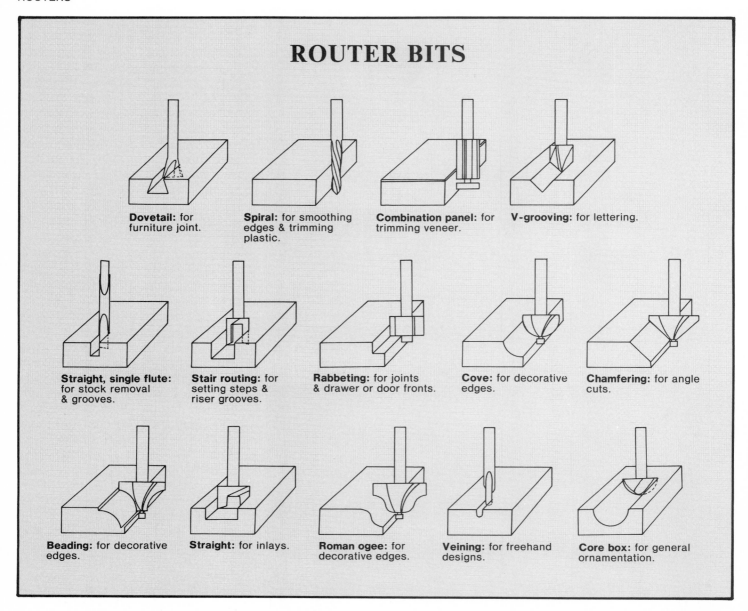

Dovetail: for furniture joint.

Spiral: for smoothing edges & trimming plastic.

Combination panel: for trimming veneer.

V-grooving: for lettering.

Straight, single flute: for stock removal & grooves.

Stair routing: for setting steps & riser grooves.

Rabbeting: for joints & drawer or door fronts.

Cove: for decorative edges.

Chamfering: for angle cuts.

Beading: for decorative edges.

Straight: for inlays.

Roman ogee: for decorative edges.

Veining: for freehand designs.

Core box: for general ornamentation.

styles: a straight bit for 90 degree edges or an angled blade bit for beveled edge cuts. If you select the beveled edge bit, be sure to set your router for a shallow cut. The pilot should be no more than 1/8 inch below the laminate. Otherwise, you'll trim off too much stock because of the angle of the blade.

OPERATING YOUR ROUTER

Make sure the router is unplugged. Then put a bit in the chuck. The bit should slip right in. If depth of cut is not a problem, insert the shank to within about 1/8 inch of the bottom of the chuck. This 1/8 inch will prevent the collet from breaking when it is tightened down. Otherwise, be sure

Unlike a drill, a router has a fixed chuck that will accept only one size shank. Normally this is a 1/4-inch diameter.

The depth of cut can be set very precisely using the gauge shown here. Work the router from the left to the right as you face the stock. In this photo the operator is pulling the router toward him.

the shank is seated at least 3/4 inch into the chuck. This allows the chuck to get a firm grip on the bit.

Now, lock the drive shaft of the router. Depending on the model, this is accomplished by pressing a button on the top of the motor; with a spring lock by the chuck; or with two flat spots on the shaft that allow you to use a wrench. If you're in doubt which method your router uses, check the instruction manual before proceeding. The shaft must be locked to prevent rotation. Next, tighten the nut on the collet. You may use your fingers initially, but the final tightening must be done with a wrench. Some routers have a second nut to tighten against the first nut as an additional back-up. Remember, your bit is going to be turning 18,000 RPM or faster, so you want it to be held tightly.

If your router has a shaft lock switch at the top of the motor, unlock it after securing the bit. Otherwise a mechanical interlock will prevent you from turning on the router.

Practice—Before starting on the doors of that beautiful oak cabinet you're building, get a piece of scrap wood and clamp it to your workbench. Always secure the wood before using the router. Adjust the router to the depth of cut you want. If the bit has a pilot, you must work on the edge of the material. If not, or if you plan to cut a dado joint, clamp a straight edge across the

scrap to act as a guide for the router.

Put your safety goggles on, plug in the router, grip the machine with both hands, and squeeze the trigger. Notice the twisting power of the router as it starts up? That torque is the reason to use both hands when starting the router—to prevent it from twisting out of a careless grip.

If you could look through the router from the top, you'd see that the motor turns in a *clockwise* direction. To make the smoothest and most efficient cut, always try to operate the router from *left to right*. This lets the cutting blades work *into* the wood and gives you better control. The router will work in the other direction, but it takes a firmer grip and more concentration to make sure it doesn't waltz off on its own, spoiling your fine cut.

Make a few passes over the scrap wood to get the feel of this new tool. You might want to lay out your house number and try working freehand to form the figures.

Some routers have a small, clear plastic window, called a *chip shield*,

that snaps into place near the bit. All it ever does for me is clog up the cutting area so that I can't see where the bit is going. If you wear your safety goggles, I don't see any benefit from chip shields.

Edge Guides—There are two types of edge guides: the kind you purchase as an accessory to the router, and the kind you make yourself, a flat, straight, wood board. Both are useful. When you are working the edge of a piece of wood using a bit with no pilot, the store-bought guide is the answer. However, if you must make a cut across the middle of a board, a flat, straight board and a couple of C clamps are the best guide. Use a ruler to measure the distance from the edge of the base plate to the closest tip of the cutting blade. Then, when you've marked where you want your cut to go on the board, add the measurement and clamp the straight edge to those marks. Work the router from left to right and you will have a perfect cut every time.

You'll need to know the distance from the cutting edge of the bit to the outside edge of the router to correctly place a straight edge guide.

Another way to get the same results is with a store-bought edge guide.

As you can see, I added the measurement from the previous illustration and clamped the edge guide to the stock to be dadoed.

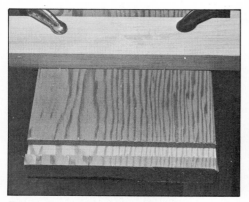

This is the result, a perfect dado.

The inlay joinery on this table was done with a router and a very sharp wood chisel. You can acquire the skill to do the same thing through patience and practice.

Inlays—Inlay work takes practice and patience. First cut out the piece you want inlaid. Then, using it as a pattern, outline the area to be cut with a sharp knife. Set the router depth just a bit shallower than the thickness of the inlay. Now, put on your safety goggles and, using both hands, start the router and lower it onto the wood to be cut. Unless you've got a very steady hand and a sharp blade, work up to just short of the outline. Remove all the wood in the center with the router and finish up with a hand chisel, cutting right on the outline. Set the inlay in place. It should be just slightly higher than the surrounding surface. That's okay because when you get through sanding the inlay with a finish sander, it will be a work of art. Practice this before trying it with expensive woods. Once you acquire the knack, it should be a snap for you to turn out exquisite design work.

Reliefs—Relief cutting is just the opposite of inlay work. You want the design to stand out from the rest of the background. Say you've decided to make a plaque with your street number on it. First, lay out the numbers—make them about 3/4 inch wide. Then, outline the diagram with the router to the depth you desire: 5/16 inch is a good cut. Use an edge guide for the straight lines. Next, start at the edge of the wood and rout your way toward the numbers. This way the base plate will have enough area contact to make a cut with uniform depth. A little sandpaper, some varnish and you're ready to hang the plaque proudly in front of your house.

Splitting—Wood may have a tendency to split at the edge when cutting across the grain. Therefore, whenever practical, make all cross-grain cuts first. Then cut with the grain and eliminate the loose ends.

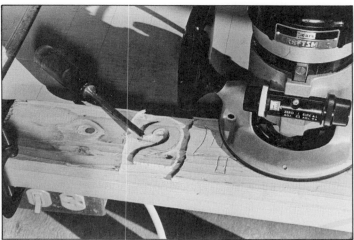

Relief work can be done freehand if you first outline the design with a chisel.

Make the first pass of a router across the wood grain.

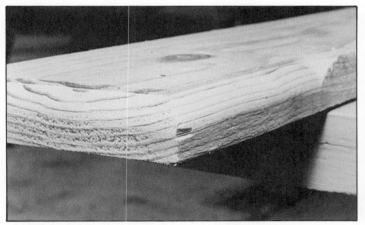

Finishing up with the grain will remove any flared edges.

This is particularly important when you are making rabbet joints.

Templates—You can use your router and make a template to repeat the same design over and over. Lay out your pattern on 3/4-inch plywood. Cut it as perfectly as possible. Sand and fill any voids in the inner facing so that it is smooth. This is your template. Clamp it to the bottom of the material to be cut. Use a straight bit with a pilot and set the depth so the pilot will ride on the inside of the pattern. Drill a hole through the wood to be cut that is big enough to allow the router bit to fit through. Start the

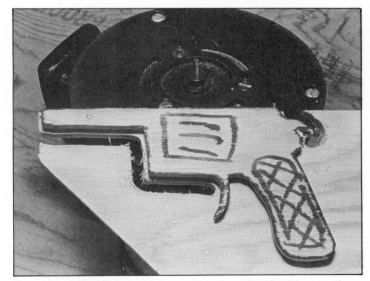

From the photo above you can see how template bushings perform. Similar to a pilot, they allow you to make identical, repetitive designs. However, notice the original pattern must be somewhat smaller than your final product.

router and work from left to right. The pilot will keep you from working outside the template and you'll have as many perfectly matched parts as you want.

Another way to use a template is by mounting it on top of the material you want cut. This lets you see what the router is doing. Buy a set of *template guide bushings* and make your template out of 1/2-inch stock. The guide bushings attach to the router's base plate with the bit in the center. No pilot is required. The bit is always smaller than the ring bushing and you must allow for this when making your pattern, especially if you are working to close tolerances.

STATIONARY MOUNTING

Sometimes it's more convenient to secure the router and pass the stock over it, rather than vice-versa. Anytime you want to use the router on long strips of wood, such as making molding you may want to mount the router upside down on your workbench. Use a long piece of wood as a rip fence. By clamping the straight edge to the workbench at whatever distance you need from the bit, you are assured of a precise cut every time. This is not only an advantage for cutting molding, but also handy in making borders and parallel cuts. A tabletop operation also gives you excellent control when making several identical cuts on different boards. If you cut a semi-circle at the midpoint in your straight edge to house the bit, you can use the router as a shaper or edge planer.

ACCESSORIES

Some accessories, like the board used as an edge guide, are very simple. You need only a steel rod, a nail and the router to make perfect circles. Drill a small hole, big enough to hold the nail, in one end of a steel rod. One of the rods that comes with the store-bought edge guide is perfect. The nail goes through the hole and into the center of the circle you plan to cut. Use a bit without a pilot. Your

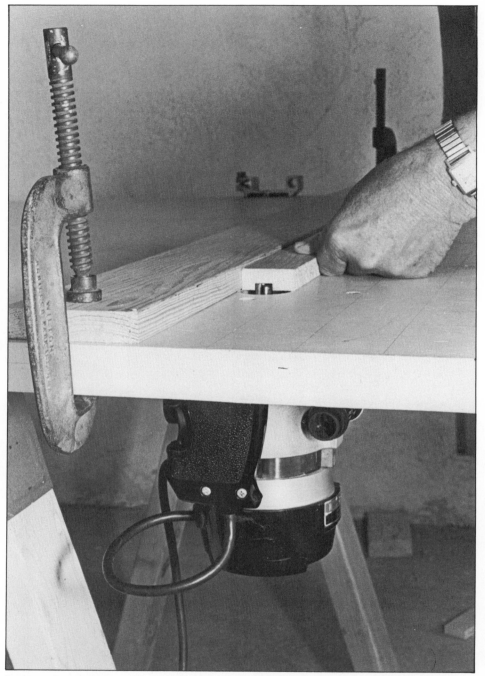

I mounted the router upside down under my workbench, added a straight edge, and came up with an acceptable shaper. You can too—the plans are in Chapter 11.

router will cut a perfect circle with any radius you desire by pivoting around the nail.

Dovetail joints become much simpler to make if you have a *dovetail bit* and a *dovetail jig*. Both Sears and Black & Decker sell excellent models at a reasonable price, as do several other manufacturers. Follow the directions supplied with the unit

and do a little practicing before tackling that expensive piece of mohagany.

For jobs requiring precision freehand work, consider adding a small light that shines right in the area being cut. Not all manufacturers offer this accessory, so before buying a router, check whether this extra is available.

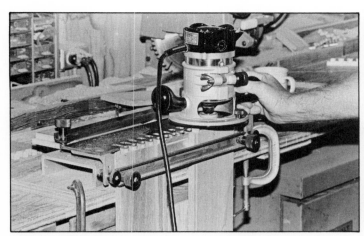

Here is a store-bought dovetail jig. The factory instructions take thinking about. Initial set up is slow.

Once you've got everything adjusted, you can make two or two hundred identical joints with ease.

And just look at the finished product. They will fit perfectly.

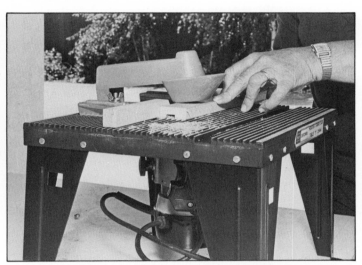

If this looks like the same table you saw in the saber saw chapter—it is. Sears makes a good one.

Small tables can be purchased to facilitate handling small wood parts, but be careful. Some tables are hardly more than toys and don't deliver the accuracy they should. Buy a good one; it will pay in the long run. Or, you may want to make the worktable I've designed in Chapter 11.

A bit sharpener is a very worthwhile investment. It will save you real dollars when your bits begin to lose their sharpness. Instead of throwing them away, you can restore their sharp edges. A bit sharpener consists of a small grinding wheel mounted in the router chuck and a device attached to the base plate to hold the bits. The router is secured upside down and the cutter blades are ground razor sharp by the high-speed grinding wheel.

If you want to do a lot of work with names and numbers, there is a lettering accessory that produces

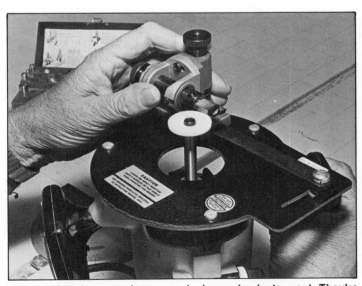

This tool bit sharpener is an amazingly precise instrument. They're priced at just under thirty dollars. Depending upon how much work you do with a router, you'll have to decide which is cheaper, the accessory sharpener or the local professional saw sharpener.

figures about 2-1/2 inches high. All you have to do is set up the name or number you want with the template letters on the wood of your choosing. Use a template guide bushing on the router and outline the template.

Sears makes a tool called a *Router Crafter* that lets you use your router as a wood lathe. It won't do everything a lathe will do but it is ideal for making table legs or divider posts inexpensively. If you're interested in making your own furniture, it is definitely a good investment, particularly when compared to the cost of a lathe.

MAINTENANCE

Maintenance for your router is very similar to other power tools. Keep the cooling vents clear and free of sawdust. On most units the bearings are sealed for the life of the unit. If you have a machine with lubrication holes, 2 or 3 drops of light oil after every 3 to 5 hours or operation should be sufficient.

Brushes that are readily accessible should be checked every 50 hours of operation. Replacement is easy. Simply remove the plug on the outside of the motor housing and pull out the spring and carbon brush. Always replace both brushes and springs at the same time.

Want a wood lathe and can't afford it? This gadget does what a lathe would do, using a router as the cutting base. It's a very clever accessory.

One other thing: Keep your router bits clean. Because of the high speed and the heat generated, the cutting edges tend to acquire a gum build-up that will soon spoil their effectiveness. Use solvent or acetone and a coarse cloth to remove that accumulation.

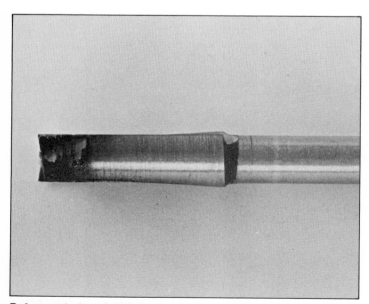

Before and after. A little kerosene dissolved the gum buildup.

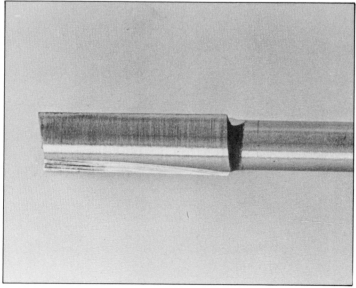

Clean cutters make clean cuts.

ROUTERS

MAKE/MODEL	HP	AMP	RPM	USE	FEATURES
Black & Decker					
7616	1.00	5.0	22,000	Heavy	
7625	1.25	5.5	22,000	Heavy	
Millers Falls					
6800	.34	3.0	30,000	Heavy	
7200	.88	6.0	22,000	Industrial	
7290	1.25	9.0	24,000	Industrial	
7800	.88	6.0	22,000	Industrial	Rotating pistol grip
7900	1.25	9.0	24,000	Industrial	Rotating pistol grip
Penney					
2892A	.50	3.8	27,000	Medium	
2587A	1.00	5.5	22,500	Heavy	
1668A	1.10	7.0	22,500	Heavy	
Rockwell					
4601	.50	3.5	28,000	Light	
4620	.63	3.5	28,000	Medium	Edge guide
4676	.88	6.5	20,000	Heavy	Ball bearing drive
4682	1.25	7.5	22,000	Heavy	Ball bearing drive
4684	1.50	8.0	22,000	Industrial	Ball bearing drive; Detachable handle
4674		3.8	28,000	Industrial	Ball bearing drive; Laminate trimmer
Sears					
1735	.50	4.5	25,000	Heavy	Ball bearing drive
1736	.88	6.0	25,000	Heavy	Ball bearing drive
1737	1.00	6.5	25,000	Heavy	Ball bearing drive
1738	1.00	6.5	25,000	Industrial	Ball bearing drive
Shopmate					
T2700	.63	5.0	23,000	Heavy	
T2701	1.00	6.0	23,000	Heavy	
Skil					
548	.50	3.8	27,000	Medium	
295	.75	5.5	22,500	Heavy	
297	1.00	7.0	22,500	Heavy	
293	.50	3.8	27,000	Heavy	Laminate trimer
Stanley					
90-092	.75	8.0	18,000	Heavy	1/2 collet; Ball bearing drive
90-051	1.25	8.0	18,000	Heavy	1/2 collet; Ball bearing drive
90-150	1.67	9.0	23,000	Industrial	1/2 collet; Ball bearing drive
90-088	.88	6.0	23,000	Industrial	Ball bearing drive
91-264	1.00	6.0	23,000	Industrial	Ball bearing drive
91-267	1.50	9.0	27,000	Industrial	Ball bearing drive
Ward					
90002	.73	4.5	30,000	Medium	100% Ball bearing drive
90003	.75	5.0	30,000	Medium	100% Ball bearing drive
90004	1.10	5.0	23,000	Heavy	
Wen					
1700	.67	4.0	25,000	Medium	

9
Miscellaneous Tools

SHOP VACUUMS

A vacuum is something you think you don't need until you own one. But they are almost indispensable for cleaning up. Not only that, they are useful as a dust-removal tool when sanding and painting.

The basic vacuum is available in two designs: *Dry*, or *Wet & Dry*. I recommend the Wet & Dry model because it can ingest water accidentally or intentionally without shorting out the mechanism. Not only will it suck up shop dust and litter like patio leaves, the vacuum cleaner can be used to clean up kitchen spills or even for shampooing carpets and rugs. Either design can be used as a blower as well as a vacuum.

A wide variety of accessory nozzles are available to help you clean up wood shavings, rugs, walls, car cushions, radiator fins, tight crevices, hardwood floors or fireplace ashes, to name just a few applications.

Most cleaners are adaptable for 1-1/4-inch or 2-1/2-inch hose. The larger size is best for dry materials; the smaller hose is best for wet pickup. You can use the 1-1/4-inch hose for the shop, but it will clog when picking up wood chips.

Vacuums are usually offered in 5-gallon and 8-gallon sizes. The 5-gallon should be sufficient for most home uses and is easy to carry around the house or out to the car. Both sizes may be bought with wheels, so the vacuum will follow you around as you work.

Outside, in the car, or around the house, a shop vacuum will more than prove its value and justify your expenditure.

Very cheap cleaners have no attachments and should be avoided because of the cost of buying those attachments separately. Deluxe 8-gallon units feature everything but the kitchen sink and are best for light industry or people with lots of bucks. I bought my 5-gallon on sale for a very reasonable price. It is a Wet & Dry model with wheels, and a modest set of 1-1/4-inch accessories. I wish I'd purchased one years ago, as I use it continuously around the shop and garage.

And my wife is much happier not having to look at a messy garage all the time.

ELECTRIC SCREWDRIVER

A two-speed screwdriver with a rechargeable powerpack is available from Disston. It works at either 160 RPM or 45 RPM. Both speeds are on the slow side but the high torque of the motor delivers enough power to get the job done. One advantage of the slow speeds is that the driver is less likely to

An electric screwdriver comes with 3 screwdriver bits, a drill bit and a rechargeable powerpack.

SHOP VACUUMS

MAKE/MODEL	HP	AMP	CAPACITY	HOSE DIAMETER IN INCHES	USE	FEATURES
Black & Decker						
7651	.75	5.2	5 gal	2-1/2	Medium	Dry; Optional wheels
7656		6.0	5 gal	2-1/2	Medium	Wet & Dry; Wheels
7665		6.0	8 gal	2-1/2	Heavy	Wet & Dry; Wheels
9322		3.5			Light	Dry; 12v; For auto
9321			1 qt		Light	Dry; Cordless
Penney						
3477A	.93		5 gal	2-1/2	Medium	Wet & Dry
1844A	.93		8 gal	2-1/2	Medium	Wet & Dry
1224A	.93		12 gal	2-1/2	Medium	Wet & Dry
1208A	1.20		6 gal	2-1/2	Medium	Wet & Dry
1216A	1.20		10 gal	2-1/2	Heavy	Wet & Dry
3360A	1.20		16 gal	2-1/2	Heavy	Wet & Dry
Rockwell						
4800	1.0			1-1/4	Light	Dry; Portable; Accessories
1060	1.0	6.0	5 gal	2-1/2	Medium	Dry; Wheels
1064	1.25	6.0	8 gal	1-1/2	Heavy	Wet & Dry; Wheels
1066	2.0	6.0	10 gal	1-1/2	Industrial	Wet & Dry; Dolly
Sears						
17844			8 gal	2-1/2	Light	Dry; Wheels
17855			8 gal	2-1/2	Heavy	Wet & Dry; Wheels
Ward						
5320M	1.25		6 gal	2-1/2	Medium	Wet & Dry
5321A	1.25		10 gal	2-1/2	Heavy	Wet & Dry
5375R	1.7		8.5 gal	2-1/2	Industrial	Wet & Dry; Accessories
5326M			5 gal	2-1/2	Medium	Wet & Dry

slip off the screw head and damage the screw and the surrounding wood. It will drive screws and small nuts and bolts. The screwdriver will reverse and can be used for both driving and withdrawing.

Using this tool with one hand is awkward and I recommend you use both hands to exercise the control necessary to work effectively.

The rechargeable powerpack will deliver up to one hour of service for each 16-hour charge. In the high-speed mode, this is enough to drive 50 #8 1-inch screws into solid pine without predrilling, according to the manufacturer. The powerpack is also interchangeable with other Disston portable tools, including a lantern, a soldering gun and hand-held garden tools.

Included with the screwdriver is a pilot-hole bit, a Phillips-head bit and two conventional slotted screwdriver bits. A seven-piece socket set with an adapter is also available.

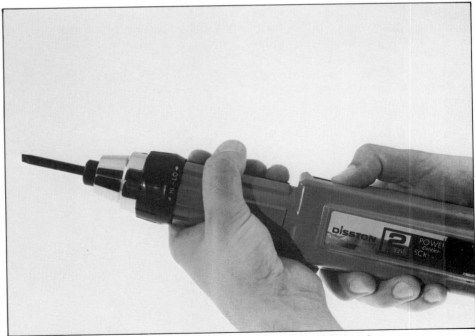

As you can readily see, the electric screwdriver is a two-handed tool.

A typical home grinder is relatively inexpensive and yet valuable to own.

BENCH GRINDER

A bench grinder is not portable, but is very useful. Until you have one you won't realize how many jobs it can do.

The first use that comes to mind is sharpening blades. Chisels, knives, planes—many hand tools have blades that must be kept razor-sharp to do their job efficiently and safely. The grinder helps to keep that sharp edge without excessive time spent over a flat wetstone. However, you need to know that a grinding wheel, because it is round, produces a *hollow-ground* edge. A wetstone gives a *flat-ground* edge.

What about screwdriver tips? A worn-out screwdriver tip can slip and ruin the screw slot and sometimes damage the wood or even your hand. A good screwdriver is really a precision instrument. The blade is meant to fit exactly into the screw slot. Instead of throwing old screwdrivers away, you can use a grinder to restore the tool in a minute. You must hold the tip at exactly 90 degrees to the wheel or it will not produce a flat tip.

A grinder is also ideal for sharpening drill bits of *all* sizes. Twist drills are the most common, but the grinder will also sharpen the edge of spade bits as well.

A grinder with a wire wheel gives you the ability to clean rusted parts or tools quickly. Something that would take all evening to clean can be dressed up in a few minutes.

Even though most home shop projects are done with wood, the grinder can help when it comes to hinges that don't fit just right. Or, what about the occasional use of metal bars or straps—a grinder deburrs the edges after they've been cut with a hacksaw.

Yard tools such as hoes and shovels occasionally need the touch of a grinder to keep them sharp.

About this time you may be thinking all this could be accomplished with a drill motor and a small grinding wheel, and you're partly right. However, the advantage of owning a grinder is you don't have to set up the drill motor when you may have other uses for it. The fact that the grinder is there

Garden tools work better if kept sharp with a grinder.

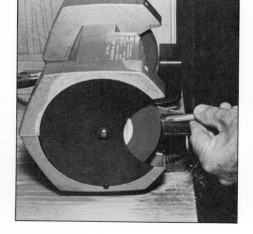

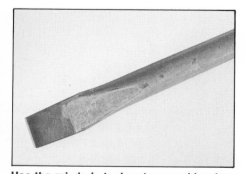

Use the grinder's tool rest as a guide when dressing up a screwdriver blade. The finished product will be easier to use and work better with screwheads.

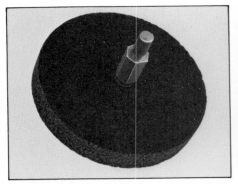

Grinding wheels are easily replaced. Make sure you select the type that is right for the work you want to do.

This drill-sharpening jig described in the text is simple to build and easy to mount. Place the bit to be sharpened against the guide. Twist and pull to the line as you sharpen the point.

means you'll be using it more often—keeping your tools sharp and safe. Also, the average grinder delivers a lot more power and speed than the drill/grinder combination, so you can do the work quicker and with less physical effort.

Grinders are measured by grinding-wheel diameter: 5 to 7 inches is the average range for home use. Larger wheels are for industrial use. Grinding wheels are identified by grit, much like sandpaper. Coarse-grit sizes range from 12 to 24; medium ones are 30 to 60 grit; and fine ones range from 70 to 120. Wheels are also graded from *soft* to *hard,* indicating the bond strength holding the abrasive together. A hard wheel is used on soft metals, while a soft wheel is used with hard materials. Most grinders are sold with a general-purpose wheel of medium grit and medium-soft bond. These wheels are not suitable for grinding aluminum, brass or other soft metals which will clog the wheel and make it unusable.

If you inadvertently grind soft metal and clog the wheel, don't despair. A carbide *wheel dresser* will clean off the jammed grit. A wheel dresser can be purchased at most hardware stores.

When using a grinder, it is usually better to grind slowly instead of taking out large chunks by forcing the tool. If the metal being worked on turns blue, you've gone too fast and gotten the part too hot. The blue indicates the area has lost its *temper,* or hardness. Dip the part in water to cool it and slowly grind

away the colored area. Dip the part in water repeatedly during grinding to keep the temperature down. This is particularly true when sharpening drill bits.

A couple of simple jigs will help when sharpening drill bits on a grinder. Cut a 3-inch by 4-inch base from 1/4-inch plywood. Cut a slot in it to fit around the grinding wheel and attach it with clamps or screws to the grinder's tool rest. Measure in 1 inch from the edge of the base along the side of the wheel and draw two lines, one at a 45° angle to the wheel and the other at

59°. Glue a small block of wood on the 59° line. Make a second jig with another piece of plywood, only set the angles at 55-1/2° and 67-1/2°. Glue another block of wood along the 67-1/2° line. This gives you two guides that will help you maintain the proper angle for either 118° or 135° on drill points. Because you're only sharpening half the drill at one time: 59° is half of 118°; 67-1/2° is half of 135°.

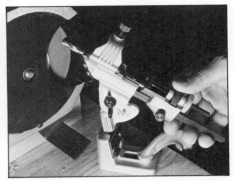

You can purchase a compact, sophisticated drill sharpener for about fifteen bucks.

Inspect a twist drill bit carefully and you'll notice the two lips of the drill bit that are the actual cutting surfaces. The balance of the tip tapers away at about a 12° angle. This is the necessary angle to let the lips bite into the material. Therefore, when sharpening a twist drill bit, place it against the block of the appropriate jig with one of the lips barely touching the revolving wheel. Twist the drill counterclockwise as you grind, and pull the shank of the drill away from the block to the second mark. Then turn the bit and sharpen the other lip.

This is a fairly delicate procedure. I suggest you first try the twisting and pulling routine with a new 1/2-inch drill and the grinder turned off. If you practice with an already-sharp drill you'll quickly see how the movement works.

Wood chisels and plane blades are generally sharpened on a flat stone. However, when a nick appears in the blade, it's a good idea to dress up the edge on the grinder. With the power off, adjust the tool rest to the proper angle for the blade. Place the chisel's cutting edge against the wheel and tilt the tool rest until the cutting taper is flat against the wheel, with the body of the chisel resting flush against the tool rest. The radius of the wheel will produce a hollow-ground blade—which is desirable. If the blade is wider than the wheel, move the blade laterally across the face of the grinder so the blade is sharpened evenly. Hold the chisel by the body so your index finger is resting against the bottom edge of the tool guide. This will help you maintain a steady position while grinding.

When you've removed all the nicks from the edge of the chisel, finish the sharpening and deburring by hand with a flat stone. A little water on the stone helps during the final honing process. Sharpen the hollow-ground side first. Then lay the chisel flat on the stone and hone the back side. Repeat this several times until the burr has disappeared. The blade should be able to shave the hairs off the back of your hand when you've finished.

A few precautions to keep in mind when operating a grinder:
• ALWAYS wear safety goggles.
• Never operate a grinder with a cracked or chipped wheel.
• Make sure the grinder speed doesn't exceed the speed marked on the wheel.
• Leave the paper bushing on the wheel—this acts as a gasket to ensure even pressure on the wheel.
• Tighten the wheel nut finger-tight, plus a half a turn. Do not over-tighten or you may crack the wheel.
• Keep the tool rest within 1/16 inch of the wheel. This prevents the part being ground from catching between the wheel and the tool rest.
• Bolt or screw the grinder to your workbench to prevent it from moving around.

The price of a bench grinder depends upon the size of the wheel and the power of the motor. Available accessories are minimal: several different style wheels and brushes,

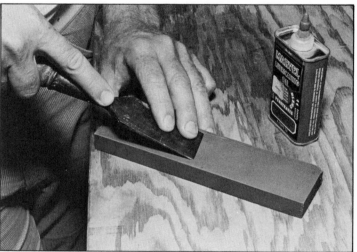

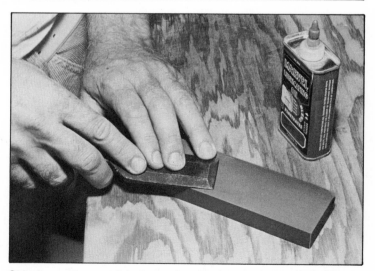

Chisels require careful sharpening. Remove nicks on the grinding wheel. Notice how the forefinger and the tool rest provide a guide to help the operator get an even surface. Finish up by hand using a quality flat stone with a little oil or saliva as a lubricant. Carefully sharpen the beveled side first, then the flat side. Repeat the last two steps back and forth until the chisel blade is surgically sharp.

BENCH GRINDERS

MAKE/MODEL	HP	AMP	RPM	WHEEL DIAMETER IN INCHES	USE	FEATURES
Black & Decker						
7900		2.2	3600	5	Light	Tilting tool rest
7908		2.2	3600	5	Light	Tilting tool rest; Water tray
7916		4.6	3600	6	Medium	Tilting tool rest; Lamp
7917		4.4	3600	6	Heavy	Tilting tool rest; Lamp
Penney						
1692A	.34	3.2	3500	5	Light	Tilting tool rest
1718A	.25	8.0	3450	6	Heavy	Tilting tool rest
2843A	.50	4.0	3550	6	Medium	Tilting tool rest
Rockwell						
4760		3.0	3450	5	Light	Water tray
1049	.34		3450	6	Heavy	Tilting tool rest
Sears						
1931			3580	5	Light	Tilting tool rest
1932	.25		3580	6	Medium	Tilting tool rest; Water tray; Lamp
1933	.34		3580	6	Medium	Tilting tool rest; Water tray; Lamp
1934	.50		3580	6	Heavy	Tilting tool rest; Water tray; Lamp
1935	.75		3580	7	Industrial	Tilting tool rest; Water tray; Lamp
Shopmate						
T2601		3.2	3500	5	Light	Tilting tool rest; Water tray; Lamp
T2602		8.0	3450	6	Medium	Tilting tool rest; Water tray; Lamp
T2602-13		8.0	3450	6	Heavy	Tilting tool rest; Water tray; Hone attachment
Ward						
89003		2.2	3600	5	Light	Tilting tool rest
89004		2.2	3600	5	Light	
8137M	.34		3450	6	Medium	
8134A	.50	4.0	3450	7	Heavy	
8135R	.75		3450	8	Industrial	All extras
Wen						
1800	.25	4.0		6	Heavy	Double-insulated; Tilting tool rest; Water tray; Electric brake

a drill bit sharpener jig, a tool jig that holds blades at the exact angle needed for optimum grinding, and a wheel dresser to true the wheel and clean the clogged surface of the wheel. Some models have a vacuum to pick up dust and dirt.

WORKMATE

Black & Decker has come up with a really practical shop tool for the weekend craftsman. It's called the *Workmate*. It is a two-level, collapsible workbench, with the entire table top working as a unique adjustable vise. Two handles drive independent wormgears at each end of the table top—making a vise that works on parallel flat shapes and on tapered material. The vise opens to 5-1/4 inches. In addition, four swivel grips can be placed in holes

Workmate is a combination vise and sawhorse.

It folds for compact storage.

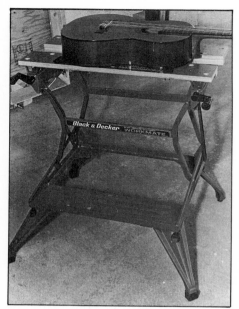

It will hold odd shapes or round stock.

on the table top to increase the clamping capabilities up to 24 inches diagonally. This means you can clamp even an irregular shape, like a guitar, if need be. Or, you could hold a 1x12 board securely during planing or sanding operations. Anything that needs holding can be gripped on the Workmate. Bicycles, chairs—you name it—Workmate will hold it at a level where you can work on it. The table has built-in grooves for handling pipe in both horizontally and vertically for cutting or threading. The Workmate will even hold a cumbersome full-size door.

Legs of the Workmate are adjustable. The lower level measures 23-1/4 inches from the floor, making it ideal as a sawhorse. The upper level of 31-3/8 inches which allows you to use it as a bench.

Black & Decker has suggested an inexpensive way to mount portable tools on the bench to give you stationary power tool precision. Cut several 12-inch squares out of 3/8-inch plywood stock to use as mounting pads for your portable power tools. Bolt each pad to a 2x4x6-inch block and a 3x3-inch square of 1/4-inch plywood for a retaining board. This portable tool mounting board is held onto

the Workmate by the table vise. You're now all set for a stationary operation. A clever idea.

Several accessories are available. *Mitermate* is used with a circular saw for making precision miter cuts. *Routermate* gives you a steady platform when doing delicate router work.

Because of the size and weight of the Workmate, it can be *brought* to the job, instead of the other way around. If you have a project in the kitchen, or on your boat, or by your car, that requires a workbench, you can easily and conveniently use the Workmate instead of carrying the parts back to your workbench for repair.

I should also stress the Workmate is a *sturdy* platform. It doesn't wobble or tip, even if the floor is uneven, assuming you've adjusted the legs. And there's a place to put your foot to hold down the bench when you're working on a job requiring a lot of muscle.

To top it off, Workmate can be collapsed and hung flat against the wall when not in use. All in all a very fine tool, deserving of your attention.

A staple gun is a fast, inexpensive way to perform light-duty tacking operations.

STAPLE GUNS

Staple guns are not new. The hand-powered models require a strong grip and are very fatiguing if you have a job that requires a lot of staples.

Good news! There's an electric staple gun made specifically for home use. Fumbling with small nails can be eliminated. Electric

stapling is far easier than the old mechanical method, and much more efficient.

At first you may think of the electric staple gun as little more than a toy. This is definitely not the case. Once you handle the electric model you will discover all sorts of everyday uses for the gun. Upholstery and insulation are common materials that can be stapled. What about window screens, ceiling tile and carpeting? Or weather stripping, fencing, laths and even shelf paper. Many small projects can be neatly put together with staples and glue. I assembled the Doghouse shown in the Projects Chapter using a Sears Electric Staple Gun and 1/2-inch staples. This lightweight, heavy-duty model performed faultlessly. The unit weighs under two pounds and is well-balanced for extended use. the gun will accept 1/4-, 5/16-, 3/8-, 1/2- and 9/16-inch staples in magazines of about 84 each. Additional staples can be purchased in boxes of 1000.

There are very few moving parts to replace, so the stapler should give years of trouble-free service. Sear's unit has only three moving parts: a spring pusher assembly, a 10-amp solenoid to drive the staples, and a trigger switch.

Glue guns apply hot glue safely, but you must work quickly.

GLUE GUNS

The simplest glue guns have no moving parts. They use household current to heat a stick of solid glue resembling a piece of chalk. You use your thumb to push the glue to the heating element which turns the glue to a liquid that flows out the tip. There is plenty of insulation to protect your thumb from coming in contact with the hot glue. Deluxe models have a trigger that provides a semi-automatic feed.

The glue gets very hot. It has a temperature of 380°F at the tip—hot enough to blister skin if it contacts the liquid. You cannot spread the glue beyond the bead that the tip makes. As it leaves the tip, you have about 15 seconds to lay the bead and clamp whatever you're gluing. In 60 seconds the glue has reached 90% of its holding strength. That's not much working time, so you have to work fast and bond small areas only. This is both good and bad. It's good if you only want to tack something until you can drive some screws in. It's very bad if you need to position or move a part around before the glue sets.

The brochures state the glue will bond wood, ceramics, Formica, leather and fabrics. This means you can repair furniture, toys, upholstery, shoes, luggage, models and even flooring tile.

I've used both types of guns and found that they perform well. I think they are best suited for repairs rather than for original construction because of the short working time allowed by the glue.

Therefore, select the job to suit the tool.

POWER PLANES

These handy power tools will perform any operation a block plane can do, but better and faster. The close tolerances and tight fit of cabinet work make an electric plane a welcome addition to any workshop. Sticking drawers that bind or a pesky door that always sticks need only a few passes of the electric plane to free them. If you find you've made an uneven cut, or made a piece just a touch too big, a couple of swipes with a plane will reduce the material to a straight line or perfect fit.

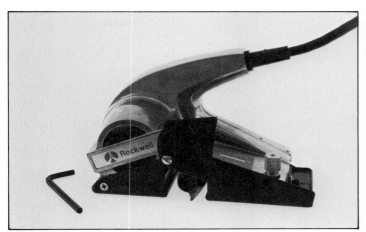

Power planes are fast and efficient.

Power planes are very useful on long cuts where you need to remove a lot of stock.

POWER PLANE

MAKE/MODEL	HP	AMP	RPM	DEPTH IN INCHES	WIDTH IN INCHES	USE	FEATURES
Penney 1832A	.50	4.0	14,500	1/16	2-1/8	Medium	Miter guide
Rockwell 4690		2.5	2400	1/64	1-13/16	Industrial	
4692	1.50	7.0	25,000	3/32	2-13/16	Industrial	Guide fence
Sears 1732	.38	4.5	15,000	0-1/16	3-5/8	Heavy	Ball-bearing drive
Shopmate T2710	.38	3.0	14,000	1/64-1/32		Medium	Guide fence
Stanley 91-258	1.00	6.0	23,000			Industrial	Complete builder's kit
Ward 85005	.50	4.0	14,500	1/16	2-1/8	Medium	Miter guide
85001	.50	3.7	15,000	0-3/64	3-5/8	Heavy	Bevel fence guide
Wen 931		4.0	14,500	0-1/16	2-1/8	Medium	Guide fence

Most power planes come with a guide fence, but it is very easy to inadvertently tilt the plane, particularly when working with thin stock, which creates a bevel cut. To prevent this, I always draw a line on *both* sides of the board I'm planing, and cut down to that line.

Start your cut with pressure on the front of the tool and finish with the weight on the rear. This allows the spinning blade to make its initial cut and prevents it from gouging the wood at the end of the board.

You may not use the power plane constantly, but it's nice to have available when you *do* need it.

RECIPROCATING SAW

The reciprocating saw has the power and work capacity of the circular saw, yet the agility of the saber saw. Think of the reciprocating saw as a big brother to your saber saw; it will perform heavy tasks the other two saws can't do.

The reciprocating saw is the best tool for remodeling where it's necessary to remove a wall or cut out a space for a door or window. Scroll or circle cuts in really thick plywood that are impossible for a circular saw, and difficult for a saber saw, are effortless for a reciprocating saw. This saw will also cut through water pipes and light steel.

Because the blade is mounted horizontally instead of vertically, the saw will cut flush to another surface, such as a wall, with no problem. The saw accepts blades up to 12 inches long, making it possible to cut through stock a foot thick with the larger, more powerful models. Cutting stroke varies from 3/4 inch to 1-1/4 inch. Single-speed, two-speed and variable-speed models are available.

Models built for home and light industrial use have a power range of less than 3 amps for light-duty work to 8 amps for a saw that can be used to construct buildings. A reciprocating saw is not a tool you would necessarily include in your basic workshop inventory, but it is something you should consider the next time you face a remodeling or heavy-duty project requiring a lot of sawing.

RECIPROCATING SAWS

MAKE/MODEL	HP	AMP	STROKES PER MINUTE	STROKE IN INCHES	USE	FEATURES
Black & Decker						
7554	.5	4.2	2600	1	Medium	Single-speed; Detachable cord
7574	.5	4.5	0-2600	1	Medium	Variable-speed; Detachable cord
7585		6.0	1100/2200	1	Industrial	Two-speed; 10-foot cord
Millers Falls						
SP550K		5.0	2500	5/8	Industrial	Single-speed
SP9551		4.4	1500/2500	5/8	Industrial	Two-speed
SP9771		5.0	0-2500	5/8	Industrial	Variable-speed
Penney						
0516A	.67	4.0	2200/ 3000	1	Heavy	Two-speed
Rockwell						
4392		8.0	2400	1	Industrial	Single-speed
Sears						
1706	.5	3.8	0-2000	1-1/4	Heavy	Variable-speed; Ball bearing drive
Skil						
577		3.0	0-2000		Medium	Variable-speed
472		6.0	2400		Industrial	Single-speed
474		5.0	0-2400		Industrial	Variable-speed
Stanley						
90-459		2.7	0-2300	3/4	Medium	Variable-speed
Ward						
81402	.5	4.2	0-2600	1	Medium	Variable-speed
Wen						
1600	.67	4.0	2200/3000	1	Heavy	Two-speed

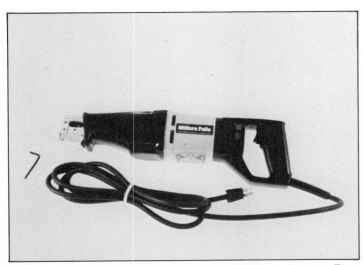

Think of a reciprocating saw as a giant, heavy-duty saber saw. Then think of where you could use a tool like this around your home.

Reciprocating saws are commonly used by the construction industry, plumbers and home remodelers.

PORTABLE POWER

One thing any backwoodsman should consider before building a cabin is a portable generator. There are several makes on the market and they all do a fairly good job. With portable electricity you can use all your power tools for construction and still have lights and refrigeration for the evening meal.

It would take a real traditionalist using just hand tools to build a cabin today. It's tough enough building from scratch; without adding the burden of not being able to use power tools. I would definitely want a small generator to help me with this job.

Because cost and watts are directly related when pricing generators, decide how big or small will work for you? That's easier to do than it sounds. You'll probably be using only one power tool at a time. Therefore, read the amperage of the largest tool you own. Multiply that times the voltage and the answer is the wattage you will require. Add a couple of hundred watts for safety and that's the capacity of the generator you should buy. For example: A 2hp, 7-1/4-inch circular saw draws 10 amps. Multiply this times 110 volts and it equals 1100 watts. Add a safety cushion, and a 1200- or 1300-watt generator will be what you need to do the job. Anything smaller won't allow you to use the saw. Anything larger will cost you extra money.

Of course, if you're going to build in a remote area, there's a good chance you're going to want electricity for the cabin after you've finished the construction. In that case, figure what you'll need for the house and use the same generator for the cabin powerplant when you're finished building.

If all this sounds a little expensive, buy a small saw, work slower, and use a smaller generator. With electricity, you can't make a dime spend like a dollar.

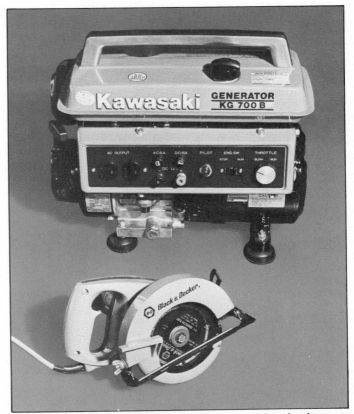

This light-duty 700-watt generator will power the circular saw shown here as well as a drill and some routers. But not at the same time.

10 Repairs

MAINTENANCE

Everyone uses tools at a different rate. One person may use a saw 100 hours per year, while another user will only use his tools 10 hours during the same period. So, it's difficult to offer hard and fast guidelines for preventive maintenance. However, I recommend you inspect the brushes and repack the gear train of your power tool after 25 to 30 hours of continuous use. In most cases, this works out to once a year. A light SAE 20 oil should be applied every 10 hours to the various external lubrication points on the tool.

Eventually, no matter what make or type of power tool you own, it's going to need repair. When this happens you'll be faced with two choices; take it to a repair shop and be prepared for a long wait to get the tool back; or analyze what's wrong and fix it yourself. Fixing most power tools is not as hard as it may sound, and you can save both time and money.

If you elect to make the repair yourself, you again have two choices; is the breakdown electrical or mechanical? Making this determination is not as difficult as it sounds at first.

ELECTRICAL PROBLEMS

Electrical problems are the most common repairs and they are the same with all power tools. So start looking for the trouble in this area first. Plug the tool into an electrical

When replacing a bad plug, peel the outer insulation of the cord 2-1/2 inches back from the end. Strip about 1/2 inch of insulation from the end of each wire. Poke both wires through the bottom opening of the plug and tie them in a simple knot. Wrap each wire around a prong and a screw in a clockwise direction. The knot will help secure the cord to the plug and ease the strain on the screw should the plug be jerked by the cord. A clockwise wrapping of the wires around the screw is compatible with the direction the screw is tightened.

outlet and turn the switch or squeeze the trigger. If the motor doesn't run or even hum, the problem is electrical.

Because most electrical failures are external—outside the body of the tool—review this area first. How about the outlet? Is there power to it? If you're using an extension cord, go all the way back to the wall outlet for your test. Use a lamp or another tool that you know works and check for power. If you get a negative response, check out the fuse or circuit breaker—maybe you've overloaded the system. If the wall outlet is okay, test the extension cord using the same method.

Examine the power tool plug and cord. Connect the tool to a power source you know is working and turn it on. Wiggle the cord by the plug to see if you can get an inter-

mittent start. Check the cord for possible breaks; twist it to check for broken wires. Look for any broken insulation.

If the inoperative tool is a reversible drill, make sure the forward/reverse switch is in the proper position. On some makes it's possible to accidently move the lever into neutral, which will not allow the drill to run.

Unplug the tool and rotate the fan blades a quarter turn. Reconnect to a power source and try the tool. If the motor runs, this indicates a bad commutator, part of the motor's armature, and means disassembly is mandatory.

Remember, before you start taking the tool apart, look for the obvious break outside. If you have no luck locating the trouble, begin a more detailed examination.

It is easy to rotate the fan on a drill by just turning the chuck, but on other power tools you may have to use this method.

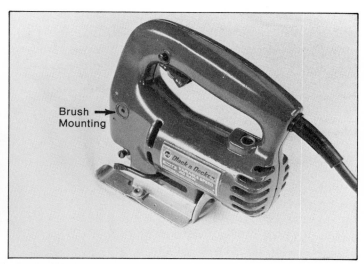

This saber saw has a clamshell case. Notice too, the external brush mounting for easy inspection and maintenance.

The modular construction on this drill allows you to work on either the electrical or mechanical portion of the tool without having to completely disassemble it. Note the lack of external brush mountings; they're internally mounted.

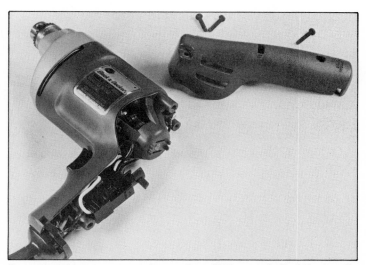

Removing three screws and snapping off the rear half of the handle exposes the entire electrical part of the drill.

TAKING YOUR TOOL APART

Each tool is taken apart differently. If you've kept the original directions, review the instructions and drawings before you start. If you've lost the directions, you can order duplicates from a service center. Exploded-view drawings help immensely in disassembly and assembly and in identifying the parts so you can order any piece that's needed to make the repair.

The motor housings of all power tools are designed in three fashions; *clamshell, stack* or *modular,* and a *combination* of both. The clamshell design comes apart by removing all the exterior screws and lifting off one half of the housing. A stack arrangement has a back, middle and front held together with very long screws. Sometimes one set of screws attaches the back to the middle, and another set attaches the front to the middle. The combination type is where one portion of the housing breaks apart like a clamshell and the rest of the unit has a modular powerhead.

Disassembly should be planned. Initial neatness and laying out the parts in an orderly fashion are essential for the reassembly process. Clean off the work area to be used. Spread out an old towel or pillow case, preferably a white one. This will keep the little parts and screws from getting mixed up and lost.

Make sure the tool is unplugged from any power source before starting disassembly.

As you take the tool apart, place each screw, spring and part in a line—either vertical or horizontal—across the towel. This establishes the order of disassembly. With this method there's no need to remember every little detail of the operation. Don't force the parts. Use gentle pressure taking the tool apart. If it gets stuck, look for a screw or clip you may have missed.

INTERNAL ELECTRICAL PROBLEMS

Practically all power tool problems are electrical. And these troubles are common to *all* types of power tools, from drills to sanders. So go ahead and finish checking out the electrical portion of the tool before moving on to the mechanical descriptions of each specific tool at the end of this chapter.

With the parts of the tool laid out on the towel, recheck the cord and plug using a volt/ohmmeter. If there's a clean break, twisting the cord may not necessarily establish contact.

Next check the switch. Usually the two wires from the cord are plugged or screwed into the switch on the side marked Line. After passing through internal contracts, the wires will leave the switch on the side marked Load. The wires are different colors for ease of identification. Using the color coding, follow each wire to the appropriate brush and field connections. Variable-speed motors have a *rheostat* built into the switch. Make sure

you mark where each wire goes to ensure proper reassembly. By inserting one probe of your volt/ohmmeter in the white Line side and the other probe in the white Load

hole and turning the switch ON, you can check the integrity of that portion of the switch. Repeat this procedure on the black-wire side and you've tested the switch.

To remove the wires from this type of switch, insert a paper clip and push while gently pulling on the wire to be removed. Care must be taken not to push too hard on the paper clip, which will remove the wire but stick the clip. If this happens, use another clip to free the first one. Note that the wires from the *cord* are plugged into *Line* and the wires to the *motor* are inserted in *Load*, black to black and white to white.

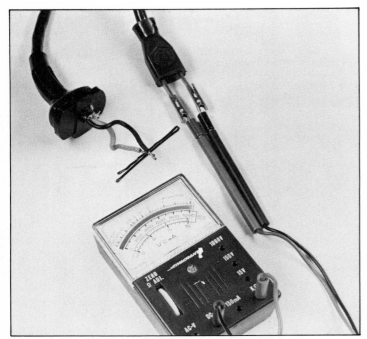

Hold the two bare wires with a bobby pin or a paper clip and you can touch the two probes to the plug prongs and check the cord and the plug in one move. I use alligator clips on the probes but needle prongs work just as well.

Use a screwdriver to remove the wire clip from the back of the brush holder.

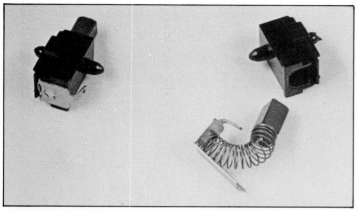

This is what internal brushes look like after they're removed from the drill case. Make sure you replace them so the curved radius of each brush seats against the round commutator.

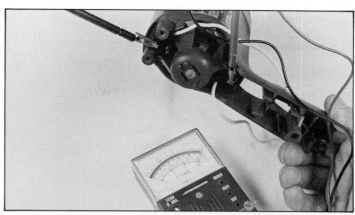

Hook the probes directly to the brushes to eliminate the possibility of broken wiring. Rotate the armature by turning the chuck. The volt/ohm meter should give a constant reading.

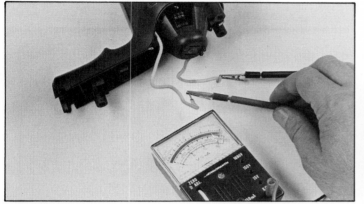

Check the field by attaching the two wires that lead into the case to the volt/ohm meter.

I removed the armature so it could be photographed better. You can perform this bar-to-bar communtator test by working through the drill case and turning the armature by turning the chuck.

BRUSHES

Look at the brushes. If they're worn down to the point where they are only as long as they are wide, replace them. Attach a probe to each of the brush leads and rotate the armature. The needle should swing towards zero and remain there as the armature is turned. If this is not the case, check for a dirty commutator. You can clean this with electrical contact cleaner.

Broken wire leads to the brushes are another thing to look for.

Finally, check out the field and armature. Connect a probe from your volt/ohmmeter to each of the field wires. You should get a near zero reading on the meter, indicating all the windings are intact. Carefully inspect the wires around the commutator for breaks. Put the probes on adjacent bars for a bar-to-bar check. A very high reading is a sign of an open circuit or broken

wire, which means you must replace the armature. Work the probes all the way around the commutator. The reading on the meter should be about the same for all bars. This ends field and armature testing.

That's it. If your tool has an electrical malfunction, you should have discovered the fault these during these checks. If you haven't, the trouble is probably mechanical. The Trouble-shooting Chart at the end of this chapter provides a quick reference for future use.

MECHANICAL PROBLEMS

The following applies to all power tools when trouble shooting. First, look for the obvious problems. Internal mechanical faults are fairly easy to spot and fix because you can readily see the break, or chipped tooth, or jammed bearing when you open up the tool.

A common malady to all power tools is excessive vibration. This is

caused by bent or improperly installed bits, screws that have loosen internally, or worn out bearings. If you are working with a drill, first check the bit to make sure it's true and centered in the chuck. Next, look for loose screws or nuts inside the case. If that doesn't solve the vibration problem, check the bearings. They probably need to be replaced.

If the motor hums but won't run, the first thing to do is turn the fan about a quarter turn and try the motor again. If it runs, the commutator is bad. If that doesn't work, let the motor cool down. Maybe you've overloaded it by pushing it too hard. Wait five minutes and give it another try.

If you can't turn the fan in the first place, that tells you there's a broken part somewhere inside the tool. You'll have to dismantle it to make the repair.

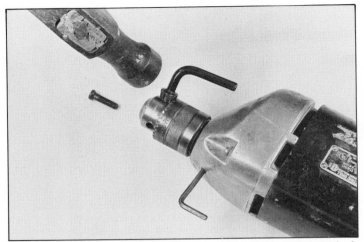

First remove the chuck screw. Because this drill has a place to lock the spindle, I've installed a hex wrench for that purpose. A light tap of the hammer will loosen the chuck.

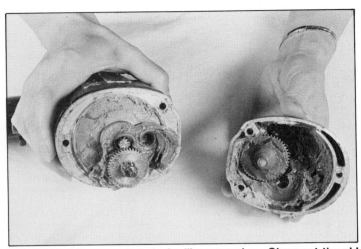

This is what the gear train looks like opened up. Clean out the old grease and inspect the gears for cracks, chips or missing teeth. Check the bearings for wear. Repack with fresh grease before reassembly.

DRILLS

Removing the chuck is the first step in disassembling a drill. If the drill is reversible, open the jaws fully and unscrew the chuck screw. This screw has *left-hand* threads and must be turned *clockwise* for removal. Next, insert the chuck key in the chuck and strike the key a sharp blow with a hammer, directing the force in a counter-clockwise direction as you look into the chuck. Some drills have a hole in the top of the gear case where a small drill bit or hex wrench can be inserted to lock the spindle the chuck is threaded into. If you own a drill of this type, rotate the chuck until the bit or wrench locks the shaft. Then remove the chuck. After the chuck has been loosened with the hammer, it can be unscrewed by hand.

Remove the forward part of the housing from the drill frame to inspect the gear train. Check each gear for missing teeth or other damage. Inspect the fan. Make sure there are no foreign objects wedged between the fan and the case. Finally, test the bearings for smooth movement. It is possible for a bearing to seize from age and overwork. Bearing and fan replacement usually requires a small *puller* to prevent damaging the shaft. Gears can be ordered from a service center.

As you reassemble the drill, make sure everything turns freely after each step. Clean the old grease from the gear box and repack with fresh grease. Use either a factory-recommended product or one of the non-staining white greases on the market. Outboard marine engine dealers handle white grease.

VIBRATOR SANDERS

Most sanders are of modular design. If the problem is electrical you can open the top section and expose the entire wiring. When there is a mechanical fault, remove the lower unit to gain access to the eccentric gear train. Check the bearings and gears, and look for foreign objects. Check wear on the rubber cushions. If they're worn replace them and save another teardown. Look at the baseplate to see if any parts of it are broken.

The modular design lets you work on either the mechanical or the electrical area of the tool. Note the internal brushes buried in the case. Everything else electrical is in the handle.

Two screws remove the sanding pad and expose the lower bearing and eccentric flywheel. Removing the flywheel gives you access to the gear train.

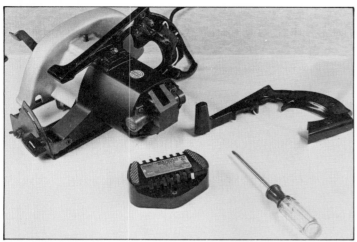

This circular saw is a combination clamshell/modular design featuring external brush mountings. The clamshell handle opens up the switch area, while the rear motor cover lets you inspect the commutator.

Lay out the parts in order of their disassembly. In this case, after unscrewing the saw blade bolt, a spring clip is snapped off to remove the blade guard and spring. Four screws hold a flange that keeps the drive gear in place.

CIRCULAR SAWS

Inspect the brushes for wear every 6 to 12 months. Also lubricate the gear train with grease. Keep the vent holes free from sawdust to extend motor life.

Motor housings of most saws are the combination type. The handle is usually a clamshell design and the motor and gear case are modular. Once the problem is isolated, you can fix it without having to tear the entire tool apart.

Worn brushes and broken switches are the most common internal electrical problems with circular saws. Mechanically, the guard spring will occasionally fail. Other than that, they're usually trouble-free. If you do not have a problem, follow procedures in this chapter.

SABER SAWS

The only mechanical problems I've ever experienced with a saber saw was a broken blade clamp, caused by tightening the blade holding screw too tightly, and a broken shaft bearing due to a lot of hard use. Both were easy to fix. The blade clamp attaches to the end of the shaft and took about two minutes to replace at a cost of 39 cents. The shaft bearing was a bit more complicated. It took 25 minutes to open the clamshell housing, change the bearing, regrease the gears and button up the unit. The cost of the repair was under three bucks. Follow the techniques given above and you should be able to repair your saber saw easily.

As you can see, doing your own repairs makes sense. It's not difficult if you have a set of drawings and exercise patience. Individual parts are usually very inexpensive. And the accomplishment gives you new practical knowledge.

If you are unsuccessful in your repair effort—all is not lost. Package the parts and send them to the nearest repair center. They are experts and will have your tool back in business in the shortest possible time.

The grease has intentionally been left in these photos to show how much lubrication is necessary and how important it is to smooth operation and long life of the tool.

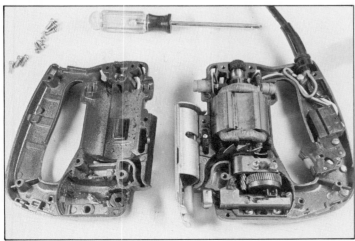

Care must be exercised when opening up a clamshell tool because everything is exposed at once and can be easily knocked out of position. Even more care must be used in reassembly.

In the front is the *shaft* and *shaft bearing assembly*. The blade clamp is to the right while the shaft is surrounded by the shaft bearing. This whole unit fits snugly in the case just ahead of the spindle gear.

TROUBLESHOOTING GUIDE

PROBLEM	DIAGNOSIS	SOLUTION
Motor won't run	Make sure the outlet has power. Test with a lamp or another tool that you know works.	Reset circuit breaker; change fuse; or check extension cord for break.
	On some variable-speed, reversing drills the forward/reverse switch can move out of the proper position. A halfway position will turn off the motor.	Make sure the switch is in the full forward or reverse position.
	Plug in tool and turn on switch: Wiggle cord near plug. Work up cord to the tool. Intermittent running indicates a broken wire in cord.	Cut cord and replace plug. If wire is broken in the middle of cord— replace the whole cord.
	If the tool is a drill, turn off and rotate the chuck by hand. If motor starts when you turn it on, the communtator on the armature of the motor may be dirty or broken. On other tools turn switch off and move fan 1/4 turn by hand. Then switch on.	Replace or clean armature with electrical contact cleaner. You might also order new bearings as preventative maintenance.
	Disassamble tool and check switch and wiring with volt/ohmmeter.	Replace whatever is faulty.
	Worn brushes and springs. Inspect brushes for pitting and wear. Check springs on the brushes.	Replace worn brushes and springs. Always change *both* brushes, even if only one is faulty.
	Broken wire in armature or field.	Check armature and field for continuity with volt/ohm meter. Replace if faulty.
Excessive vibration	Drill bit is not properly positioned in chuck.	Reposition bit in chuck.
	Bit is bent.	Replace kit.
	Interval screws or nuts are loose.	Open case and tighten fasteners.
	Bearings are excessively worn.	Replace bearings. Use a small wheel puller to extract bearings.
	Fan is worn, bent or broken.	Replace fan. Use a small wheel puller to extract fan.
Motor hums but won't run	Motor has overheated.	Let motor cool down 5 minutes. Try motor again.
	Bad communtator.	Turn fan 1/4 turn and try motor again. Clean commutator with electrical contact cleaner. If problem persists, replace armature.
	Fan is frozen.	Broken mechanical part, foreign object jamming motor, or seized bearing. Check for foreign object and remove. If problem continues, replace bearings. Use a small wheel puller to extract bearings.
Water damage [WARNING: Never pick up tool that has been dropped in water until you've unplugged the power at the main outlet!]	Exposure to fresh water.	Allow tool to thoroughly dry in a warm room, such as furnace closet.
	Imersion in salt water.	Flush completely with fresh water and allow tool to dry in warm room.
	Tool dropped in muddy water.	Tear down tool. Clean with soap and warm fresh water. Rinse and dry parts before reassembly.

VOLT/OHMMETER

You can purchase a volt/ohmmeter at most electrical supply houses. Radio stores sell an economy model that works well and will perform all of the tests you'll need while trouble shooting any of your power tools. A volt/ohmmeter gives you the capability to check *line voltages*, both AC and DC. It will also allow you to make continuity checks on switches, cords and motors, by measuring the resistance (ohms) in the circuit. Two separate wires with probes lead from the volt/ohmmeter to whatever's to be tested. If there's no break in the system, the needle in the meter will fully deflect from the left to the right and show a reading of zero ohms when properly connected. For example, twisting or clamping the two exposed wires of a power cord together and touching the two probes to each of the exposed wires on the opposite end of the cord should complete the circuit and the needle should move to zero. This indicates there is no fault in the cord. Testing a switch requires you to connect one probe to the *line* side of the switch and the other probe to the matching *load* terminal. You can tell the correct terminals by the matching colors on the wires leading from the switch. Flip the toggle or squeeze the trigger and the needle should register zero, indicating a good test. If it fails to do this, there's a break and the switch should be replaced. Using the probes on a motor will determine whether or not any of the internal wiring has broken.

The instruction sheet provided by the manufacturer of the volt/ohm meter will give you detailed steps on how to use that particular unit. Naturally, read the instructions and familiarize yourself with the meter before putting it to use.

Volt/ohmmeters work on very low voltage; either a 1-1/2- or 9-volt battery. When you test, be sure the power tool is not plugged into the outlet, so there's no chance of damaging the tool, breaking the meter or shocking yourself. Volt/ohmmeters are very safe to use and an essential addition to your tool collection if you plan on doing your own repairs.

11
Projects

The projects in this chapter were selected because they are something you and the family will enjoy when completed. They are not designed to be senseless exercises, to practice your building skills and then be discarded, or relegated to the back of the garage to be used as dust catchers. So when you build one, do it with the thought in mind that your completed work will be on display for all to see. Build it with pride.

If you can't personally use the projects contained here, consider their value as gifts. Most people love to receive hand-made presents. Something produced by hand—rather than store-bought—seems to always reflect a much more personal statement of friendship and warmth.

You should take full advantage of the opportunity to get the most out of the building process. Don't just assemble the parts following the *cookbook recipe*. Think about what you're doing so you can apply your newly acquired knowledge to creative projects of your own.

The same steps that go into building a simple doghouse can be transferred to making kitchen cabinets, or building a tool shed, or a playhouse. The picnic table is not really so different from a fence, or even a garage, as far as the basic cutting and layout is concerned. It's just a matter of changing the plans and applying the skill and knowledge.

You can't use power tools alone to build something. You will also have to use hand tools. Therefore,

This desktop bookshelf and pencil holder make an attractive addition to your study or they can be proudly offered as a gift.

your skill in this area will also increase. Always take advantage of any opportunity to learn more by trying to do your absolute best on whatever project you undertake.

PLAN TO SAVE

Too little thought is given to layout, but layout is where you either save or waste money. At the cost of lumber today, you want to get the most for your dollar. Be very careful to squeeze every penny out of the wood by careful layout. Plywood is the easiest to economize on, because you can readily visualize where each part is going to be cut. But you can save on conventional lumber by planning ahead. Notice how the cleats are cut out for the Picnic Table—that saves you money. And those big scraps. You'd be sur-

prised at how often you will need something *just that size* for another project.

Because of the cost of the material, it's important that you start your learning experience with small projects. Develop your skill before you tackle the Big One—the one you've wanted to build all along. You'll be happier with the results and it will save you money in the long run. You'll discover there is very little difference between building small and building big. Mainly, it's just a matter of repeating the same steps over, and over, and over again until the big project is completed. The projects in this book are small. Houses are big. Boats are big. Big is usually expensive. Therefore, learn small first.

PENCIL HOLDER & BOOKSHELF

Here are a couple of simple projects that are easy to make, providing you with a chance to gain some practice with your drill. The finished product will enhance your office or make a much appreciated gift for a friend.

The die is really a pencil holder, something any student—or writer?—can't do without. They're handy for anyone who has ever spent time searching for something to write with. Add a memo pad and it's a natural for phone messages.

The bookshelf is just right for a desktop, offering a very convenient place to hold those reference books that usually get temporarily stacked near the corner of the desk and wind up falling on the floor.

Die Pencil Holder

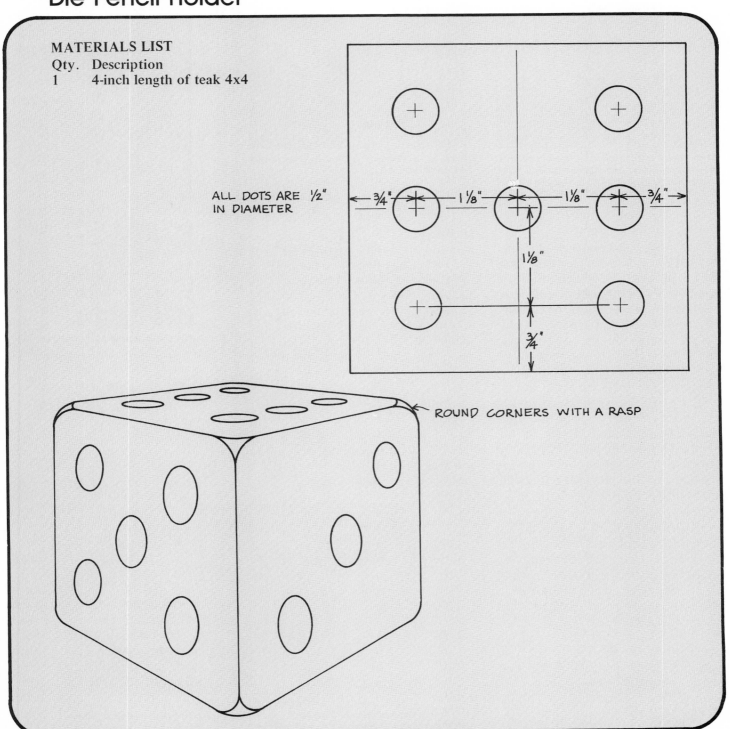

MATERIALS LIST

Qty.   Description
1   4-inch length of teak 4x4

ALL DOTS ARE ½" IN DIAMETER

¾"   1⅛"   1⅛"   ¾"

1⅛"

¾"

ROUND CORNERS WITH A RASP

After the holes for pencils are bored, you may use a rotary rasp with a rounded tip in place of a 1/2-inch bit to make the rest of the *dots*, but you should bore pilot holes first.

Use a small hand rasp to give your pencil holder its final shape.

The die can be varnished or oiled. I prefer the oil because it gives a more natural appearance to an already finely-textured wood. A little teak oil and a soft rag is all you need.

DESKTOP BOOKSHELF

The bookshelf requires just enough additional skill and concentration to hold your interest. Make this with teak wood, too. It will look warm and rich when finished.

Saw the 1x4 exactly in half. You should wind up with an overall dimension of about 11-7/8 inches.

Using a plane, trim the 1x6 down to exactly 1 inch by 5 inches by measuring 5 inches off the width on *both* sides and planing down to the line. If the plane is gouging chunks out of the wood, you're probably working against the grain. Start the plane from the other direction for smoother results. I like using a Stanly Surform hand plane for this operation; it removes the stock fast—with a minimum of effort.

When you've reached 5 inch net width, cut two 8-inch lengths. Make sure all cuts are perfectly square. Put the two boards together in a vise or C-clamp and smooth them using a rasp or plane until they are identical. Be sure and use scrap wood pads to protect the teak.

Locate the center of the 8-inch dimension and mark both ends with a pencil dot 1/2 inch up from the 8-inch bottom. Place a piece of stiff cardboard cut with a right

Ask your local hard-wood dealer to cut you a cube from a teak 4x4. The 4x4 will actually measure somewhat less, therefore you want the cut to match the dimensions of the 4x4 to form a perfect cube. Locate a pair of dice and lay out the same pattern on your block of wood. Remember, the numbers on the opposite sides of a die always add up to seven. Measure in 3/4 inch on each side to form the basic design for the *dots*. Refer to my sketch for the dimensions necessary to give the proper proportions to the die, so it looks like the real thing.

The side with six dots is where you can put the most pencils. So, let's drill it out first. Place the die in a vise and carefully bore six holes, 90 degrees to the surface and 2 inches deep, using a 3/16-inch bit. A piece of masking tape wrapped around the bit 2 inches up the shank will give you an accurate depth indicator. Or, you can buy a plastic drill guide that will do the same thing.

After you've drilled the 3/16-inch holes, switch bits and rebore the holes to 1/2-inch diameter, main-

taining the same depth. Two bits are necessary here to keep from splitting the wood and to ensure an accurate cut.

Dimple the remaining surfaces where you've laid out the dots using the 3/16-inch and the 1/2-inch bits. Be careful not to bore too deeply. You want the drill to form a 1/2-inch circle where the dot is located.

Round the corners and edges with a rasp to resemble your *model*. Smooth the dots and die with a fine sandpaper. Paint the dots with a glossy black enamel.

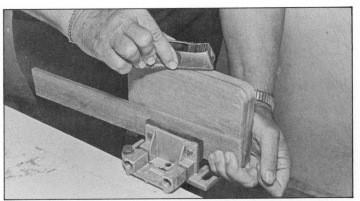

The Stanley Surform plane will help you get the final dimensions of the matched end plates. I rounded the top corners at this time, working a little ahead of the text.

Desktop bookshelf

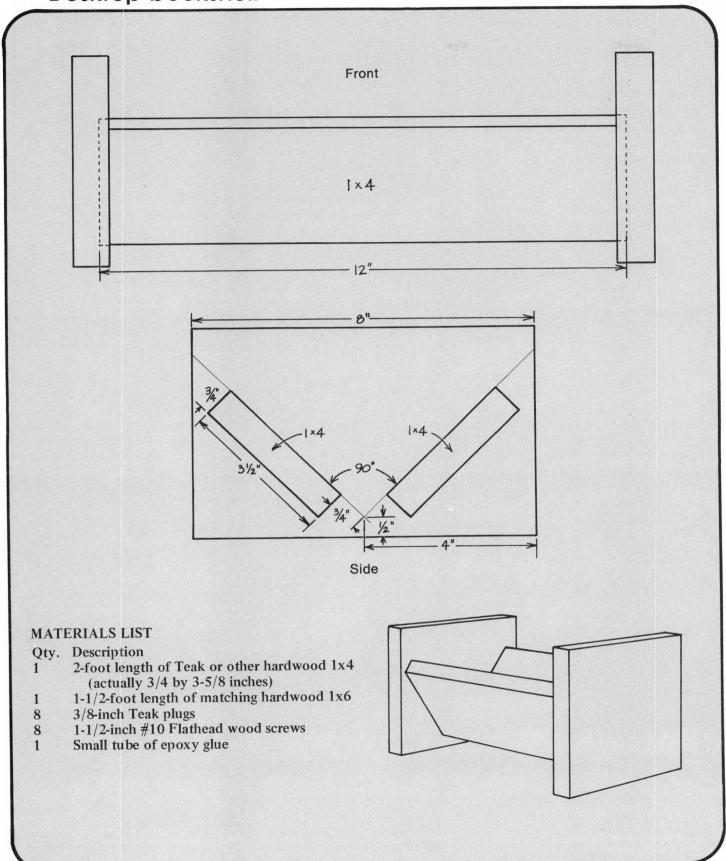

Front

1 × 4

12"

8"

3/4"

1×4

1×4

3½"

90°

3/4"

½"

4"

Side

MATERIALS LIST

Qty.	Description
1	2-foot length of Teak or other hardwood 1x4 (actually 3/4 by 3-5/8 inches)
1	1-1/2-foot length of matching hardwood 1x6
8	3/8-inch Teak plugs
8	1-1/2-inch #10 Flathead wood screws
1	Small tube of epoxy glue

angle on the teak bookend so the point of the right angle is touching the pencil dot and the sides of the right angle are equal distance from the top of the bookend. Draw a line on the teak, marking both sides of the right angle. Draw a line on the cardboard, outlining the teak. Mark the face of the cardboard A. With a pair of scissors, trim the cardboard until it exactly matches the bookend. This is the template you'll need to transfer the same angles to the other bookend.

Place the cardboard with the A face *down* on the second bookend and trace the right angle on the teak.

Measure 3/4 inch along both lines from the point of the right angle and make a small pencil mark. Do this on both bookends.

Place the end of a 1x4 alongside and below either line on the bookend. A corner of the 1x4 should be touching the 3/4-inch mark. Outline the 1x4 in the bookend with a sharp pencil. Repeat this step on the remaining three lines.

With a wood chisel, gouge out the insides of the 1x4 outline on the bookends. A shallow depth

This is what the parts will look like after you've cut and matched them.

between 1/16 and 1/8 inch is sufficient. You want to give the butt of the 1x4 a slight notch to fit into. This does two things: One, it hides the sawn end—giving you a better finished appearance, and two, it will provide a little extra strength for the 1x4 book support. A router may also be used for this step.

Using a rasp and medium to fine grit sandpaper, round off all the corners and edges to a constant radius. You can work teak par-

ticularly well in this manner—it's almost like sculpting clay.

If you don't already have one, I strongly recommend you purchase a #10 Stanley *Adjustable Screwmate*. It performs three drilling functions at once. Set it up to bore the hole compatible with the 1-1/2-inch #10 woodscrews you're going to use. Adjust the plug depth to its most shallow setting.

If you don't have a Screwmate, you'll need the following drill bits: 1/8-inch, 3/16-inch, and 3/8-inch.

Notching the bookend can be accomplished manually with chisels or with a router and a small hand chisel.

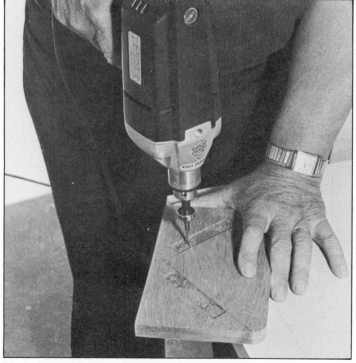

It's important that you first drill from the inside to ensure the screw holes line up.

Then reverse the end plates and drill the countersink.

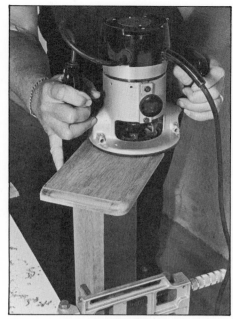

If you're fortunate enough to own a router, you may use it to round off the outside edges. If not, a hand rasp will produce similar results.

Using the smallest bit, bore two holes in each chiseled-out portion of the bookends. Locate these holes about 1-1/2 inches apart in the center of the 1x4 outline. Place the 1x4s in the notched-out bed and drill from the other side to a depth of 1-1/2 inches using a 1/8-inch bit. If you have the Screwmate, bore each hole up to the collar and you're finished. Without the Screwmate, put the 1x4s aside after the first hole. Drill a second hole through the bookends using the 3/16-inch bit. The 3/8-inch drill is used last; very carefully bore 1/8-inch deep on the outside of the bookend, using the 3/16-inch hole as a pilot. Repeat this procedure on all four notches for the 1x4s.

Mix enough epoxy glue to cover all eight surfaces. Spread a thin, even coat over the ends of the 1x4s and the notched out areas. Screw the 1x4 to the bookend until a little glue is forced out of the joint. Wipe off the excess glue with a rag wrapped around the tip of your screwdriver. Repeat this step until all four joints have been assembled.

The plugs go in easily. Use a little white glue as a sealer. Make sure the grain is lined up parallel to the grain of the bookends. If you don't have a mallet, use a large hammer with a smooth head and gently tap the plugs down until they seat against the screwheads. You can tell by the sound of the tapping when

the plug has hit bottom. After the glue has dried for a few minutes, get your largest, sharpest wood chisel and trim the plugs flush with the surface.

There's a little trick that's handy to know when you trim plugs. Start about 1/8 inch up from the base for your first slice. This cut will show you which direction the grain of the plug runs. If the plug cuts on an angle, move your chisel to where you are trimming from edge of the plug closest to the base. Rest the chisel on the surface of the bookend and make a series of small cuts with a slight sweeping motion. It's a little like slicing baloney. When you get almost even with the surface, use a scrap block

of wood and fine-grit sandpaper to finish up. Be sure and sand only with the grain.

The bookshelf can now be varnished or oiled. Naturally, I prefer the oil to match the pencil holder. Oiling just seems to do more justice to the beauty of the wood. Use a rag and wipe on several thin coats. If your local hardware store doesn't carry teak oil, check with a marine supply dealer in your area.

The bookshelf as it should appear before the finishing touches are added.

WORKTABLE

Probably 85 to 90 percent of all home craftsmen use their garage as the workshop. It's a natural place to work: convenient, usually wired for electricity, and the big garage door allows for easy access for oversize raw materials.

The main disadvantage to using the garage is the car, or cars, wind up outside in the elements, aging before their time. What to do? Does it have to be a decision between a workshop or a garage? Can't some solution be worked out without tacking on a ten-thousand dollar addition to your already over-valued, over-taxed, humble abode?

I think I've found a workable compromise. The answer to the do-it-yourselfer's space dilemma is deceptively simple. In fact, the whole concept is built around only one 4x8 sheet of 1/2-inch plywood mounted on two sawhorses. That way the worktable can be dismantled and leaned against the garage wall and the sawhorses stacked in the corner when not in use—leaving plenty of room for the car. The big plywood sheet offers far more area to work on than a conventional shop bench—an advantage when sawing oversized pieces.

Naturally the plywood sheet will need a little reinforcing and some modification before it suits your needs. The beauty of this idea is the low initial cost, the easy adaptability to your individual requirements, and the fact it can be readily stored out of the way when not in use—much like a collapsable ping-pong table.

If you've stayed with me this long, follow through while I describe how to build this most useful shop addition.

ACX plywood has a "good" side and a "rough" side. You want the good side to be the table top. Drill and countersink holes into the good side as shown in the plans. Space them about 12 inches apart and about 2 inches from the edge. Glue and screw the flat side of the 1x4s

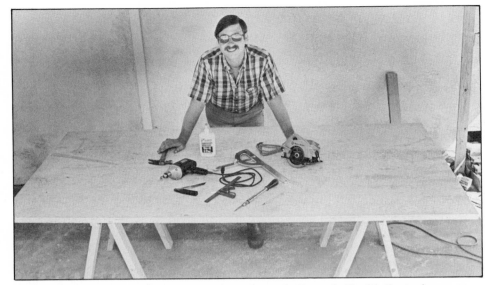

Now that's a workbench big enough to do some work. It was built with the tools you see pictured. Of course it can be collapsed and stacked against the wall when not in use.

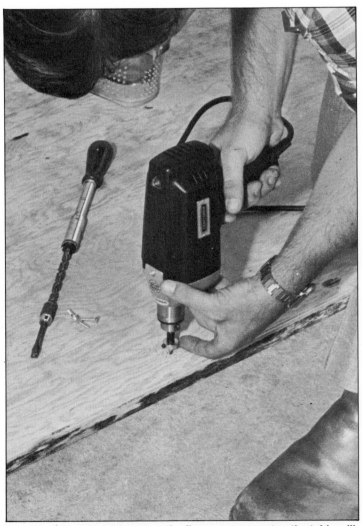

By assembling the table top on the floor, you guarantee the table will be flat after the 1x4 stiffeners are secured.

Worktable

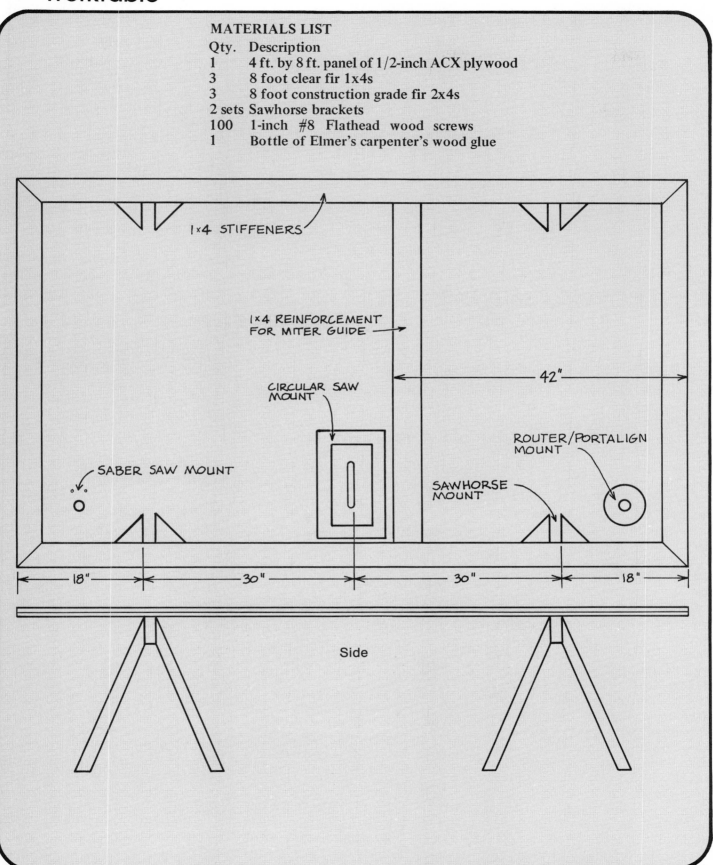

MATERIALS LIST

Qty. Description
1   4 ft. by 8 ft. panel of 1/2-inch ACX plywood
3   8 foot clear fir 1x4s
3   8 foot construction grade fir 2x4s
2 sets Sawhorse brackets
100   1-inch #8 Flathead wood screws
1   Bottle of Elmer's carpenter's wood glue

1×4 STIFFENERS

1×4 REINFORCEMENT
FOR MITER GUIDE

42"

CIRCULAR SAW
MOUNT

ROUTER/PORTALIGN
MOUNT

SABER SAW MOUNT

SAWHORSE
MOUNT

18"

30"

30"

18"

Side

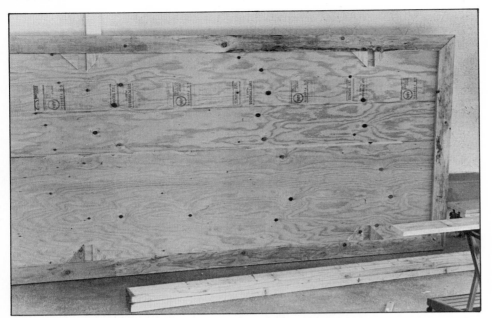

This is what the underside of your table will look like after the 1x4 doublers and cleats have been added. The cleats are the waste stock from the miter cuts of the 1x4 stiffeners.

around the perimeter of the plywood, making sure the screws bite into the fir and the heads are flush with the plywood's surface. This will give you a stiff table top. Do this on the garage floor to ensure a flat table.

Cut the 2x4s for the sawhorse so the table will measure 31-3/8 inches high. Saw the cross member of the sawhorses 41 inches long so they fit snugly inside the 1x4 framing of the table top. The sawhorse brackets are assembled according to the instructions on the package. Before final assembly, set the legs in the brackets and a cut line on their ends parallel to the floor. Trim the bottoms on this line so the legs form a steady base for your table. Assemble and nail the sawhorse and place the plywood on top of them.

Position the horses 18 inches in from the end of the table. Using scrap 1x4s, cut eight pieces 1-1/2 by 3-1/2 inches long for cleats. Place these cleats on each side of the sawhorses's cross members, against the table's framing. Attach them to the table with glue and screws. This forms a slot for the sawhorse to fit in, giving better support and perfect

alignment each time you set up the work table.

Using a dark pencil, draw a fine grid of 2-inch squares over the entire table top. The wide side of a carpenter's square is 2 inches wide and makes an excellent layout guide. Then cover the top with two coats of a clear sealer and two coats of varnish or Varathane. Sand lightly between coats. The basic table is now complete.

Now for the fun part—this is where the table will begin to show you its full potential. Almost every type of portable hand power tool can be turned upside down and mounted under the table—thus giving your hand-held machine a stationary base for more precision work. The capacity is now available to you to perform all sorts of projects that previously would have required stationary shop tools—at a considerable savings in money and valuable space.

MOUNTING A CIRCULAR SAW

If you have a 7-1/4-inch circular saw and want to convert it to a table saw, measure in 10-3/4 inches from the edge of the table and drill a

1-1/4-inch hole 4 feet from the end. Bore a second 1-1/4-inch hole in line with the first hole 20 inches from the edge. Make two plunge cuts to connect the holes. Use a straight 4 foot 1x4 board and two C-clamps to act as a guide. The cutout is where the sawblade will fit after you mount the saw under the table.

To mount the saw, flip the table over so the bottom side is on top. Place the sawblade in the cutout, making sure the blade is 90° to the edge and the bevel tilt will not bind in the slot. When you have everything aligned, trace the outline of the baseplate on the plywood. Glue and screw 2-inch wide strips of 1/4-inch plywood around the baseplate. Some saws have two 1/4-inch holes in their baseplate for table mounting. If you have this type, mark the plywood and drill the holes. Remember to countersink the holes on the table top. Two 1/4 x 3/4 flathead machine screws with nuts and washers will finish the mounting. If your saw has no holes in the baseplate, drill four 1/4-inch holes in the plywood next to the baseplate and use large flat washers to hold the plate in position.

A radiator hose clamp or a 3-inch C-clamp and an electrical receptacle with an on/off switch will complete the table saw hookup. Wrap the hose clamp around the trigger and tighten it enough to ensure the trigger is fully depressed. Mount the receptacle on the edge of the table. Make sure the switch is OFF. Plug in the saw to the receptacle and the receptacle to the 110v wall outlet. Turn on the switch and the saw should work. Turn off the saw, flip the table and you're in business.

The C-clamps and the straight edge can be used as a rip fence for later operations. If you want to get fancy, dado out a 3/4-inch wide by 3/8-inch deep channel 6 inches to the left of the slot cut for the saw. Reinforce the cut with a piece of 1x4 under the table. Next go down to Sears & Roebuck and buy a miter guide. You now have both rip and miter cutting potential, plus the

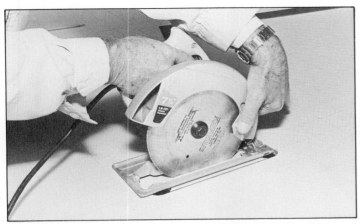

After the holes are drilled for the saw opening, a simple plunge cut will connect the two. Use the procedure discribed on page 52.

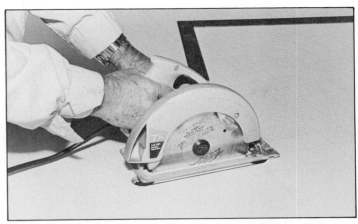

I painted the tabletop an off-white so the 2-inch grid would show up better in the photographs. You may or may not want to, depending on the contrast the natural grain plywood will reflect after it's varnished.

Nothing difficult about that. Make sure the 1/4-inch plywood cleats fit snugly against the saw's baseplate. A small strip of plywood placed between the sawblade and the cutout will ensure perfect alignment of the blade to the table.

This is what the saw looks like in position.

ability to make bevel cuts by tilting the saw blade—in short, you have all the features of a table saw. And it's mounted on a big 4-foot by 8-foot table. By mounting the saw in the middle of the table, you will be able to cut a full sheet of plywood with accuracy, safety and control—a trick that's almost impossible with a standard model table saw.

MOUNTING A SABER SAW

The saber saw should be attached about 9 inches in from the edge. This will serve as your jig saw for handling small projects and doing scroll work. The rip fence will be available to you regardless of where the saw is located. Saber saws can be mounted to the table using large flat washers and 1/4-inch bolts.

A straight board clamped to the table makes an ideal rip fence.

Inverted mounting of the saber saw is no problem at all.

Removing a layer of plywood around the base of the router before you mount it will give a firmer fit.

MOUNTING A ROUTER

If you have a router, it can be mounted on one end of the table by cutting a 2-inch hole in the table top 9 inches in from the edge. Remove the router's baseplate and use it as a template for hole alignment. Mount the router against the table using the already threaded screw holes in the frame and longer flathead machine screws. This, together with the straight edge board from the saws, becomes your shaper.

MOUNTING A BELT SANDER

Pick a corner on the opposite side from the router to install a belt sander. The sander will be mounted on its side, lying on top of the table. Make sure you cut a ventilation hole in the table top for the sander's motor. Use cleats to position the sander 1 inch from both edges.

MOUNTING A DRILL

In the Accessories chapter, page 36, we discussed a tool called *Portalign*. Attaching it to your drill will let you mount it upside down on the table and use it as a sanding drum, a shaper of passable quality, or a rotary rasp. Mount the drill on the same end as the belt sander, only on the other corner—9 inches in from the edges.

Detailed drawings for this worktable will help you in setting up switches and tool locations. As you study the plan, you will readily see the simplicity and merit of this shop project.

The size of the table is a two-fold advantage; it's excellent when working with large parts, and it will allow you to perform several operations at once without having to tear down your original setup. Notice the tools are purposely scattered over the entire surface of the table to allow you a lot of *elbow room* when working.

Also note that you don't have to mount every tool when you set up the table. Sometimes you'll only need to mount one or two tools. Other times, you may not need any—just the use of the surface and maybe a vise clamped to the edge. You don't *have* to mount every tool every time—but you *do* have the *capability* to broaden your shop uses, when the need arises, making your tools do more work for you.

And when you're finished, the table stacks neatly in the corner, out of the way. The best of both worlds—a shop and a garage.

The Portalign fits nicely in the same hole as the router.

The tools are all mounted. Turn the table over and get to work.

SHOP CADDY

At first glance, this Shop Caddy appears to be just another storage case to hold small power tools and accessories, with a small table top for doing little jobs. True, you can use it for the above, but the primary use is to hold large plywood sheets as they're sawn.

There is nothing more cumbersome than a 4x8 sheet of plywood before you've cut it down to size. The first cut is usually the hardest. Most of the sheet is resting on the worktable or sawhorses, while the piece being cut is left out in space to split or be damaged when the saw finally cuts all the way through.

To avoid this damage, many people perform a juggling act that would do credit to a circus midway star. With the Shop Caddy, this folly is no longer necessary. The Caddy's table is purposely built to the same height as your worktable or sawhorses. The plywood overhang will rest comfortably on the Caddy top while being cut, eliminating the need for gymnastics. You and your insurance carrier will both breathe easier when you use this simple shop addition.

The pegboard is for storing tools. The two pockets are for power tools. But the main function of the Shop Caddy is to hold the loose end of plywood as it is being cut.

To build this lifesaver will require a circular or saber saw, a drill and a few hand tools. It can be cut and assembled in an evening.

Decide what height you want to make the Shop Caddy. The table top should be the same distance from the floor as whatever you use to support your plywood sheeting for sawing. Because my worktable is 31-3/8 inches high, that is the height on these plans. The thickness of the 1x10 fir is 3/4 inch. This is deducted from the 31-3/8 inches to get the required length of the sides—30-5/8 inches.

Cut two pieces off the 1x10, 30-5/8 inches long. These are the sides. Cut another piece 40 inches long. This will be the top.

The Shop Caddy is a natural companion to the workbench—not only as a support for material, but as a convenient storage for tools being used on the job at hand.

With the 3/4-inch brads and glue, attach two quarter-round cleats 9-1/8 inches long across the bottom of each side. Measure up the center of each side and fasten a 30-inch cleat with one side touching the middle measurement. Rest the cleat on a pegboard spacer to leave room for attaching the bottom later in assembly. Nail a second cleat parallel 1/8 inch from the first strip, forming a channel for the center piece.

On the opposite face of the sides, screw and glue the 9-inch and 24-inch 2x2 supports across the top and bottom. Make sure both pieces are centered and flush with the edges.

Place the bottom pegboard in place on both sides. Secure it with brads and glue. Slide the center piece into position and measure the distance between the two sides. Trim four of the 24-inch cleats to fit that length, with 45° ends.

Cut the remaining two 24-inch quarter-round stock to the same dimenions as the cleats above. Install them together with the four 6-inch cleats on the front and back pegboards. Position the two pieces in place and secure them to the sides and bottom.

Set the Shop Caddy upright and screw down the table top, being careful to center it in all directions.

From the 2x2 stock cut two pieces 2 feet long. These form the base. Saw two more pieces 9 inches long, on a 45° angle. These will support the top.

Lay out the pegboard following the plans.

After cutting out the parts, clamp the front, back and bottom to the center piece. Make sure all the parts are the same width. Use a Surform block plane if necessary to equalize the parts. Repeat this step with the front and back clamped together to assure the same height.

Cut the side as shown in the drawing. If you're cutting with a saber saw, use it to make the curves. If you use a circular saw, you will need a rasp to make the curves.

From the quarter-round strips saw:

2 9-1/8-inch pieces
4 6-inch pieces 45° on one end
4 30-inch pieces 45° on both ends
6 24-inch pieces (approx.)

Paint your Shop Caddy or leave it natural. Painting will preserve it longer. Fasten the four furniture glides with a hammer to the bottom supports and you're all set to go. The next time you've got a large sheet of plywood to cut, you won't have to risk life and limb to do it.

Shop Caddy

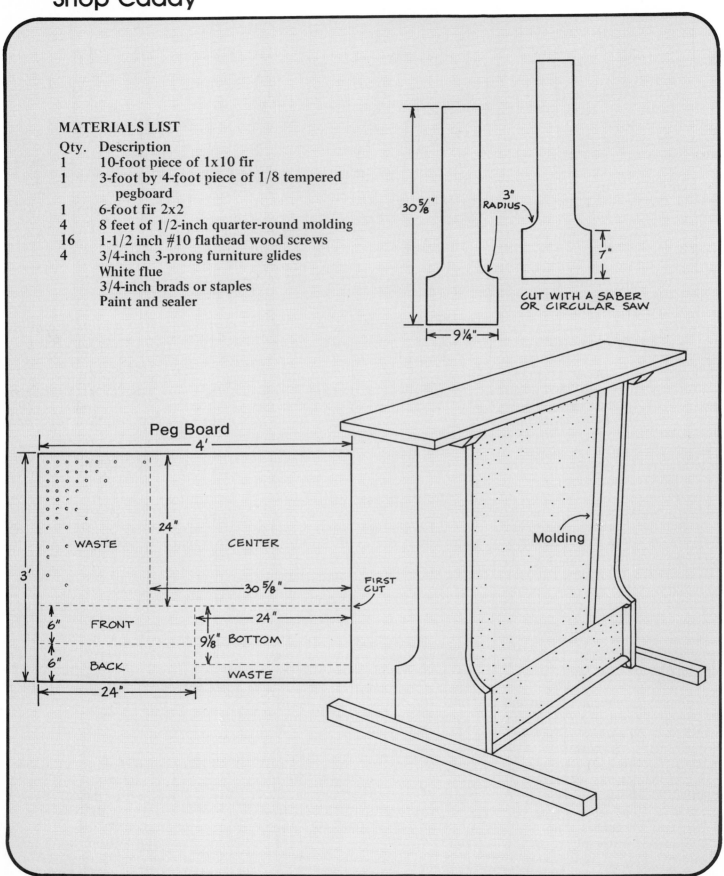

MATERIALS LIST

Qty.	Description
1	10-foot piece of 1x10 fir
1	3-foot by 4-foot piece of 1/8 tempered pegboard
1	6-foot fir 2x2
4	8 feet of 1/2-inch quarter-round molding
16	1-1/2 inch #10 flathead wood screws
4	3/4-inch 3-prong furniture glides
	White flue
	3/4-inch brads or staples
	Paint and sealer

$30\frac{5}{8}$"

$9\frac{1}{4}$"

3" RADIUS

7"

CUT WITH A SABER OR CIRCULAR SAW

Peg Board

4'

3'

24"

WASTE

CENTER

$30\frac{5}{8}$"

FIRST CUT

6" FRONT

24"

$9\frac{1}{8}$" BOTTOM

6" BACK

WASTE

24"

Molding

PET SHELTER

If this pet shelter seems to bear a close resemblance to Snoopy's Doghouse, it's because I got the idea while reading Charles Schultz's famous cartoon strip. Actually, the structure is good for any small pet— cat or dog—and it can be placed inside or outside the home.

The design is simple yet clever. There's plenty of roof overhang for shade and to keep your pet out of the rain. The vent holes near the peak of the roof cool the shelter. The porch provides a place for food dishes. When I was through building the new residence for our animal, my wife insisted I add a scrap of shag carpeting for warmth and wall-to-wall luxury. Later my daughter pirated an old heating pad to warm the house on cold winter evenings. A bit much, I thought—but the cat loved it.

After studying the plans and layout of the parts on the plywood sheets, cut the necessary dimensions one at a time. Do this because you'll lose a little wood due to the kerf. This will throw off your dimensions if you lay out everything at once. Clamp a good straight edge to the plywood to act as a guide for your saber saw when cutting the straight lines. Use a fine-tooth wood blade to cut the plywood. A medium-tooth wood blade is okay for the fir.

Remember, ACX plywood has a finished and a rough side. As you build the pet house, you'll want to wind up with the finished side out so it will be easier to paint. Also, as I mentioned in the chapter on Saber Saws, the sawblade leaves a rough edge on the top of the material and a smooth cut underneath. Therefore lay out and cut the plywood with the *good* side down. Assemble with the *good* side out.

Start with the roof first. Cut the first side 19 inches wide and the full width of the plywood sheet. Mark it A. The second piece will measure 19-1/4 inches wide. Saw it the full width of the plywood sheet also. Mark it Z. It is the larger of the two. Clamp both roof parts

This boy built a home for his best friend.

together, rough side up. Make sure the two parts are perfectly lined up on three sides. Measure 41 inches and saw both pieces at the same time, giving you a matched set, except for the 1/4-inch extra width of Z.

Measure 18 inches down the remainder of the plywood sheet and saw across the entire width of the plywood. Cut the 18-inch piece exactly in half lengthwise and clamp the two halves together, again with the rough side up. Match them carefully and plane until they are the same length. The dimension will be a little less than 24 inches because of the saw cut and planing.

Go back to what's left of the quarter-inch plywood sheet and saw 24 inches off the 48-inch width. Mark that piece with an F for Front. Measure 24-1/2 inches from the remaining stock and carefully cut off the small scrap strip. Label this piece B for Back.

To make the peaked roof, clamp F on top of B so the B overlaps 1 inch at the bottom, and F overhangs B on both sides by 1/4 inch. Use a piece of scrap plywood for this alignment. It is important this be done carefully and accurately; otherwise the roof will not be true.

Measure 12 inches in from the 24-inch width of F and 29 inches

Match the edges where you need to by using Surform plane.

Clamp the front and back together when cutting the roof line.

up from the bottom—make a cross with your pencil at the intersecting dimensions. That's the center of your roof.

Make a mark 17 inches up each side from the bottom of F. Draw two lines connecting these marks to the top center cross, this forms

Pet Shelter

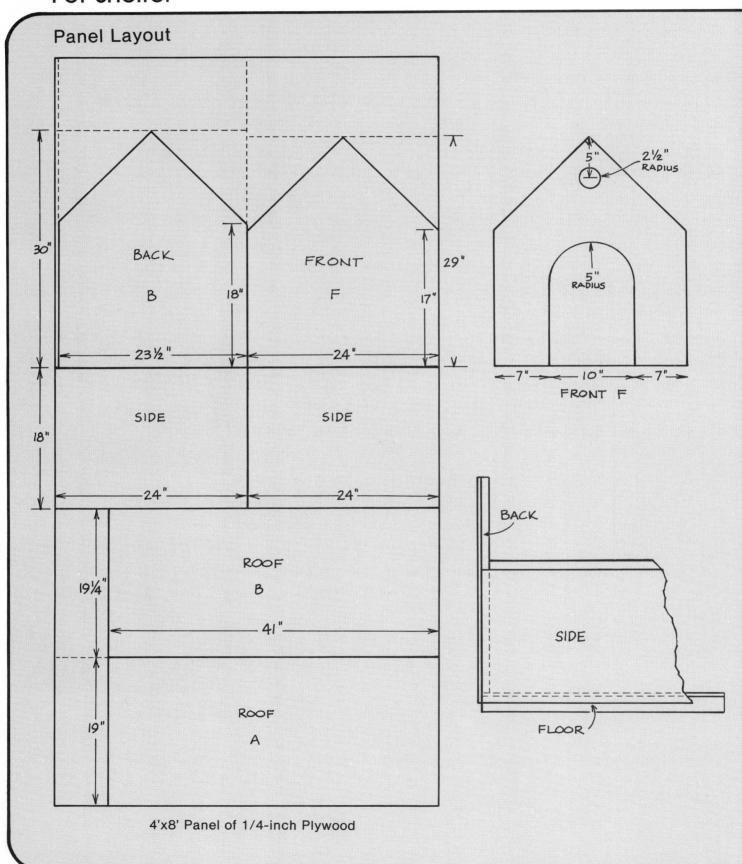

Panel Layout

BACK

B

FRONT

F

30"

18"

29"

17"

23½"

24"

SIDE

SIDE

18"

24"

24"

ROOF

B

19¼"

41"

19"

ROOF

A

4'x8' Panel of 1/4-inch Plywood

5"

2½" RADIUS

5" RADIUS

7"   10"   7"

FRONT F

BACK

SIDE

FLOOR

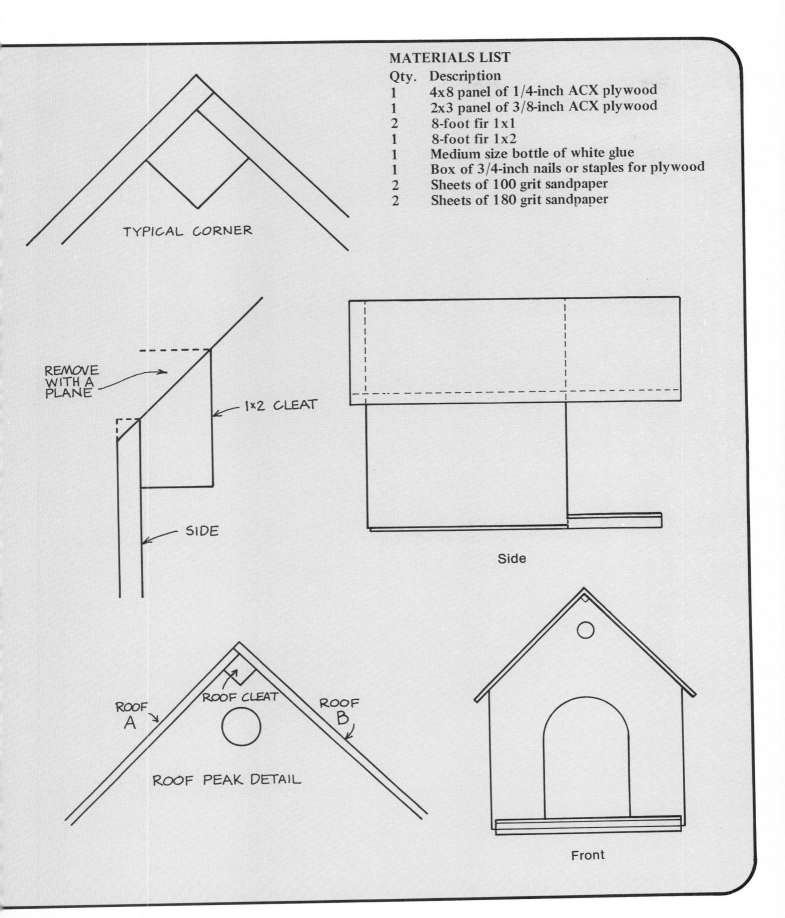

TYPICAL CORNER

REMOVE
WITH A
PLANE

1x2 CLEAT

SIDE

Side

ROOF
A

ROOF CLEAT

ROOF
B

ROOF PEAK DETAIL

Front

MATERIALS LIST

Qty.	Description
1	4x8 panel of 1/4-inch ACX plywood
1	2x3 panel of 3/8-inch ACX plywood
2	8-foot fir 1x1
1	8-foot fir 1x2
1	Medium size bottle of white glue
1	Box of 3/4-inch nails or staples for plywood
2	Sheets of 100 grit sandpaper
2	Sheets of 180 grit sandpaper

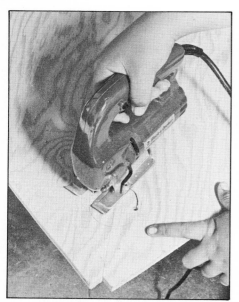

The vent holes may also be cut together. Start the hole by drilling a pilot hole to fit the sawblade.

Clamps are a must for positioning your work accurately before you secure it with nails.

Final assembly will go quickly once you get the back and one side in place.

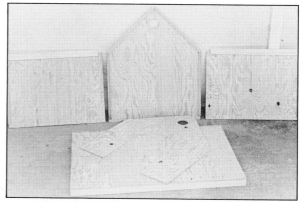

The pre-assembled panels should look like this.

your roof outline. The roof has a 45-degree pitch. If you own a framing square you can check the angle for accuracy.

Saw the peak. Place a 1x1 on edge at the peak and outline with a pencil. Cut out the outline. This will be where the roof rafter rests.

Before unclamping F and B, measure 5 inches down from the peak and draw a 2-1/2-inch circle. Cut out the circle in both parts for ventilation.

Now, working only with F, measure and cut out the doorway. The entrance is 10 inches wide by 16 inches tall, with the radius at the top being 5 inches. Locate the center of F and measure 5 inches on each side. Draw two 11-inch parallel lines from the bottom up. Connect the top of the two lines with a third line and divide it in half—it should be 10 inches long. Using a compass, spread it to 5 inches and put the point on the center mark of the 10-inch line and draw a half circle. Both sides of the circle should connect to both sides of the two 11-inch lines. The top of the circle forms the arched doorway.

Cut the floor from the 3/8-inch plywood. It should be 23-1/2 inches by 26 inches. Make sure the corners are square.

Cut 4 feet off the 1x2 fir strip. Set your saw for a 45° bevel and rip one side the full length. This completes cutting the parts.

Glue-nail 1x2 fir strips all the way around the border of the 3/8-inch plywood floor. Clamp the strips with the 1-inch surface against the plywood. Drive the nails through the plywood into the fir. Butt joints may be used on the corners, but miter cuts make a nicer-looking finish.

Measure up 1 inch from the bottom of the back piece B, and glue-nail 1x1 cleat strips all the way around the outside edge of the *rough* side.

On the side pieces, measure up 1 inch from the edge that will be the front and glue-nail a 1x1 strip to the *rough* side. Fasten a 1x2 strip along the top edge so the 45° bevel cut is flush with the top edge of the side. Before nailing this piece in place, measure the width of the 1x1 cleat and the plywood on the back

piece you just finished. Deduct this measurement from the length of the 1x2 with the front end up against the forward side cleat. This will make room for the back wall to fit into the sides.

Glue-nail the back wall to the floor, letting the cleats rest against the top surface of the floor. The sides of the back should be flush with the width of the floor.

Glue-nail both sides to the back wall and the floor. Overlap the back edges of the sides against the back wall, to form a corner. The three sides should be perfectly square and should support each other.

Set the front piece in place. Mark where the side cleats end, so you'll know how long and what angle to cut the forward roof strips. Mark the opening on the floor and draw a line from both sides, using a straight edge. Remove the front wall and attach the roof cleats to it.

Fasten two 1x1 strips to the floor on each side of the opening.

The old Surform will nicely trim the excess off the sides, allowing the roof to fit snugly.

You are now ready to seal and paint the inside of the doghouse.

He ought to look proud. He's done a fine job.

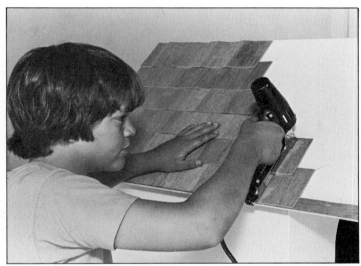

For a really deluxe finish, attach *shakes* to the roof. Add two bedrooms and I'd move in myself.

Set the front wall in position. Nail it to both sides and the floor. The front panel should overlap the sides to form a square corner.

Using a rasp or a Surform plane and a bevel square, file down the top edge of the sides to match the angle of the roof line and the 1x2 cleat.

Fasten a 1x1 strip the full length of roof A on the *rough* side. Set the roof on the house. Line up roof A so it overhangs the back side by 2 inches, and nail it down.

At this point I'd recommend you stop the construction and paint the inside with a good sealer. Mask off the areas where you're going to glue roof Z in position before you start to paint. Also mask roof Z where it will be glued, and paint it with sealer. Painting the inside of the house will protect the wood.

Roof Z should overlap A at the peak to form a square, flush top. Nail roof Z on the house.

Sand, fill and paint the outside with two coats of sealer and two coats of a color of your choice. Sand between each coat. Use a sanding block of scrap 1x4. 100 grit should be used for the sealer and 180 grit for the finish coats.

A swatch of carpeting on the floor and you're all set to move your pet inside—although it's a good idea to wait a few days to allow the paint smell to go away.

One other thought: If you've ever wondered how to shingle a roof, this is a nice size to use to learn. Buy some thin decorative veneer wooden wall strips. They're about 4 inches wide, 1/8 inch thick, and 4 feet long. Starting at the bottom of the roof, tack or staple a 1 inch wide strip the length of the roof. Then cut 4-inch lengths and tack them to the roof so the ends of the first course just overhang the bottom edge. Before starting the second layer, split one 4-inch length and fasten it so it overlaps the first layer by 2 inches. That will give you a staggered effect and the overlap will set you up for the next layer. Repeat this alternately starting with a half panel until you get to the peak. Finish off with two strips 1-1/2 inches wide the length of the roof. Make sure one strip overlaps the other at the peak. Now you've really got first-class accommodations for your pet.

END TABLE

Here's a nice simple, yet attractive table you can make with a few sticks of wood, some glue and screws. Depending on the length of legs it can either be a classy end table or a low poolside drink stand. Except for the varnishing, you should be able to complete this project in an evening of relaxed enjoyment. You'll need a Stanley Screwmate #10 and a 3/8-inch plug cutter.

When you pick up the pine and redwood, if the edges are rounded, ask the lumberman to run them through a saw to give you nice sharp corners. This will save you a lot of sanding later.

Cut both pine and redwood into 23-inch lengths. Lay all the boards on edge and square them up with a circular or saber saw. Mark a line across the boards and clamp a straight edge on top to act as a guide for your saw. Crosscut all six boards at once, using a fine-tooth blade. Repeat this until you have twenty-four pieces, 23 inches long.

Square alignment for the table top will be much easier if you build the following simple jig. With a framing square, lay out a 90° corner on your workbench or a piece of plywood. Clamp or nail two scrap 2x4s to your bench along the lines of the 90° corner. Now you can assemble the table top by lining up and drilling each piece in the jig.

End Table

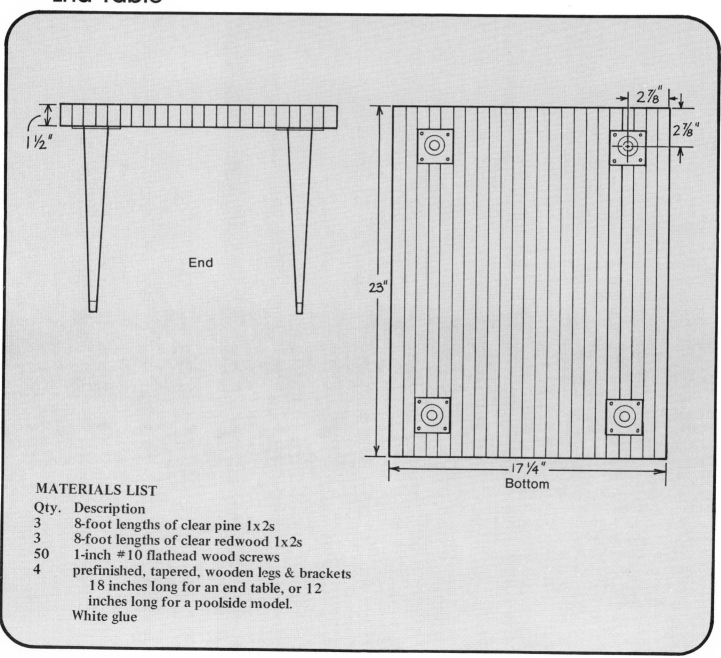

MATERIALS LIST

Qty.	Description
3	8-foot lengths of clear pine 1x2s
3	8-foot lengths of clear redwood 1x2s
50	1-inch #10 flathead wood screws
4	prefinished, tapered, wooden legs & brackets 18 inches long for an end table, or 12 inches long for a poolside model.
	White glue

This procedure ensures the table will be square.

To get the table started, glue and clamp one redwood and one pine piece together. Make sure the ends are flush with each other. On the redwood part measure in 4 inches from each end and drill holes using the Screwmate for the 1-inch #10 screws. Drill another hole in the middle, about 11-1/2 inches from the end. Make sure you countersink the holes deep enough to plug later. Screw the two pieces together and remove the clamps.

Attach alternate redwood and pine strips to the first redwood piece which becomes the outside border of the table. Stagger the screw holes between 3 and 5 inches from the ends and plus or minus 1 inch at the center. Be sure and keep the ends even. Otherwise you'll wind up with a parallelogram, instead of a rectangle.

Use up all the redwood parts. There'll be one extra pine piece left over. If you want a narrower table than the plans show, leave off a couple of boards to suit your individual taste.

The last redwood part should match the first piece. So make sure the holes on the last board are drilled 4 inches in from the end and 11-1/2 inches at the center.

Cut six plugs from redwood scrap. Coat the sides of the plugs with a little glue and tap them into the end pieces, making sure the grain of the plug is lined up with the rest of the redwood. Trim the plugs using a 1-inch, or larger, wood chisel.

If you have a belt sander, smooth the rough-sawn edges. Draw a line along the edge on both sides of the wood to act as a guide when you sand. Be careful to hold the sander even with the wood. A belt sander can take off a lot of wood in a very short time and, once it's off, you can't put it back.

If you don't have a belt sander, use a wooden block. Start with 60-grit sandpaper to dress up the ends.

The legs are easily attached. Screw the brackets to the bottom corners and twist the legs into the brackets.

Smooth the top and sides with a vibrator sander. Paint the table with a good clear sealer. Sand again and follow with two or three coats of varnish or Varathane for a mirror-like finish, sanding between coats with a fine sandpaper.

If after the final coat a little dust settles on the varnish—don't worry. Pumice powder and a soft cloth, or fine polishing compound will remove the particles, leaving a very professional-looking table.

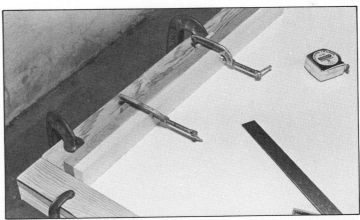

Go slow as you glue-screw each board into position. Careful initial assembly is important to establish the correct pattern.

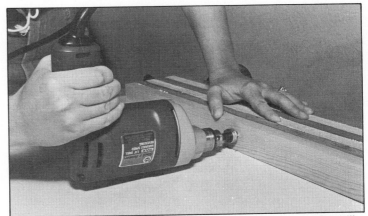

Your drill will work just as well upside down as right side up. By drilling and assembling the tabletop in the jig, you assure a square, flat surface.

A large 2x4 block makes it easier to keep the surface flat when sanding.

PICNIC TABLE

This picnic table will become the backyard entertainment center all summer long.

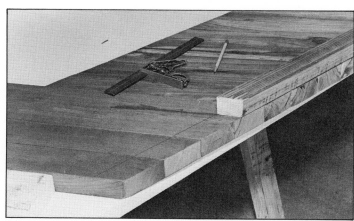

After cutting the legs, line them up for cutting the miter-rabbet cut. Use a 1-5/8-inch board as a guide so the cut will fit exactly during final assembly.

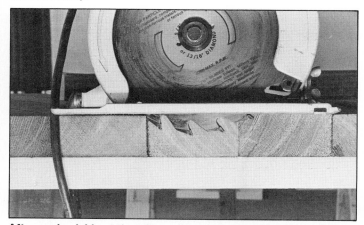

After you've laid out the miter-rabbet, set the saw depth by adjusting the baseplate.

A redwood picnic table is something nice to have in the backyard for summer barbecues and lawn parties. Buying one completely assembled will cost from eighty to over one hundred dollars at today's market. However, with an electric drill, a circular saw, and a few hand tools, you can make a first-class table with benches for about forty bucks and an afternoon's work.

Use the materials list on page 120 to get an estimate from the lumberyard. Some yards won't sell in the lengths or size you'll need, which means you might have to substitute or rearrange your layout to get the best economy.

Using a saw guide, rip two 2x4s in half lengthwise. You now have four 72-inch long 1-5/8 x 1-5/8 boards.

Cut two 28-inch lengths and one 10-inch length with 35° angles on each end, using one of the 1-5/8-inch square pieces as shown on the cutting diagram.

Cut another 28-inch length and four more 10-inch pieces with 35° angles from another square board.

Saw one 23-inch and four 10-inch lengths on a 45° angle with the third board.

From the last square board cut one 23-inch length, 45° at both ends, and one 10-inch piece with 35° ends.

You should now have the following list of parts:

Qty.	Measurements	Angles
6	1-5/8 x 10 inches	35°
4	1-5/8 x 10 inches	45°
3	1-5/8 x 28 inches	35°
2	1-5/8 x 23 inches	45°

These are the cleats that will support and brace the table and benches.

The table legs are next and you'll be using the 2x3s. Cut four legs 33-33-1/2 inches long with opposite 35° angles on each end. The legs should resemble a parallelogram when you're finished. You should get two legs from each 2x3.

Saw eight 17-1/4-inch bench legs with opposite 35° angles from the remaining 2x3s.

Lay the 2x6s and 2x4s flat on the floor to use as support for the legs. Place the legs on top so they cross the boards. Line up all the legs so that the 35° ends form a straight line. Use clamps or drive a couple of nails in the boards to keep the legs from moving once you have the straight line established. Take a 28 by 1-5/8-inch part and place it on top of the legs, parallel to the straight line and flush with the edge for a marking guide. Draw a pencil line along the

Make the full measurement cut on all the legs first. Then use random cuts to eliminate unwanted stock.

Finish up by cleaning the joint with a hammer and chisel. That completes cutting the legs.

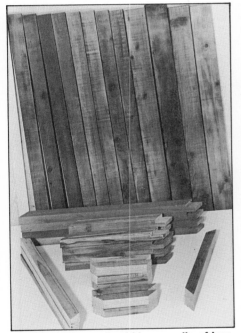

At this point you should have a pile of lumber that resembles this.

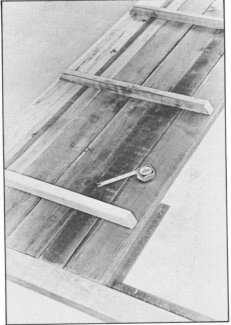

Use a straight edge and a framing square to make sure the table and bench tops are rectangular.

If you don't own any long clamps, do what I've done: Secure a piece of scrap to a long 1x4, squeeze the table top together and clamp the opposite side. This will work until you can firmly attach the cleats with glue and 2-inch #12 screws.

edge of the guide across the entire group of legs.

Set your circular saw blade to cut half the thickness of the legs. Adjust the saw guide so the blade will cut on the line you've just drawn. Crosscut all the legs at one time, on the line. Now, make repeated parallel cuts outside the original cut, until you've formed a rabbet half the thickness of the 2x3 legs, and the width of the 1-5/8-inch square cleat. Remove the nails and stack the legs.

Lay the four 2x6s and two 2x4s flat on the floor in the alternating pattern shown in the plans. Square the boards to form an even rectangle. Measure in 9 inches from each end and glue-screw two 2-5/8 by 28-inch cleats. Attach the third cleat half-way between and parallel to the two outside cleats. You've now built the table top.

Lay out three of the remaining 2x4s on the floor, squaring the corners. Glue-screw a 10-inch cleat with 35° ends 7 inches in from each end. Locate a third 10-inch cleat with 35° ends in the middle for additional bracing. Repeat this step with the three remaining 2x4s and you've assembled both bench tops.

With the last bench still on the floor, place two of the short legs so that the rabbets straddle each side of the outside cleats. The legs should cross each other.

Picnic Table

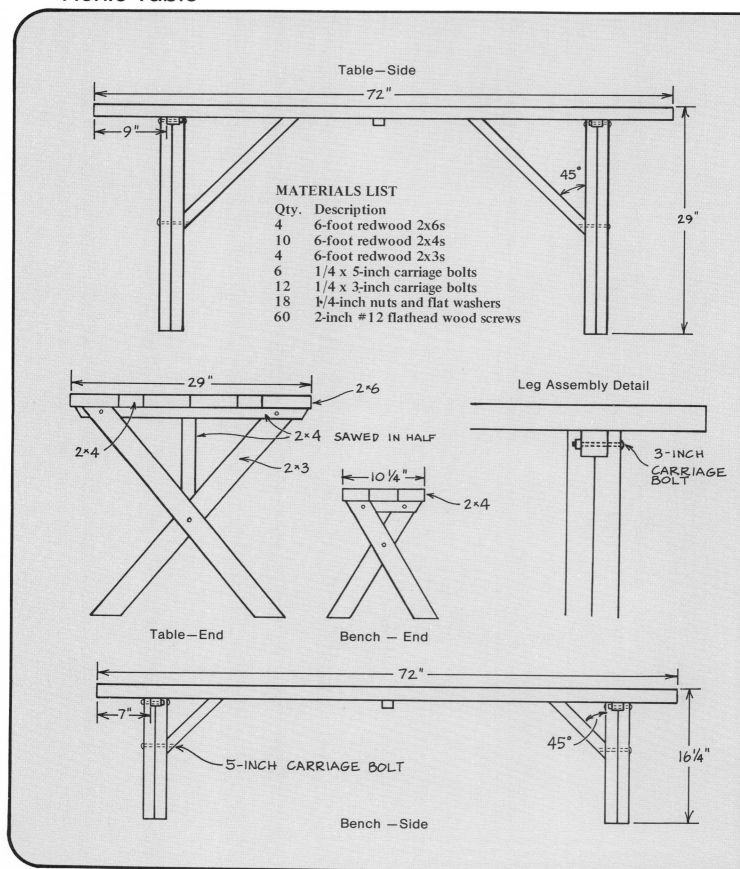

Table—Side

72"

9"

45°

29"

MATERIALS LIST

Qty.	Description
4	6-foot redwood 2x6s
10	6-foot redwood 2x4s
4	6-foot redwood 2x3s
6	1/4 x 5-inch carriage bolts
12	1/4 x 3-inch carriage bolts
18	1/4-inch nuts and flat washers
60	2-inch #12 flathead wood screws

29"

2×6

2×4 SAWED IN HALF

2×4

2×3

2×4

10 1/4"

3-INCH CARRIAGE BOLT

Leg Assembly Detail

Table—End

Bench — End

72"

7"

45°

5-INCH CARRIAGE BOLT

16 1/4"

Bench —Side

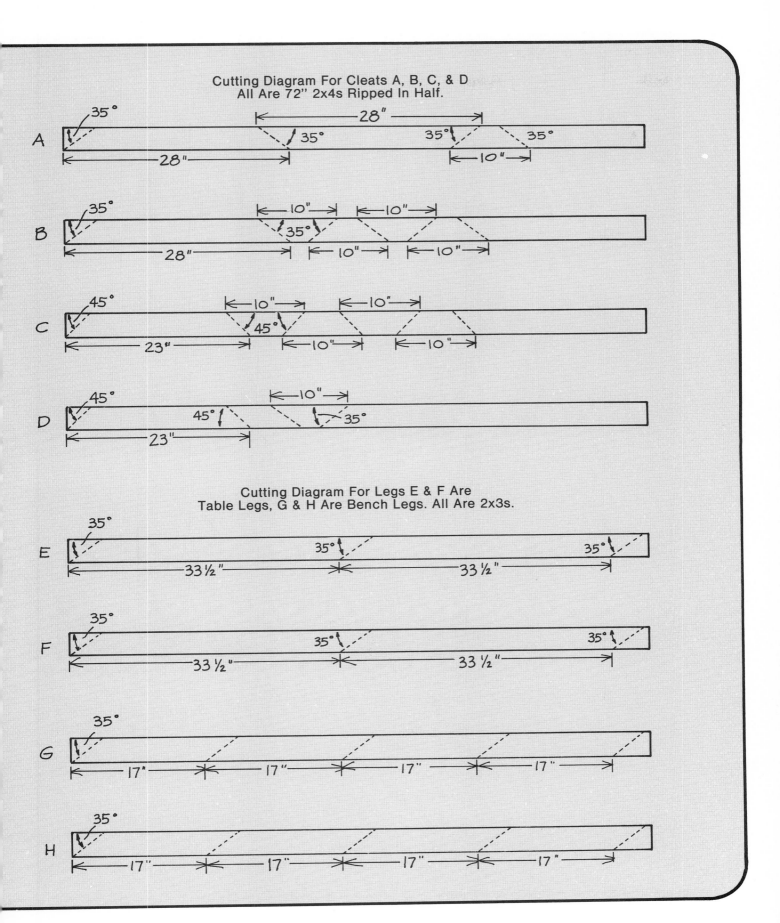

Cutting Diagram For Cleats A, B, C, & D
All Are 72" 2x4s Ripped In Half.

Cutting Diagram For Legs E & F Are
Table Legs, G & H Are Bench Legs. All Are 2x3s.

Bore from this direction for a more accurate hole.

After the hole is made, chisel out enough stock to ensure a flat surface for the washer and nut.

Once the table is set up, check to make sure it's square. If not, or if some boards are longer than others, use your saw to correct the situation.

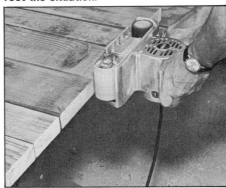

A belt sander will smooth out the saw cut.

You'll need three 4-inch C-clamps to hold the legs in position while you align them and drill the necessary holes. Loosely clamp the two rabbets to the cleat, with the legs equidistant from the sides of the bench top. Place a scrap board across the tops of both legs. Move the legs until the scrap board lies flat on the 35° miter cut, then tighten down the two clamps.

Secure a third clamp where the two legs cross. Drill a 1/4-inch hole through each leg and cleat. Fasten with a 1/4 x 3-inch bolt, washer and nut.

Take one of the 10 x 1-5/8-inch supports and place it so one end rests where the legs cross and the other end is flat on the bench. Use a framing square to make sure the legs are 90 degrees to the bench. Mark the bench with a pencil where the support meets it.

Drill a 5/32-inch hole through the support and into the bench. Countersink a 2-inch #12 screw into the support and bench. Do not glue.

Bore a 1/4-inch hole through the support and the crossed legs. Using a 3/4-inch wood chisel, cut a notch in the support where you just drilled the 1/4-inch hole. The chiseled-out area should be wide enough to accept a 1/4-inch washer and nut. One side of the notch should be parallel to the bench legs.

Re-position the support and fasten it to the crossed legs with a 1/4 x 5-inch bolt. Rescrew the other end of the support into the bench. Duplicate this operation on the rest of the benches.

Measure 3 inches in from each side to properly locate the table legs and repeat the same steps as you did with the bench legs.

Set the table and benches right side up. Round off the corners and any sharp edges with a Surform

Use a Surform plane, a rasp or sandpaper to round the edges.

plane. Sand the tops and sides with a medium to fine grit sandpaper.

Paint the tops and sides with two coats of clear sealer and two coats of clear Varathane or varnish. Sand between coats. It is not necessary to paint the bottom and legs of redwood (although you can do it if you so desire), as the wood has a natural resistance to weather. The tops and sides need painting to protect the user from splinters and scratches.

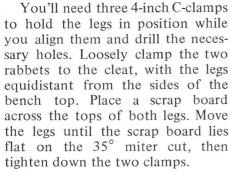

WALL HUTCH

This one's a little like assembling an erector set. It goes together with threaded rods and nuts. The warm, natural beauty of redwood gives the unit its character.

The thing I like about this design is the versatility you can build into it. There's no need to stick exactly to the plan. You can custom tailor the shape to suit your personal needs, once you understand the basic construction procedures. The unit can be made to mount flush against the wall, or be used as a room divider. It can be large or small, tall or short. Let your imagination do a little wandering and you'll come up with something just right for you.

The actual material list will vary, depending upon what design you finally select. However, since we've got to start with something to illustrate the procedures, I'm going to base the construction on the large wall model. It measures 8 feet wide by 6 feet high. You should have a drill press for this project to ensure accuracy.

I built this project for the book. After it was finished my wife insisted we keep it, and I must admit I like it too. The warmth of the wood and contemporary design blend in perfectly with our decor.

If you've already built the workbench, by all means use it instead of a floor. Use 1x4 scrap and clamps to help get the proper alignment when laying out the initial holes.

Cut out the redwood to make:

14	8-foot lengths for top and bottom shelves.
12	4-foot lengths for three middle shelves.
6	6-foot lengths for two main verticals
10	2-foot lengths for stub verticals Use the waste from the six footers.
20	3-inch spacers.
6	1-1/2-inch spacers

If the final lengths are a little short due to the waste of the saw cut, don't worry. The final assembly will compensate for the slightly smaller sizes. The important thing is that each set of parts is exactly the same length after the ends have been sanded smooth. Take your time here; it will pay you big dividends during assembly.

Lay all the cut parts flat on the floor. If they are not perfectly

Wall Hutch

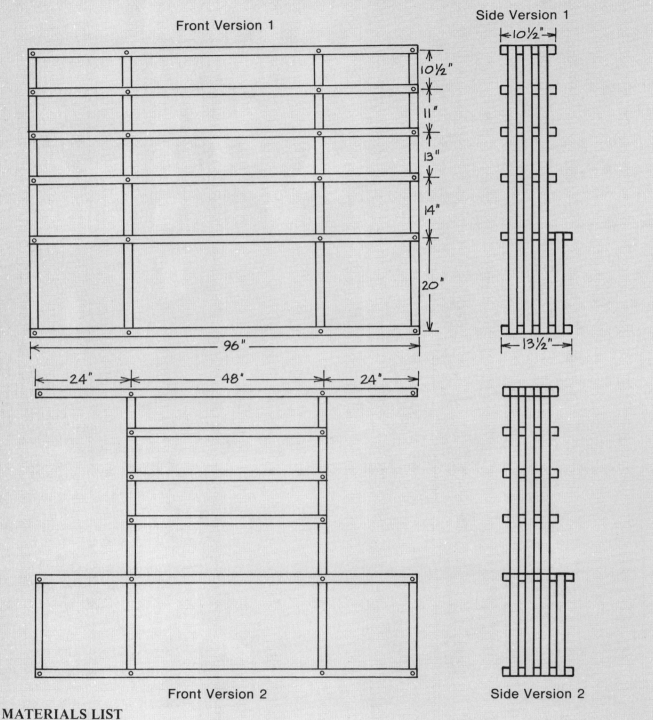

Front Version 1

Side Version 1

Front Version 2

Side Version 2

MATERIALS LIST

Qty.	Description
28	8-foot lengths of redwood 2x2 milled to 1-1/2 by 1-1/2 inches
9	3-foot lengths of threaded 5/16-inch rod
48	5/16-inch nuts
48	5/16-inch washers

This shows only two of the many possible versions of this hutch. Arrange the shelves to suit your needs.

This simple jig and drill press sped up the drilling process. But it's still a good idea to have each hole marked to confirm the accuracy of the guide.

A Portalign attachment may also be used to bore the holes precisely if you don't have a drill press.

Note the support at the end of the board being drilled. This is required to keep the holes perpendicular to the surface.

When making the inner holes, use the connecting pieces as a jig to insure perfect alignment.

square, turn them until all the pieces are even with each other. Keep all the like parts together. Line them up so the butt ends form a straight line. Using a combination square, measure in 3/4-inch on every end of every piece, except the spacer blocks, and draw a line with a sharp pencil. Locate the halfway point on the 4-foot and 8-foot parts and mark them.

Remeasure the four footers; they may be slightly less than 48 inches. If so, figure out what half the distance is and mark that measurement on each side of the center of the 8-foot pieces—less 3/4 inch. Because you're going to drill your holes 3/4 inch in from the end of the boards, this measurement must also equal the same spot on the four footers.

Check the length of the 2-foot stub verticals and measure up from one end of the 6-foot pieces that distance, less 3/4 inch. From that point mark off 14 inches, 13 inches and 11-1/2 inches on the six footers.

Mark the center of all the 3-foot spacers.

All the holes have to be drilled with a high degree of accuracy. Use a combination square to mark each hole on the boards. It is also best to make a guide to ensure precision duplicating. Clamp a piece of scrap wood to the table of the drill press. Take a waste 1-1/2-inch square and draw a line down the middle of one

side. Place the line directly under the center of the drill bit. Slide the scrap wood to be used as a guide snug against the 1-1/2-inch square and clamp it tightly to the drill press table. That will give you a guide for properly centering the holes on the boards.

To enusre that the holes are the right distance from the board ends, turn the waste square 90° so the butt end is resting against the guide. Make sure the drill bores in the middle. Clamp another piece of scrap on the right side of the waste square. This will give you a right-angle jig to fit the ends of each board for drilling.

Now you're ready to bore the end holes. Start with six 8-footers and six 4-footers. These should be drilled with a 3/4-inch bit, 5/8 inch deep to form a counterbore to hold the nuts on the finished project.

Then replace the 3/4-inch bit with a 5/16-inch bit and rebore the 3/4-inch holes all the way through. Drill the rest of the end holes with the 5/16-inch bit.

To make the holes in the middle of the boards, remove the second piece of scrap from your jig and drill where you've marked the redwood parts using the 5/16-inch bit. The jig should center them exactly.

Before cutting the threaded rods, measure your redwood boards. If the redwood is not exactly 1-1/2

inches square, measure the total thickness of seven and nine boards placed side-by-side. Deduct 1/2 inch and this will be the required length of the threaded rods.

If your redwood is 1-1/2-inches square, cut the threaded rods into two 10-1/4-inch lengths and one 13-1/4-inch section until you have fourteen 10-1/4-inch pieces. Saw the remainder of the threaded stock in 13-1/4-inch lengths until you have ten. A saber saw with a hacksaw blade is a good tool for this operation.

You are now ready to start the final assembly. Put a washer and

Clamp the threaded rod between two pieces of scrap wood to protect the threads. Masking tape marks a 90-degree cut. I found that a hand saw works almost as well for this operation. Your choice—power or manual—you've got a lot of cutting to do.

At first it seems like a giant tinker toy. Take it slow. Be careful of the ends; they'll chip if the boards are angled too far on the rods.

Make sure you've squared up the unit before you cinch down the nuts. A parallelogram makes the rest of the room look crooked.

nut on the end of each threaded rod. Starting with three 4-foot and 8-foot parts that have 3/4-inch holes, carefully tap the 10-1/4-inch rods through until the nut is recessed into the 3/4-inch counterbore. The 13-1/4-inch rods should all be inserted into two of the 8-foot pieces. These will become the bottom shelves. It will be a tight fit, so use a mallet or a hammer and a block of wood to prevent damaging the threads.

Next, tap two 6-foot pieces down the rods—2 feet in from each end of the 8-foot pieces. Position the 3-inch spacers in the middle of the 4- and 8-footers. Drive the three 4-foot parts onto the 6-foot pieces from the rear. Alternate 8-foot and 4-foot lengths with 6-foot verticals. The stub verticals go on the ends of the bottom 8-foot horizontals—connecting the two shelves. Take your time and make sure everything fits flush. If one piece doesn't seem to line up with the others, turn it over. Maybe you didn't drill the holes exactly in the center.

When you're finished, square up the unit using a framing square. Or, if the floor is level, set the complete piece upright and use a level on the verticals to assure true alignment.

Put on the final nuts and washers and tighten everything down. A socket set comes in handy here.

If you want to cover the 3/4-inch counterbores, redwood plugs would be ideal. But they're very hard to find; 3/4-inch dowels will do an accaptable job. Cut them in 1/4-inch slices and tap them into place using a little white glue to keep them there. A good sharp chisel and some sandpaper will finish the job.

The wall unit can be either varnished, oiled or left natural. Redwood looks good any way you choose. If you select varnish, seal the wood first and use a fine steel wool between coats, instead of sandpaper. It's faster, easier, and works just as well.

Put it in place, load it with books, your stereo, and a couple of planters. It's finished and you should be proud of it.

Now that I've talked you through several projects, here are some plans you can follow on your own. With the techniques we've discussed in this book, these plans should be easy and should produce fine projects.

Because all of these plans include plywood, as will many of the plans you use in the future, let me say one or two things about working with that material.

HOW TO SELECT PLYWOOD

Plywood comes in two types: Exterior Type for outdoor uses and Interior Type for indoor use. Within each type are grades for every job. The right grade to use for each of the projects in this chapter is given in the materials list.

Additional information on selecting plywood, lumber and other materials is found in Chapter 13.

PLANNING

Before starting, study the plan carefully to make sure you understand all details. Compare the materials list with the drawings so you know exactly where each part fits on the plan.

MAKING A LAYOUT

Following the panel layout, draw all parts on the plywood panels using a straightedge and a carpenter's square for accuracy. Use a compass to draw corner radii. Be sure to allow for saw kerfs when plotting dimensions. If in doubt, measure the width of your saw cut.

CUTTING

For hand-sawing use a 10 to 15 point crosscut blade. Support the panel firmly with face *up*. Use a finetoothed coping saw for curves. For inside cuts, start the hole with a drill then use a coping or keyhole saw to complete the cut.

For power sawing, a *plywood blade* gives best results, but a *combination blade* may be used. Lay the panel *face down for a hand power saw* and *face up for a table power saw*.

Your first cuts should reduce the panel to pieces small enough for easy handling. Use scrap lumber underneath panel, clamped or

tacked securely in place to prevent splintering on back side. Cut matching parts with same saw setting.

DRILLING

Support plywood firmly. For larger holes use brace and bit. When point appears through plywood, reverse the panel and complete hole from the back. Finish slowly to avoid splintering.

PLANING

Remember, edge grain of plywood runs in alternate directions so plane from both ends toward center. Use a shallow-set blade.

SANDING

Most sanding should be confined to edges with 1-0 or finer sandpaper, before sealer or flat undercoat is applied. You may find it easier to sand cut edges smooth before assembling each unit. Plywood is sanded smooth in manufacture—one of the big time-savers in its use—so only minimum surface sanding is necessary. Use 3-0 sandpaper in direction of the grain only, after sealing.

ASSEMBLY

Assembly by sections. For example, assemble any part that can be handled separately as an individual completed unit, such as drawers, cabinet shells or compartments. Construction by section makes final assembly easier. For strongest possible joints, use a combination of glue and nails or screws. To glue-nail or glue-screw, check for a good fit by holding the pieces together. Pieces should contact at all points for lasting strength along edge of the piece to be nailed. In careful work where nails must be very close to an edge, you may wish to pre-drill using a drill bit slightly smaller than nail size. Always predrill for screws.

Apply glue to clean surfaces, according to manufacturer's instructions. Press surfaces firmly together until a bead of glue appears at the edge of the joint, then drive the nails or screws. Check for squareness, and apply clamps if possible to maintain pressure until glue sets. For exterior exposure, use resorcinol-type waterproof glue. For interior work, use liquid resin (white) or urea resin glues. Other glues are available for special gluing problems. In any case, follow the manufacturer's instructions for applying the glue.

FINISHING FOR EXTERIOR USE

Since edges of plywood absorb moisture rapidly unless sealed, coat edges thoroughly with a high-quality oil-base exterior paint primer if unit is to be painted, or a good water-repellent preservative if unit is to be stained.

For painting, always use a prime coat. Skimping on a primer can jeopardize the effectiveness of even the best top coats. Prime the unit just as soon as you can after assembly is complete. Use the painting technique described on page 61 for a really fine finish.

For rough or textured plywood, oil-base stains are the recommended finish. Semi-transparent stains allow both the grain and the surface texture to show clearly, but leave little surface film. Opaque stains hide grain pattern, but not the texture. Stains should be applied in one or two coats, and, as with paints, give best performance if applied by brush. Brushing works the finish into the wood surface.

Whatever finishing method you use—paint or stain—always use top-quality materials, and follow the manufacturer's instructions.

SLIP-TOGETHER BED/DESK

Lay out parts as shown on panel layout. Use a straight edge to ensure accuracy. Label each part for identification.

Cut out parts. Center saw blade on the lines to reduce effect of the kerf width on dimensions.

Cut out slots carefully. Use a plunge cut for interior slots.

Fill any voids in the edges with wood dough or synthetic filler. When dry, smooth with fine sandpaper.

Glue step doublers for the bunk ladder as shown on ladder side view.

Begin assembly by placing sides into slots on bottom ends.

Insert desk top and bed support.

Insert bed board. Lock all horizontal pieces in place with the tabs on each slot. Attach foot and head boards. Finish as desired.

Slip-Together Bed/Desk

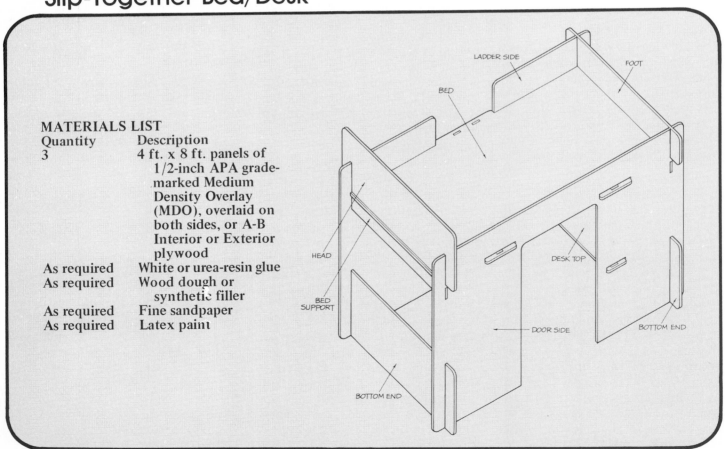

MATERIALS LIST

Quantity	Description
3	4 ft. x 8 ft. panels of 1/2-inch APA grade-marked Medium Density Overlay (MDO), overlaid on both sides, or A-B Interior or Exterior plywood
As required	White or urea-resin glue
As required	Wood dough or synthetic filler
As required	Fine sandpaper
As required	Latex paint

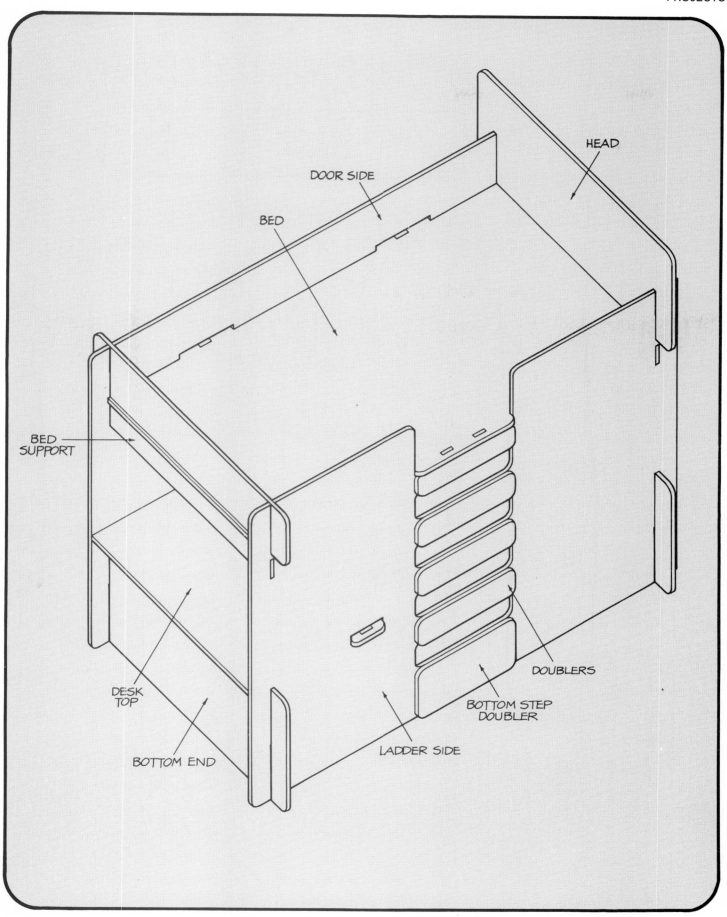

HEAD

DOOR SIDE

BED

BED SUPPORT

DESK TOP

BOTTOM END

LADDER SIDE

BOTTOM STEP DOUBLER

DOUBLERS

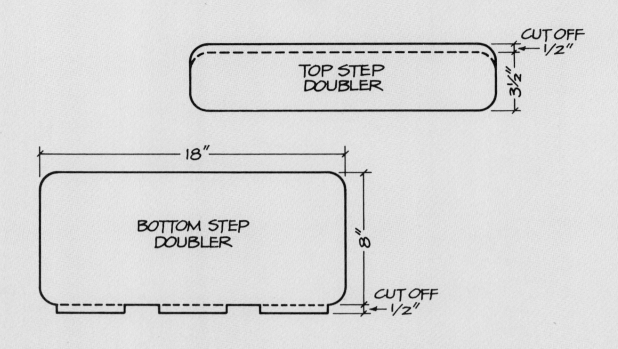

Panel Layout

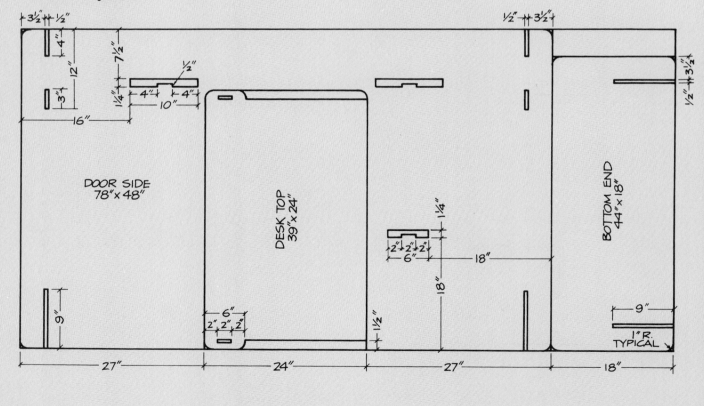

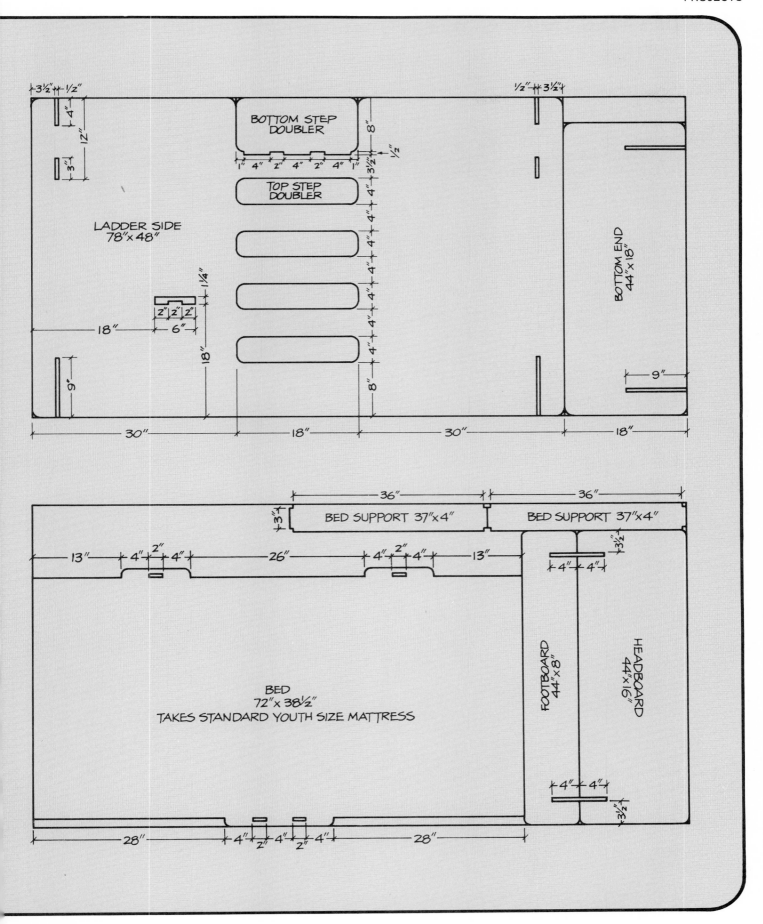

LADDER SIDE
78" x 48"

BOTTOM STEP
DOUBLER

TOP STEP
DOUBLER

BOTTOM END
44" x 18"

BED SUPPORT 37" x 4"

BED SUPPORT 37" x 4"

FOOTBOARD
44" x 8"

HEADBOARD
44" x 16"

BED
72" x 38½"
TAKES STANDARD YOUTH SIZE MATTRESS

DESK/DRAWING TABLE

Lay out parts as shown in panel layout. Use a straight edge for accuracy.

Cut out parts. Center saw blade on cut lines to minimize the effect of kerf width on dimensions. Take special care when cutting slots to ensure a tight fit when assembling.

Fill any voids in edges with wood dough or synthetic filler. When dry, sand smooth with fine sandpaper.

Assemble as shown in plans. Choose position 1 or 2 according to your needs. The angled drawing surface G can be held in place by dowels inserted into the top edges of sides A and B and the bottom of G. Or, G can be held by using non-permanent-stick adhesive strips such as Velcro tape.

Finish desk as desired.

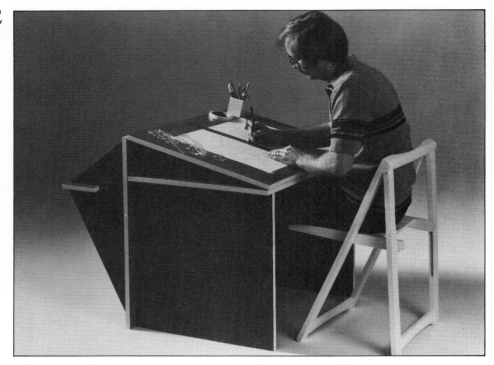

Desk/Drawing Table

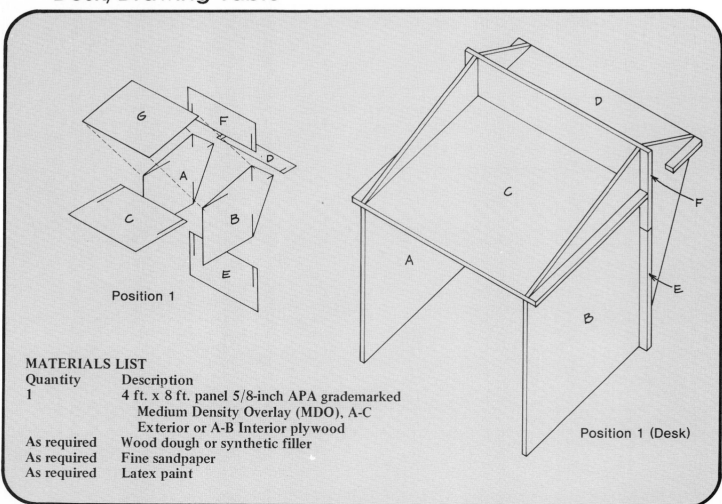

Position 1

Position 1 (Desk)

MATERIALS LIST

Quantity	Description
1	4 ft. x 8 ft. panel 5/8-inch APA grademarked Medium Density Overlay (MDO), A-C Exterior or A-B Interior plywood
As required	Wood dough or synthetic filler
As required	Fine sandpaper
As required	Latex paint

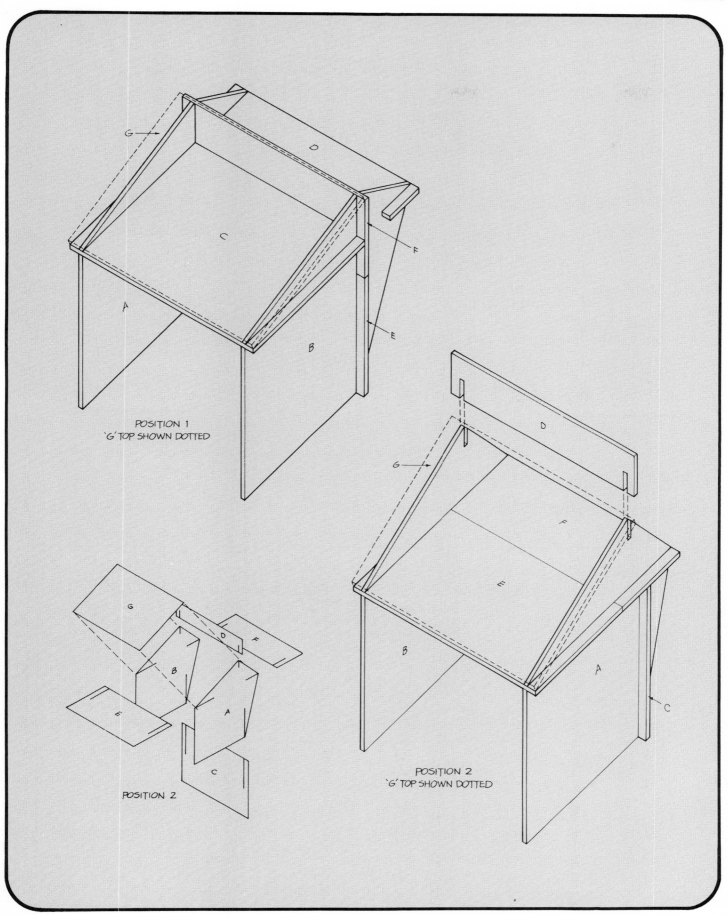

POSITION 1
'G' TOP SHOWN DOTTED

POSITION 2

POSITION 2
'G' TOP SHOWN DOTTED

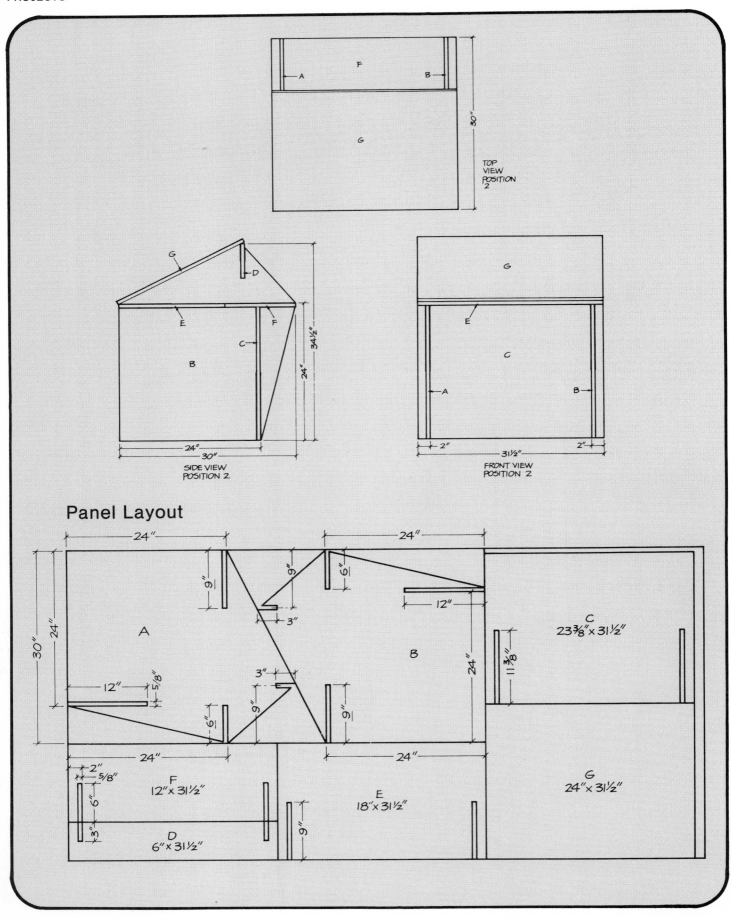

TOP VIEW
POSITION 2

SIDE VIEW
POSITION 2

FRONT VIEW
POSITION 2

Panel Layout

A

B

C
23⅜" x 31½"

F
12" x 31½"

E
18" x 31½"

D
6" x 31½"

G
24" x 31½"

PATIO TABLE & CHAIRS

Lay out parts as shown in panel layout. Use a straight edge for accuracy. Label parts for easy identification.

Cut out parts. Center saw blade on cut lines to minimize the effect of kerf width on dimensions.

Fill any voids in edges with wood dough or synthetic filler. When dry, sand smooth with fine sandpaper.

Glue chair seats and back to one side and clamp. When glue is dry, glue other side in place and clamp.

Glue-screw chair braces into place.

Finish chairs as desired.

Match different width table legs in sets of two. Glue together at right angles with wide leg overlapping edge of other leg. Clamp and let glue dry.

Place table top down on a clean, flat surface. Glue one leg assembly at each corner. Glue-screw leg brace in place. Let glue dry.

Glue table edges into place. Two longer edges should go on opposite sides and overlap the ends of shorter edges.

Finish table as desired.

Build lazy Susan as shown in detail using 6-inch bearing. Lazy Susan can be attached permanently to table with glue or left unattached, if you prefer.

Patio Table & Chairs

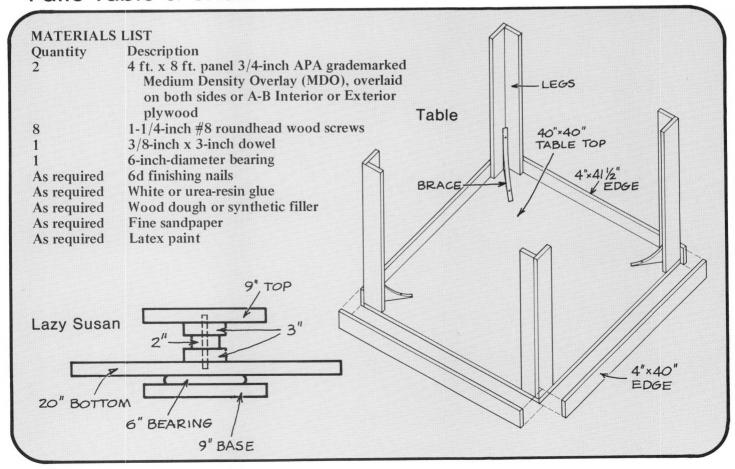

MATERIALS LIST

Quantity	Description
2	4 ft. x 8 ft. panel 3/4-inch APA grademarked Medium Density Overlay (MDO), overlaid on both sides or A-B Interior or Exterior plywood
8	1-1/4-inch #8 roundhead wood screws
1	3/8-inch x 3-inch dowel
1	6-inch-diameter bearing
As required	6d finishing nails
As required	White or urea-resin glue
As required	Wood dough or synthetic filler
As required	Fine sandpaper
As required	Latex paint

135

Chairs

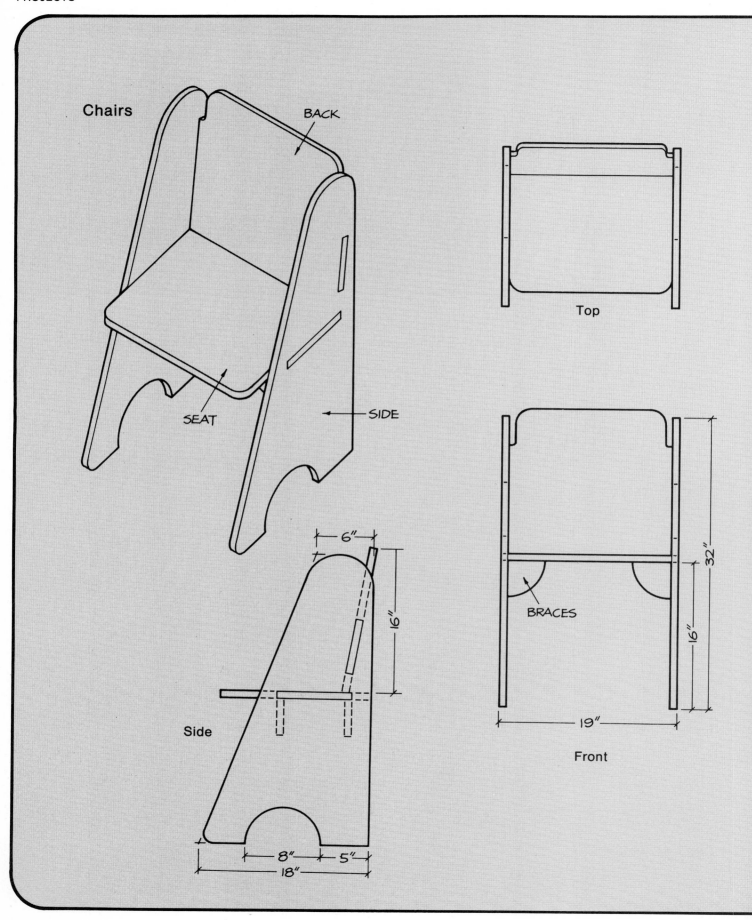

BACK

SEAT

SIDE

Top

6"

16"

Side

8"   5"

18"

BRACES

32"

16"

19"

Front

Panel Layout

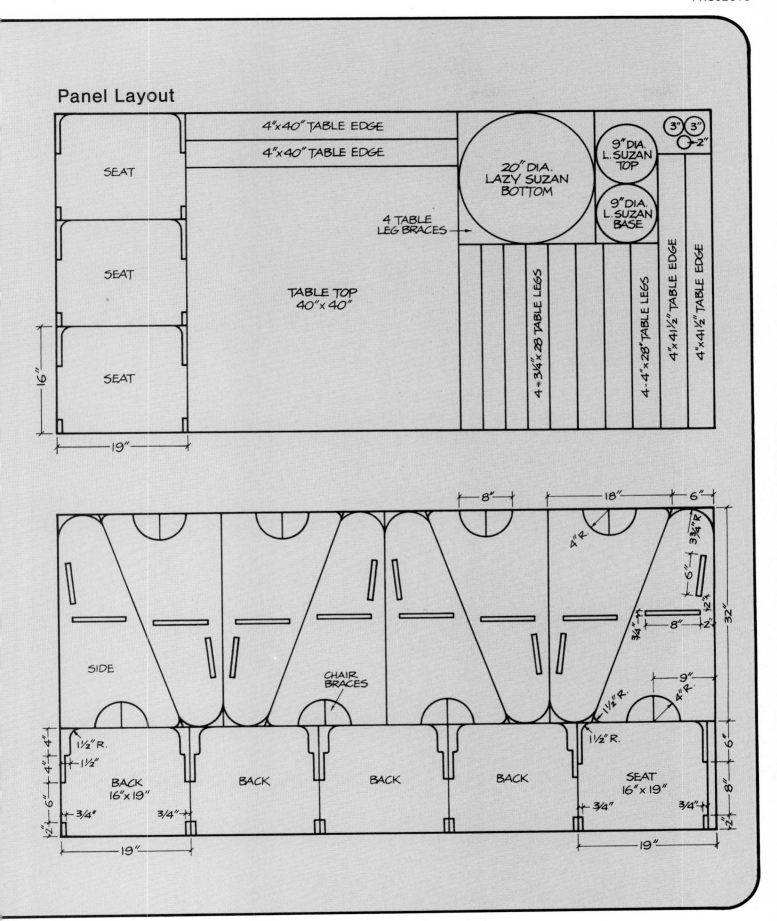

CHILDRENS' TABLE & STOOLS

Lay out parts as shown in panel layout. For accuracy, it is best to make a template out of cardboard for the table parts and another for the stools. Use a straight edge and compass for accuracy.

Cut out parts. Center saw blade on cut lines to minimize the effect of kerf width on dimensions.

Clamp like pieces together and sand to make equal. Fill any voids in edges with wood dough or synthetic filler. When dry, sand smooth with fine sandpaper.

Assemble table top and stool tops as shown in plans. Glue-nail framing into position.

Legs for both table and stools are held together with hinges so they

can be folded and stored. Use 4 butt hinges and 2 loose-pin hinges for each set of legs as shown in the plans.

Lock each loose-pin hinge together with a bent nail. It can be removed easily for folding.

Finish table and stools as desired.

Childrens' Table & Stools

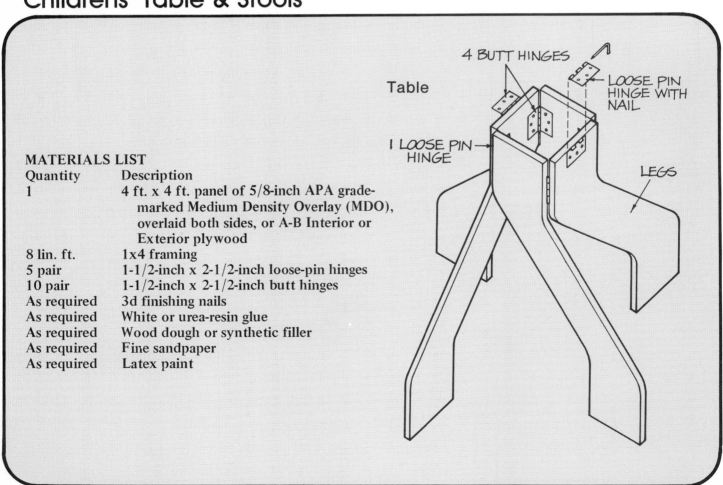

MATERIALS LIST

Quantity	Description
1	4 ft. x 4 ft. panel of 5/8-inch APA grade-marked Medium Density Overlay (MDO), overlaid both sides, or A-B Interior or Exterior plywood
8 lin. ft.	1x4 framing
5 pair	1-1/2-inch x 2-1/2-inch loose-pin hinges
10 pair	1-1/2-inch x 2-1/2-inch butt hinges
As required	3d finishing nails
As required	White or urea-resin glue
As required	Wood dough or synthetic filler
As required	Fine sandpaper
As required	Latex paint

Table

4 BUTT HINGES

LOOSE PIN HINGE WITH NAIL

I LOOSE PIN HINGE

LEGS

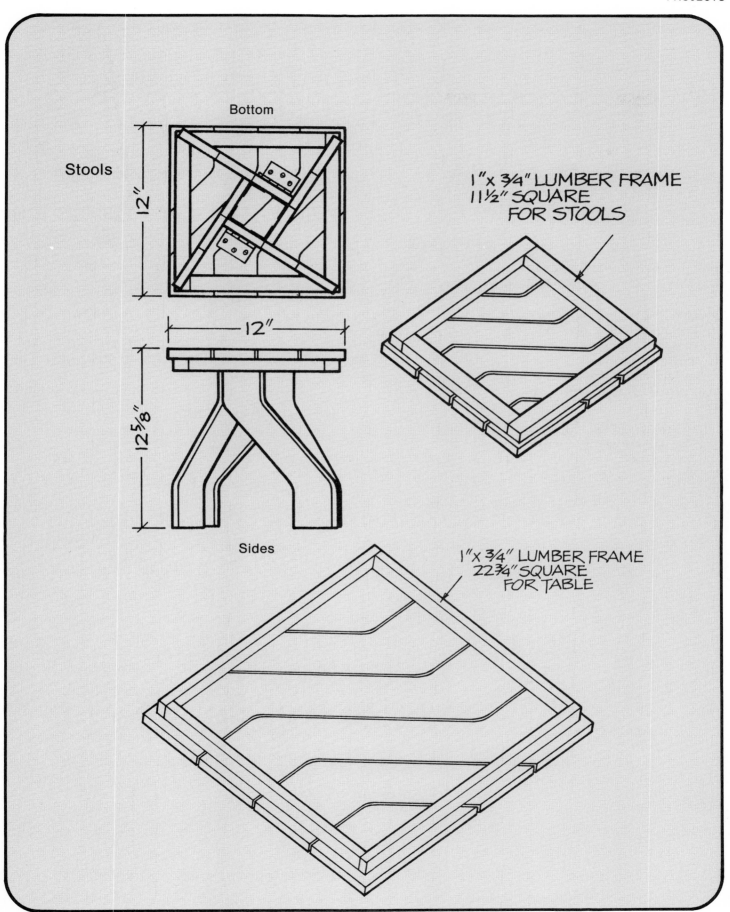

Stools

Bottom

12"

12"

12⅝"

Sides

1"x ¾" LUMBER FRAME
11½" SQUARE
    FOR STOOLS

1"x ¾" LUMBER FRAME
22¾" SQUARE
    FOR TABLE

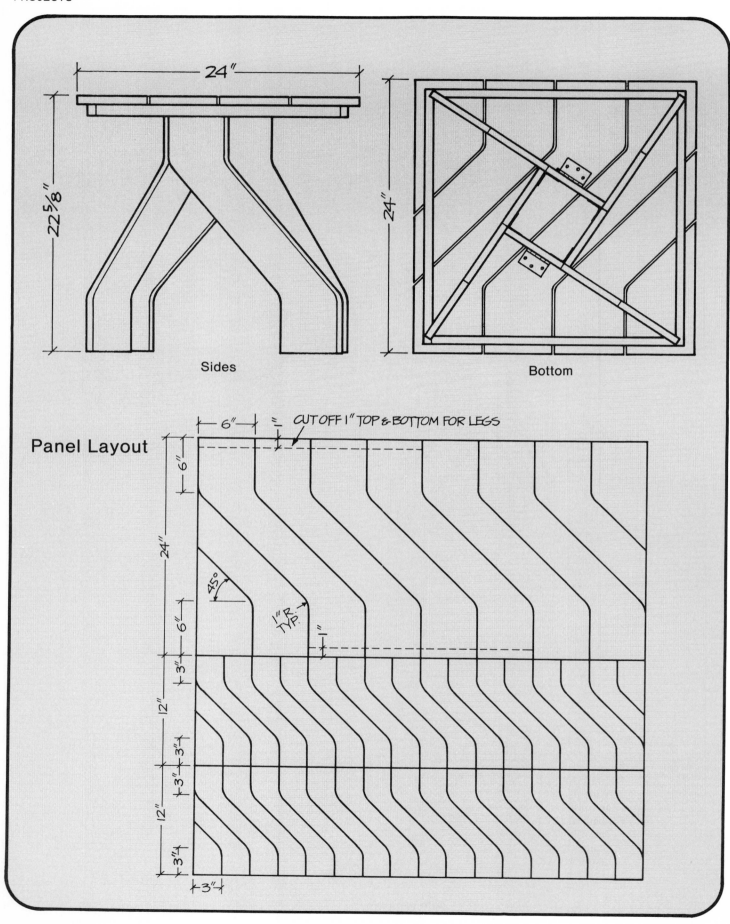

24"

22 5/8"

Sides

24"

Bottom

Panel Layout

6"

CUT OFF 1" TOP & BOTTOM FOR LEGS

6"

24"

45°

6"

1" R. TYP.

3"

12"

3"

3"

12"

3"

3"

PATIO BARBECUE STAND

Lay out and mark parts as shown in panel layout.

Cut out panels. Center blade on cut line between parts to minimize the effect of kerf width. Note that textured sidings are manufactured with shiplapped edges so that grooves occur at edge joints. Follow cutting plan carefully.

Assemble 2x4 framing with 10d common nails as shown in plans.

Attach doors to end pieces with butt hinges.

Nail bottom, dividers and 2 back pieces to frame with 8d nails.

Nail front to frame.

Nail ends to frame so they overlap both front and back.

Nail top in place. Glue Formica to top.

Fill any visable edge with wood dough or synthetic filler.

Finish as desired.

Patio Barbecue Stand

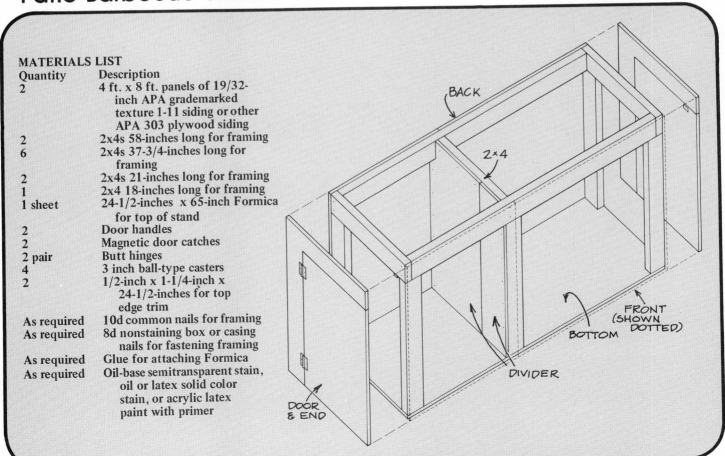

MATERIALS LIST

Quantity	Description
2	4 ft. x 8 ft. panels of 19/32-inch APA grademarked texture 1-11 siding or other APA 303 plywood siding
2	2x4s 58-inches long for framing
6	2x4s 37-3/4-inches long for framing
2	2x4s 21-inches long for framing
1	2x4 18-inches long for framing
1 sheet	24-1/2-inches x 65-inch Formica for top of stand
2	Door handles
2	Magnetic door catches
2 pair	Butt hinges
4	3 inch ball-type casters
2	1/2-inch x 1-1/4-inch x 24-1/2-inches for top edge trim
As required	10d common nails for framing
As required	8d nonstaining box or casing nails for fastening framing
As required	Glue for attaching Formica
As required	Oil-base semitransparent stain, oil or latex solid color stain, or acrylic latex paint with primer

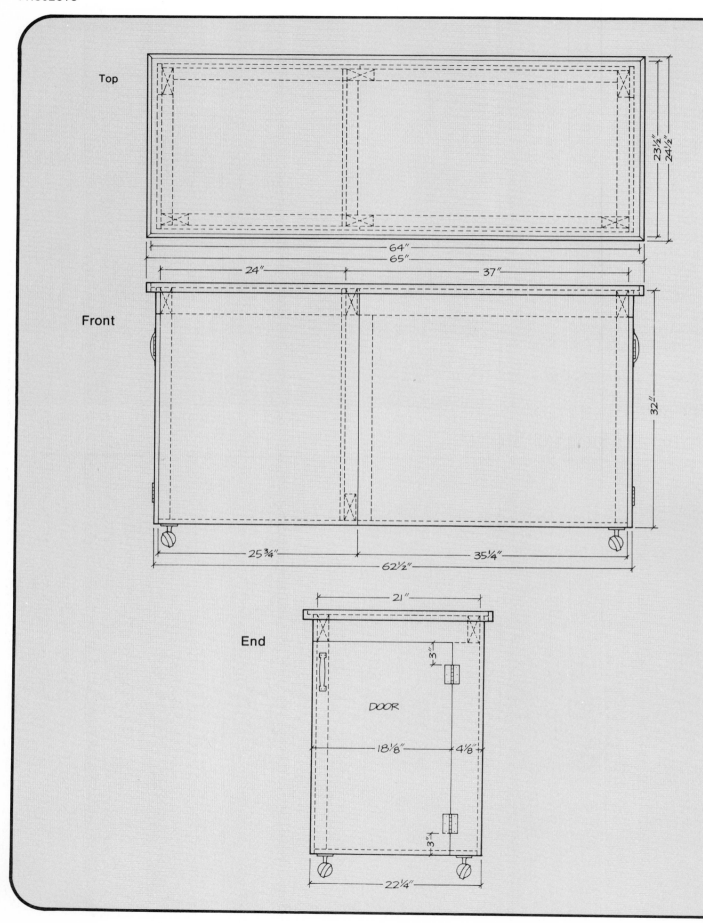

Panel Layout

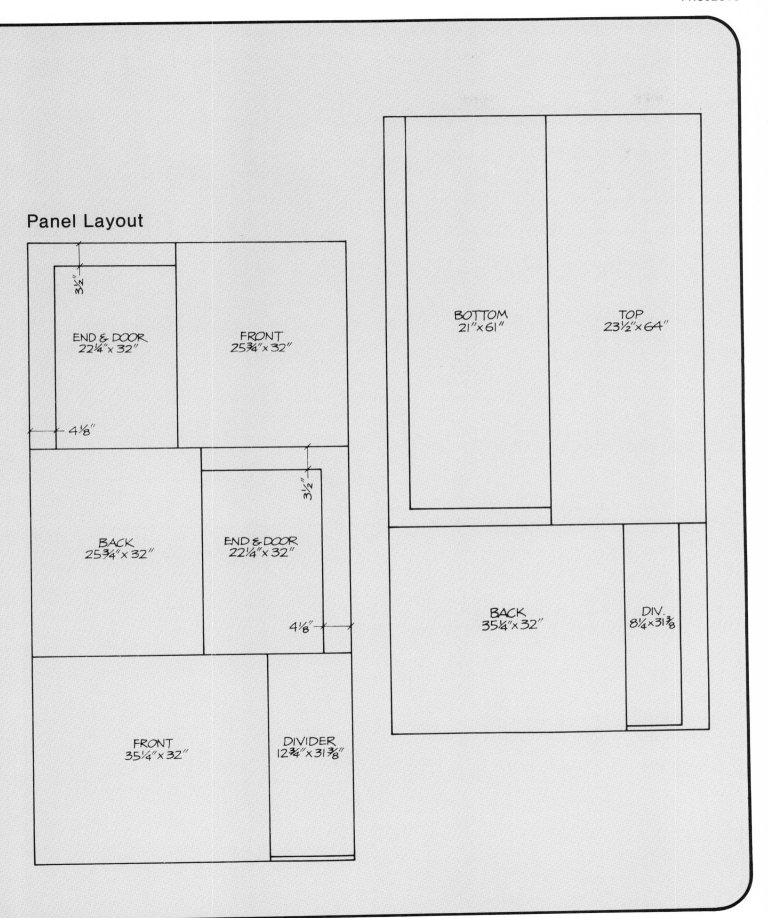

END & DOOR
22¼" x 32"

FRONT
25¾" x 32"

3½"

4⅛"

BACK
25¾" x 32"

END & DOOR
22¼" x 32"

3½"

4⅛"

FRONT
35¼" x 32"

DIVIDER
12¾" x 31⅜"

BOTTOM
21" x 61"

TOP
23½" x 64"

BACK
35¼" x 32"

DIV.
8¼ x 31⅜

ROCKING CHAIR

Lay out parts as shown in panel layout. Use a straight edge and compass for accuracy. Follow side detail for establishing proper curves. Label parts for easy identification.

Cut out parts. Center saw blade on cut line to minimize the effect or kerf width on dimensions.

Clamp sides A and B together and sand so all edges are equal.

Fill any voids in edges with wood dough or synthetic filler. When dry, sand smooth with fine sandpaper.

The back (F1 & F2) and the seat (D, E1 & E2) are attached to the sides with dowels. Drill matching 7/8-inch-deep holes into the ends of the back and seat pieces, and in the sides as shown in the plans. Round the outer edges of pieces E1, F1 and F2 with a file or sandpaper.

Glue dowels in place in the back and seat. Allow glue to dry.

Glue center brace C and the seat and back in position on side A.

Glue side B into position and clamp or press until dry.

Finish as desired.

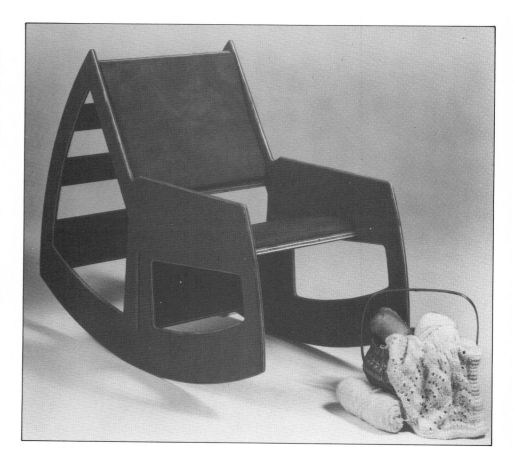

Rocking Chair

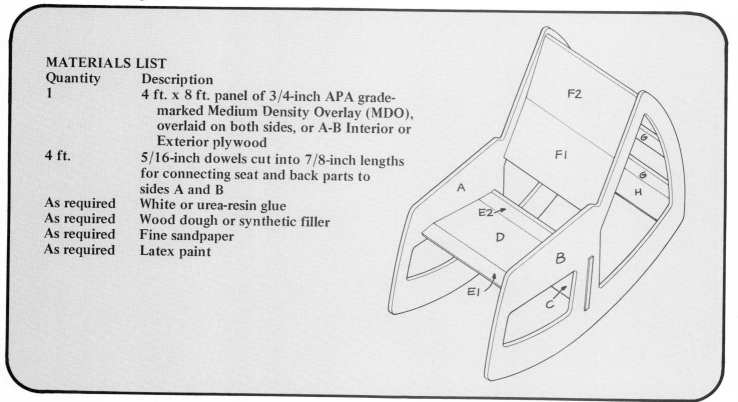

MATERIALS LIST

Quantity	Description
1	4 ft. x 8 ft. panel of 3/4-inch APA grade-marked Medium Density Overlay (MDO), overlaid on both sides, or A-B Interior or Exterior plywood
4 ft.	5/16-inch dowels cut into 7/8-inch lengths for connecting seat and back parts to sides A and B
As required	White or urea-resin glue
As required	Wood dough or synthetic filler
As required	Fine sandpaper
As required	Latex paint

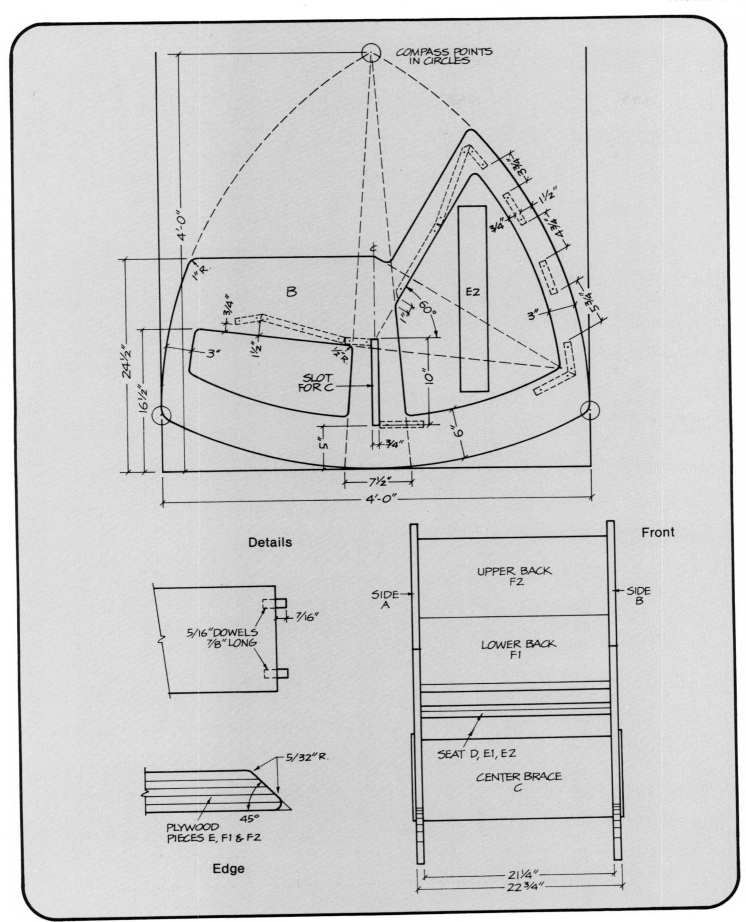

COMPASS POINTS IN CIRCLES

4'-0"

1" R.

B

24½"

16½"

3/4"

1½"

3"

½" R.

SLOT FOR C

5"

3/4"

7½"

4'-0"

E2

60°

1"

10"

6"

3/4"

1½"

3/4"

4¼"

3"

5¾"

Details

5/16" DOWELS 7/8" LONG

7/16"

5/32" R.

45°

PLYWOOD PIECES E, F1 & F2

Edge

Front

UPPER BACK F2

SIDE A

SIDE B

LOWER BACK F1

SEAT D, E1, E2

CENTER BRACE C

21¼"

22¾"

Panel Layout

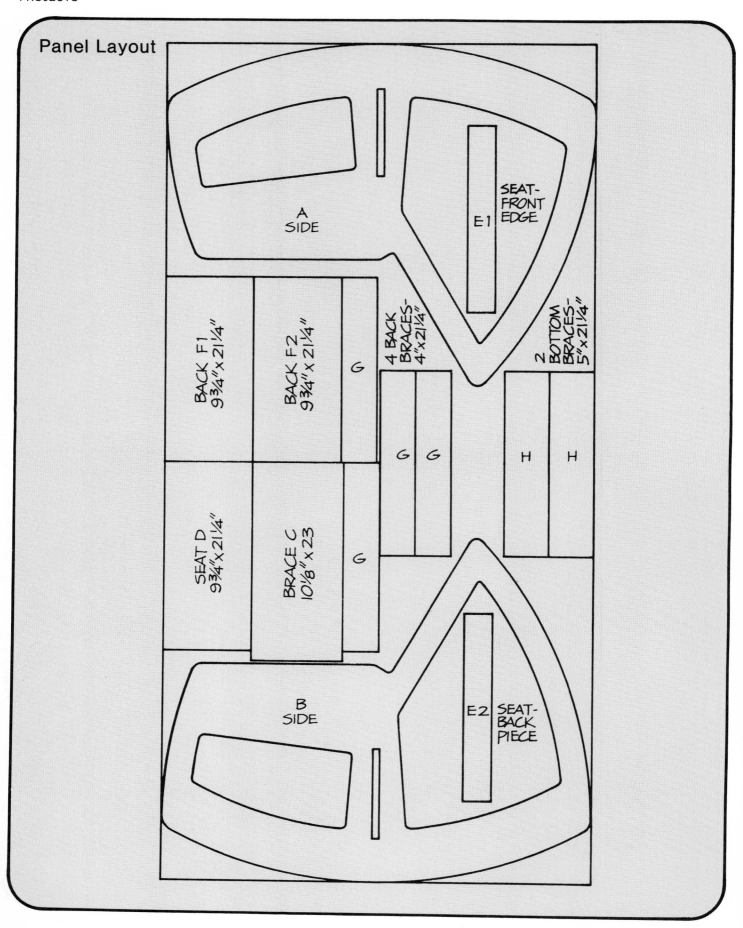

A SIDE

SEAT-FRONT EDGE

E1

BACK F1 9¾" x 21¼"

BACK F2 9¾" x 21¼"

G

4 BACK BRACES— 4" x 21¼"

2 BOTTOM BRACES— 5" x 21¼"

G   G

H   H

G

SEAT D 9¾" x 21¼"

BRACE C 10⅛" x 23

G

B SIDE

E2 SEAT-BACK PIECE

MULTI-WIDTH TABLE

Lay out parts as shown on panel layout. Use a straight edge to insure accuracy.

Cut out parts. Center saw blade on cut lines to minimize the effect of kerf width on dimensions.

Fill any voids in edges with wood dough or synthetic filler. When dry, sand smooth with fine sandpaper.

Attach large and small top braces to the center support with continuous hinges.

Attach large and small top to center top with continuous hinges.

Lay the top face down on a clean surface and set brace assembly into position. Glue-screw center support to the center top with the method shown in the detail.

Glue 1/8-inch shims into position to stabilize braces. Let glue dry.

Finish as desired.

Multi Width Table

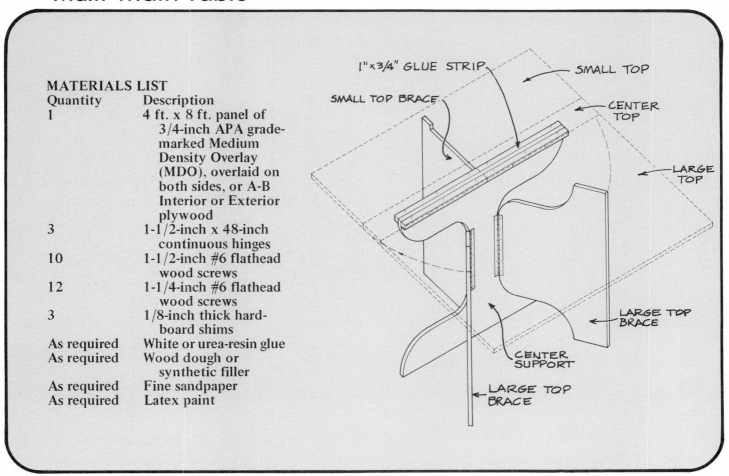

MATERIALS LIST

Quantity	Description
1	4 ft. x 8 ft. panel of 3/4-inch APA grade-marked Medium Density Overlay (MDO), overlaid on both sides, or A-B Interior or Exterior plywood
3	1-1/2-inch x 48-inch continuous hinges
10	1-1/2-inch #6 flathead wood screws
12	1-1/4-inch #6 flathead wood screws
3	1/8-inch thick hardboard shims
As required	White or urea-resin glue
As required	Wood dough or synthetic filler
As required	Fine sandpaper
As required	Latex paint

Diagram labels: 1"x3/4" GLUE STRIP, SMALL TOP, SMALL TOP BRACE, CENTER TOP, LARGE TOP, LARGE TOP BRACE, CENTER SUPPORT, LARGE TOP BRACE

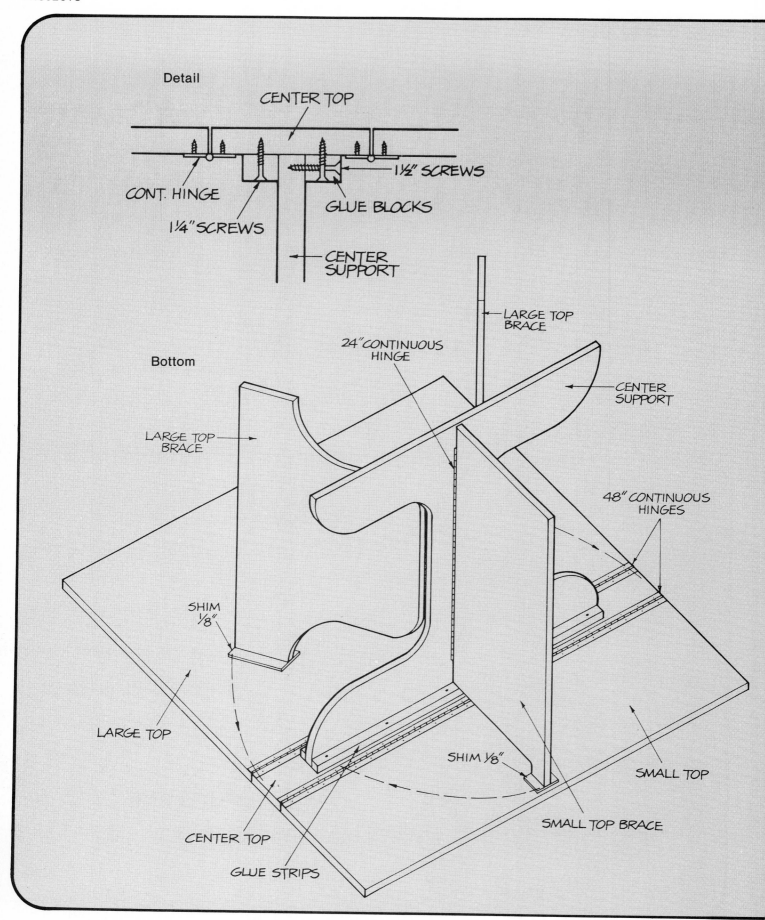

Detail

CENTER TOP

CONT. HINGE

1¼" SCREWS

1½" SCREWS

GLUE BLOCKS

CENTER SUPPORT

LARGE TOP BRACE

24" CONTINUOUS HINGE

Bottom

CENTER SUPPORT

LARGE TOP BRACE

48" CONTINUOUS HINGES

SHIM ⅛"

LARGE TOP

SHIM ⅛"

SMALL TOP

CENTER TOP

SMALL TOP BRACE

GLUE STRIPS

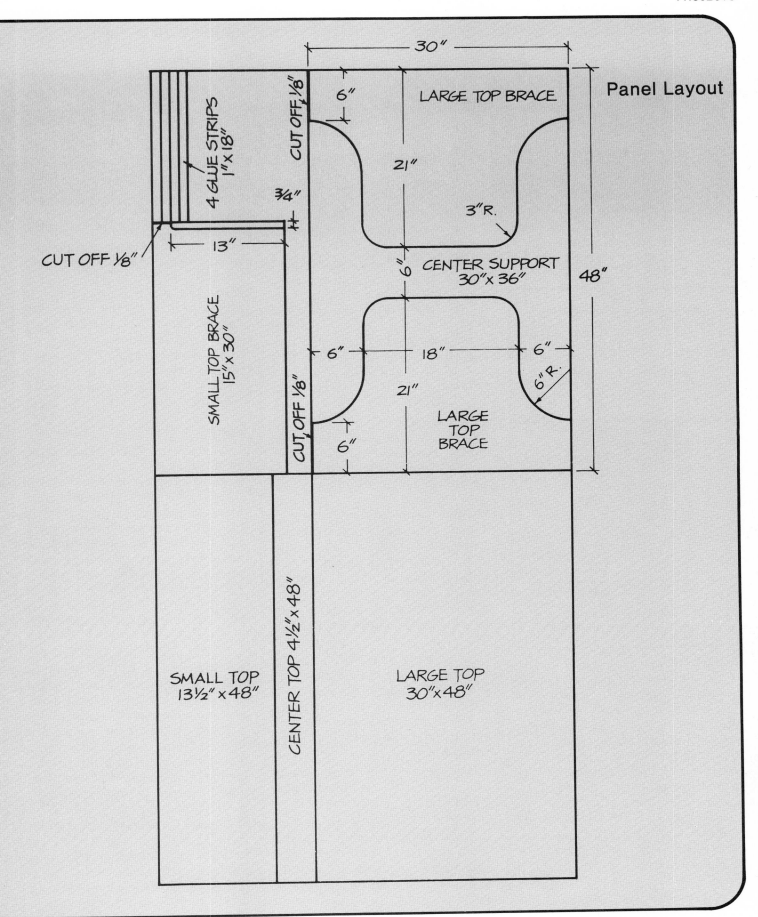

Panel Layout

- 30"
- LARGE TOP BRACE
- 6"
- 21"
- 3" R.
- CUT OFF ⅛"
- 4 GLUE STRIPS 1" x 18"
- ¾"
- CUT OFF ⅛"
- 13"
- CENTER SUPPORT 30" x 36"
- 6"
- 48"
- SMALL TOP BRACE 15" x 30"
- 6"
- 18"
- 6"
- CUT OFF ⅛"
- 21"
- 6" R.
- LARGE TOP BRACE
- 6"
- SMALL TOP 13½" x 48"
- CENTER TOP 4½" x 48"
- LARGE TOP 30" x 48"

13
Shop Reference

LUMBER GRADES

Lumber has two classifications: *Select*, top quality, used where appearance is important, and *Common* construction or utility quality which has some defects. These two classifications are further divided into various grades of lumber. The chart below will help you understand what to buy the next time you have something to build.

SELECT		
Grade	Idaho White Pine	Characteristics
B & better	Supreme	Clear, with only minute blemishes.
C	Choice	Minor defects, small knots.
D	Quality	Larger defects, can be hidden with paint.

COMMON LUMBER		
Grade	Idaho White Pine	Characteristics
1	Colonial	Few defects, tight knots, OK for natural finish or paint.
2	Sterling	More defects, larger knots. OK for natural finish or paint.
3	Standard	Many flaws, loose knots. OK for shelving, fencing.
4	Utility	Low quality. OK for subflooring, crating and forms.
5	Industrial	Lowest quality. Poor strength and appearance.

SOFTWOODS

Generally, softwoods are used in construction and utility functions. The wood is comparatively low in price and is commonly available. Except for redwood and cedar, softwoods have a very low resistance to weather and should be protected by either varnishing or painting. Posts should be chemically treated to guard against rot and insect damage prior to imbedding in the ground.

Because of the loose grain, softwood often splits at the end of a board. Therefore, it is a good idea to order sizes five to ten percent longer than you actually need.

Redwood is a slightly different breed of softwood. It is highly resistant to rot and insects. The color makes beautiful trim, both inside and outdoors. Redwood panelling will warm an otherwise ordinary room. It is also excellent for lawn furniture because of its weather-resistant properties.

Cedar is another softwood that is unique. It gives off a strong, sweet odor that protects clothes and fabrics from moths and silverfish. Cedar chests, or a closet lined with cedar is an excellent place to store infrequently used clothing. It is easy to work and fairly inexpensive to buy.

HARDWOODS

This is where you'll spend some money. Hardwoods are the costliest of the woods. They are also the most elegant, the most durable, and the strongest. Boats, furniture, flooring, and choice cabinetry should be made of first quality hardwoods. Guitars and other musical instruments are constructed using hardwoods. The decorative possibilities are endless with hardwoods because of the tight grain patterns and superior finishing properties.

Your tools must be sharp to work successfully with these woods. Tungsten Carbide blades are recommended. Some of the woods—like teak—will produce sparks when cut and quickly dull a saw of lesser hardness.

Hardwoods show their beauty best when oiled or varnished. Think twice before you cover any of them with paint.

Working with these fine woods is where you'll begin to feel like a real craftsman or sculptor. The results of your efforts will oftentimes be spectacular due to the texture of the wood.

LUMBER SIZES

Lumber is measured two ways: by the running or linear foot and by the board foot. The linear foot is a measurement of length only, while a board foot is a hypothetical board 12 inches in length by 12 inches wide by 1 inch thick. To determine how many board feet is in a 2-inch by 6-inch by 6-inch piece of lumber you would multiply 2 x 6 x 6 and divide by 12. Answer: six board feet.

I have recently heard of two other ways to measure exotic hardwoods such as Burma teak. Both methods are unusual and non-standard. The wood is priced by the square foot or by the pound. The dealers using these methods say it works out the same as the traditional manner. I think the reason for the unique way of determining cost is to hide the actual board-foot price.

SIZE

At one time a 2x4 measured two inches by 4 inches. That was in the days when a dozen eggs sold for fifteen cents. Today the mill starts with a 2x4 measurement and by the time shrinkage occurs from drying, and the finish planing is done, the net size of your 2x4 has dwindled to 1-1/2 inches by 3-1/2 inches. There's nothing you or I can do about this. It's an economic fact of life. The mill passes on all the loss to you.

If you need an actual 2x4 net, the lumberyard will be happy to mill that size from a larger board, and charge you for the larger board *plus the milling costs.*

Study the chart on lumber sizes so you'll know what size you're actually buying. This information is obviously necessary to know when you're figuring a project and need to butt one piece to another. For example: If a span measures 36 inches across and you have a 1x4 on each end, the distance between the two is 29 inches, not the 28 inches you would assume, because each 1x4 measures 3-1/2 inches instead of the 4 inches advertised.

HARDWOOD SELECTION

SPECIES	CHARACTERISTICS
Mahogany:	Fine-grained; reddish brown; durable; resists swelling, shrinking, and warping; easy to work.
Walnut:	Strong; fine-textured; free from warping and shrinking; easy to work; finishes well.
Oak:	Strong; durable; good bending qualities; finishes well; resists moisture absorption.
Maple:	Strong; hard; machines well; resists shock; fine-textured; moderate shrinkage.
Cherry:	Close-grained; resists warping and shrinking; ages well; reddens when exposed to sunlight.
Rosewood:	Very hard; dark reddish brown; close-grained; fragrant; hard to work; takes high polish.
Teak:	Hard; durable; resistant to moisture and rot; resists warping, cracking, and decay.

SOFTWOOD SELECTION

SPECIES	CHARACTERISTICS
Pine:	Uniform texture; works easily, finishes well; resists shrinking, swelling and warping.
Hemlock:	Light in weight; uniformly textured; machines well; low resistance to decay; nonresinous.
Fir:	Easily worked; finishes well; uniform texture; non-resinous, low resistance to decay.
Redwood:	Light in weight; durable; easy to work; naturally resistant to decay.
Spruce:	Strong; hard; low resistance to decay; finishes well; moderate shrinkage; light in weight.
Cedar:	Fresh sweet odor; reddish color; easy to work; uniform texture; resistant to decay.

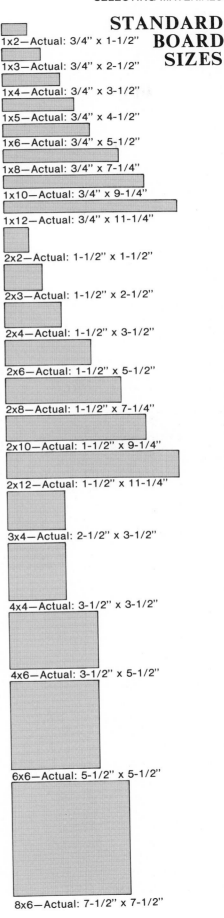

STANDARD BOARD SIZES

1x2—Actual: 3/4" x 1-1/2"
1x3—Actual: 3/4" x 2-1/2"
1x4—Actual: 3/4" x 3-1/2"
1x5—Actual: 3/4" x 4-1/2"
1x6—Actual: 3/4" x 5-1/2"
1x8—Actual: 3/4" x 7-1/4"
1x10—Actual: 3/4" x 9-1/4"
1x12—Actual: 3/4" x 11-1/4"
2x2—Actual: 1-1/2" x 1-1/2"
2x3—Actual: 1-1/2" x 2-1/2"
2x4—Actual: 1-1/2" x 3-1/2"
2x6—Actual: 1-1/2" x 5-1/2"
2x8—Actual: 1-1/2" x 7-1/4"
2x10—Actual: 1-1/2" x 9-1/4"
2x12—Actual: 1-1/2" x 11-1/4"
3x4—Actual: 2-1/2" x 3-1/2"
4x4—Actual: 3-1/2" x 3-1/2"
4x6—Actual: 3-1/2" x 5-1/2"
6x6—Actual: 5-1/2" x 5-1/2"
8x6—Actual: 7-1/2" x 7-1/2"

In buying lumber it pays to compare prices. I've seen 1x2 pine sell for 36 cents a linear foot in one store, while another shop has the same wood for 19 cents! Shop carefully.

ORDERING WOOD

Board foot, the unit used in buying lumber, equals the amount of wood in a piece of lumber measuring 1 foot long, 1 inch thick, and 12 inches wide. To calculate the number of board feet, multiply length in feet by *nominal* thickness and width in inches and divide by 12. Thus, the number of board feet in a piece of lumber 6 feet long, 2 inches thick, and 6 inches wide would be:

$$\frac{6 \text{ ft.} \times 2 \text{ in.} \times 6 \text{ in.}}{12} = \frac{72}{12} = 6 \text{ board ft.}$$

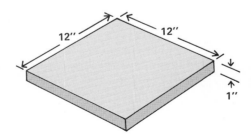

12"   12"   1"

Piece of lumber equivalent to board foot

Linear or running foot is the buying unit for such products as moldings, dowels, furring strips, railings, poles, sometimes 2x4s. Length, not thickness or width, is the only consideration. Shingles and laths are usually sold by the bundle; plywood and wallboard by the panel.

PLYWOOD

Plywood comes in two different types: *Interior* and *Exterior*. Interior plywood is laminated with moisture resistant glue, while Exterior is put together with 100% waterproof adhesive. Exterior is the more expensive of the two. Never, never use Interior where plans call for Exterior. If in doubt, buy Exterior type plywood—the few extra dollars spent will give you peace of mind, knowing the glue is not coming apart on your project.

Aside from specialty plywoods, there are five Interior and six Exterior grades of plywood. Letter designation is used to indicate the surface quality of the wood. The two letters give a grading to both sides of the plywood. Below I've listed a short explanation of what the letters mean and how they are used in combination to grade the plywood.

A Presents a smooth surface.

B Presents a solid surface. Small filled knots.

C May have tight knots of up to 1-1/2 inches across.

D Used only in Interior plywood. May contain plugs, patches, shims, and worm or borer holes.

In addition, there are engineering and specialty grades of plywood. If you plan to build a house, or are going to use plywood forms in concrete work, consult with your local lumber dealer for a complete rundown of choices available to you.

PLYWOOD GRADES FOR EXTERIOR USES

Grade (Exterior)	Face	Back	Inner Plies	Uses
A-A	A	A	C	Outdoor, where appearance of both sides is important.
A-B	A	B	C	Alternate for A-A, where appearance of one side is less important. Face is finish grade.
A-C	A	C	C	Soffits, fences, base for coatings.
B-C	B	C	C	For utility uses such as farm buildings, some kinds of fences, etc., base for coatings.
303® Siding	C (or better)	C	C	Panels with variety of surface texture and grooving patterns. For siding, fences, paneling, screens, etc.
T1-11®	C	C	C	Special 303 panel with grooves 1/4" deep, 3/8" wide. Available unsanded, textured, or MDO surface.
C-C (Plugged)	C (Plugged)	C	C	Excellent base for tile and linoleum, backing for wall coverings, high-performance coatings.
C-C	C	C	C	Unsanded, for backing and rough construction exposed to weather.
B-B Plyform	B	B	C	Concrete forms. Re-use until wood literally wears out.
MDO	B	B or C	C	Medium Density Overlay. Ideal base for paint; for siding, built-ins, signs, displays.
HDO	A or B	A or B	C-Plugged or C	High Density Overlay. Hard surface; no paint needed. For concrete forms, cabinets, counter tops, tanks.

PLYWOOD GRADES FOR INTERIOR USES

Grade (Interior)	Face	Back	Inner Plies	Uses
A-A	A	A	D	Cabinet doors, built-ins, furniture where both sides will show.
A-B	A	B	D	Alternate of A-A. Face is finish grade, back is solid and smooth.
A-D	A	D	D	Finish grade face for paneling, built-ins, backing.
B-D	B	D	D	Utility grade. For backing, cabinet sides, etc.
C-D	C	D	D	Sheathing and structural uses such as temporary enclosures, subfloor. Unsanded.
Underlayment	C-Plugged	D	C and D	For underlayment or combination subfloor-underlayment under tile, carpeting.

Courtesy of American Plywood Association

SELECTING NAILS

This chart will help you order the right size nails, in the proper quantity. Nail sizes are gauged by a penny rating. If you go to the hardware store and ask for a 2-inch nail, the clerk will look amused and know you're a rank amateur. But if you order a 6-penny nail, he'll know right away he's dealing with a man who knows his business.

The next thing to figure out is how many you'll need. You can't say: "I want two hundred 6-penny nails," because nails are sold by the pound. A check of the lower chart reveals there are approximately 167 6-penny common nails to the pound. Therefore, to razzle-dazzle your neighbors and please the clerk, the correct thing you should say is: "I want a pound and a quarter of 6-penny common nails." You'll probably have a few nails left over for the next job.

NAIL TYPES AND USES

Common nail: General-purpose heavy-duty type used in construction and rough work. Large head won't pull through.

Finishing nail: Used on trim and cabinetwork where nailheads must be concealed. Head is sunk and then filled over.

Casing nail: Similar to finishing nail but heavier. Used for trim where strength and concealment are required.

Cut flooring nail: Has rectangular cross section and a blunt lip. Used to blind-nail flooring through edges without splitting.

Annular ring nail: Has sharp-edged ridges that lock into wood fibers and greatly increase holding power.

Spiral nails: Used in flooring to assure tight and squeak-proof joining. Nail tends to turn into the wood like a screw as it is driven home.

Square-shank concrete nail: Similar to round types used to fasten furring strips and brackets to concrete walls and floors.

Common brads: Used for nailing parquet flooring to subfloor, attaching molding to walls and furniture. Brads are usually sunk and filled.

Tacks: Made in cut or round form; used to fasten carpet or fabric to wood, and for similar light fastening jobs.

Upholstery nails: Made with both ornamental and colored heads; used to fasten upholstery where fastenings will show.

Roofing nail: Has large head, is usually galvanized. Used to hold composition roofings; design resists pull-through.

Sealing roofing nails: Have lead or plastic washer under head to provide watertight seal; used on metal roofing.

Duplex head nail: Can be driven tight against lower head, with upper head projecting for removal; for temporary work.

Barbed dowel pin: Has many purposes, such as aligning parts, serving as pivot, permitting disassembly or separation.

Corrugated fastener: Used in making light-duty miter joints, such as screens and large picture frames. Drive it across joint.

Staples: Made in many forms to hold wire fencing, bell wire, electric cable, screening, available with insulated shoulders.

APPROXIMATE NUMBER OF NAILS IN A POUND

Length of nail in inches	7/8	1	1¼	1½	1¾	2	2¼	2½	2¾	3	3¼	3½	4	4½	5	5½	6
Common nail		847	543	294	254	167	150	101	92	66	61	47	30	23	17	14	11
Finishing nail		1,473*	880	630	535*	288	254*	196	178*	124	113*	93*	65*				
Spiral flooring nail						177	158	142									
Roofing nail	246	223	189	164	145												
Square concrete nail		254	202	168	143	125	111	100	91	83							
Fence staples (bright)	122	106	87	72	61												

*Nonstandard sizes—must be specially ordered

SELECTING SCREWS

The two most common screwheads are the slotted type found in most woodworking projects, and the cross-slotted or X type, used wherever production work is done. The cross-slotted type is sub-divided into Phillips and Reid & Prince, orignally two different manufacturers. The most obvious difference between the Phillips and the Reid & Prince is the Phillips is blunted at the bottom of the slot, while the Reid & Prince comes to a sharp point. Look at the tip of the two screwdrivers designed for these screws and you'll readily see the difference.

Phillips is the most common of the cross-slotted screwheads. If you were going to drive a lot of screws with a power screwdriver or drill, the cross-slotted would be preferred over the single slot because the bit is less likely to slip off the head of the screw.

One-way screwheads are used primarily to prevent vandals from taking something apart, such as the partitions of public restrooms.

SUITING THE SCREWS TO THE JOB

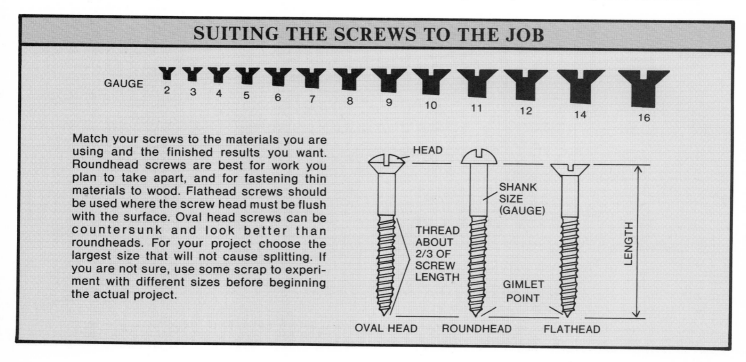

GAUGE 2 3 4 5 6 7 8 9 10 11 12 14 16

Match your screws to the materials you are using and the finished results you want. Roundhead screws are best for work you plan to take apart, and for fastening thin materials to wood. Flathead screws should be used where the screw head must be flush with the surface. Oval head screws can be countersunk and look better than roundheads. For your project choose the largest size that will not cause splitting. If you are not sure, use some scrap to experiment with different sizes before beginning the actual project.

HEAD

SHANK SIZE (GAUGE)

THREAD ABOUT 2/3 OF SCREW LENGTH

GIMLET POINT

LENGTH

OVAL HEAD   ROUNDHEAD   FLATHEAD

TYPES OF SCREWS

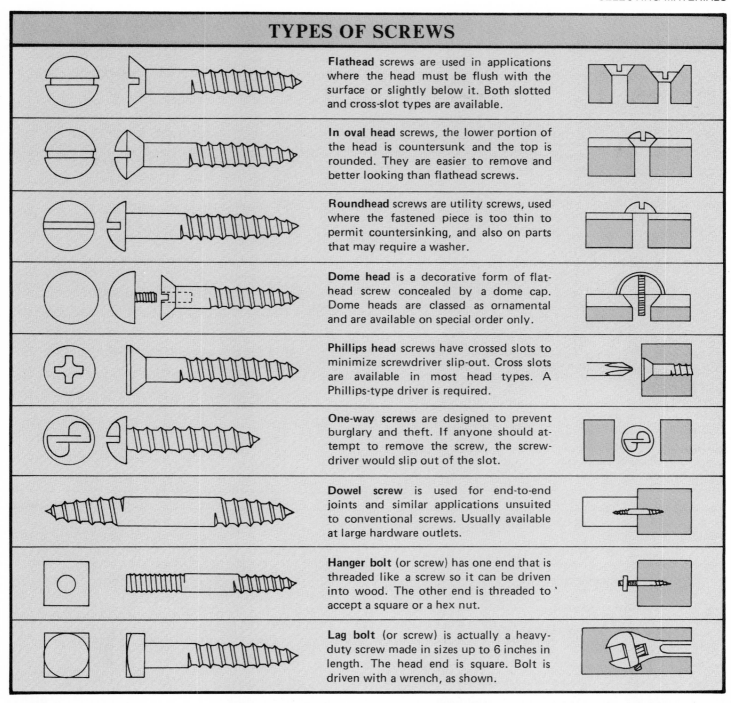

Flathead screws are used in applications where the head must be flush with the surface or slightly below it. Both slotted and cross-slot types are available.

In oval head screws, the lower portion of the head is countersunk and the top is rounded. They are easier to remove and better looking than flathead screws.

Roundhead screws are utility screws, used where the fastened piece is too thin to permit countersinking, and also on parts that may require a washer.

Dome head is a decorative form of flathead screw concealed by a dome cap. Dome heads are classed as ornamental and are available on special order only.

Phillips head screws have crossed slots to minimize screwdriver slip-out. Cross slots are available in most head types. A Phillips-type driver is required.

One-way screws are designed to prevent burglary and theft. If anyone should attempt to remove the screw, the screwdriver would slip out of the slot.

Dowel screw is used for end-to-end joints and similar applications unsuited to conventional screws. Usually available at large hardware outlets.

Hanger bolt (or screw) has one end that is threaded like a screw so it can be driven into wood. The other end is threaded to accept a square or a hex nut.

Lag bolt (or screw) is actually a heavy-duty screw made in sizes up to 6 inches in length. The head end is square. Bolt is driven with a wrench, as shown.

TYPES OF WASHERS

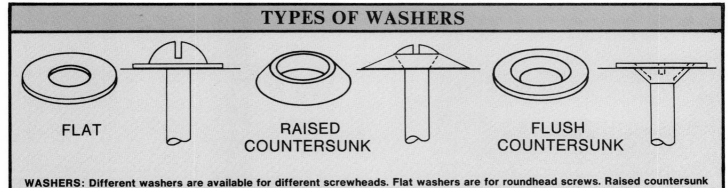

FLAT

RAISED COUNTERSUNK

FLUSH COUNTERSUNK

WASHERS: Different washers are available for different screwheads. Flat washers are for roundhead screws. Raised countersunk and flush countersunk washers are for oval and flathead screws.

QUICK REFERENCE DRILL GUIDE

If you own a modest number of drill bits—say a seventeen unit kit—this chart can get you by most situations. Using it is simplicity itself; check the size of the wood screw you want to use in the lefthand column under "Wood Screws," read the drill size required in the two righthand columns, marked "softwood" or "hardwood." For example: A #6 screw requires a 1/16-inch bit for softwood, or a 3/32-inch drill for hardwood.

DECIMAL EQUIVALENTS

This easy-to-read chart will prove very handy whenever you need to convert fractions into decimals or vice-versa. As more tools become metric, this will become a more common experience.

DRILL SIZES FOR WOOD SCREW LEAD HOLES

Wood Screw Size	Size Drill To Use		Wood Screw Size	Size Drill to Use	
	Soft Wood	Hard Wood		Soft Wood	Hard Wood
0	1/32	1/32	9	3/32	1/8
1	1/32	3/64	10	3/32	1/8
2	1/32	3/64	11	3/32	1/8
3	3/64	1/16	12	7/64	9/64
4	3/64	1/16	14	7/64	9/64
5	1/16	5/64	16	1/8	5/32
6	1/16	3/32	18	9/64	9/64
7	5/64	3/32	20	5/32	5/32
8	5/64	7/6	24	3/16	15/64

DRILL SIZES FOR SHEET METAL SCREW LEAD HOLES

Sheet Metal Screw Size	Size Drill To Use		Sheet Metal Screw Size	Size Drill To Use	
	Type A Gimlet Point Screw	Type Z Blunt Point Screw		Type A Gimlet Point Screw	Type Z Blunt Point Screw
2	1/16	1/16	10	9/64	5/32
4	3/32	3/32	12	5/32	11/64
6	3/32	7/64	14	3/16	13/64
7	7/64	1/8	14		13/64
8	1/8	9/64			

THE DECIMAL EQUIVALENTS OF MOST COMMON FRACTIONS

Fractions	Decimals	Fractions	Decimals
1/64	.015625	33/64	.515625
2/64—1/32	.03125	34/64—17/32	.53125
3/64	.046875	35/64	.546875
4/64—2/32—1/16	.0625	36/64—18/32—9/16	.5625
5/64	.078125	37/64	.578125
6/64—3/32	.09375	38/64—19/32	.59375
7/64	.109375	39/64	.609375
8/64—4/32—2/16—1/8	.125	40/64—20/32—10/16—5/8	.625
9/64	.140625	41/64	.640625
10/64—5/32	.15625	42/64—21/32	.65625
11/64	.171875	43/64	.671875
12/64—6/32—3/16	.1875	44/64—22/32—11/16	.6875
13/64	.203125	45/64	.703125
14/64—7/32	.21875	46/64—23/32	.71875
15/64	.234375	47/64	.734375
16/64—8/32—4/16—1/4	.250	48/64—24/32—12/16—6/8—3/4	.750
17/64	.265625	49/64	.765625
18/64—9/32	.28125	50/64—25/32	.78125
19/64	.296875	51/64	.796875
20/64—10/32—5/16	.3125	52/64—26/32—13/16	.8125
21/64	.328125	53/64	.828125
22/64—11/32	.34375	54/64—27/32	.84375
23/64	.359375	55/64	.859375
24/64—12/32—6/16—3/8	.3750	56/64—28/32—14/16—7/8	.8750
25/64	.390625	57/64	.890625
26/64—13/32	.40625	58/64—29/32	.90625
27/64	.421875	59/64	.921875
28/64—14/32—7/16	.4375	60/64—30/32—15/16	.9375
29/64	.453125	61/64	.953125
30/64—15/32	.46875	62/64—31/32	.96875
31/64	.484375	63/64	.984375
32/64—16/32—8/16—4/8—2/4—1/2	.5	64/64—32/32—16/16—8/8—4/4—2/2—1	1.000

Suppliers

The following companies assisted in the production of this book. We gratefully acknowledge their help and recommend their products.

American Plywood Association
Tacoma, WA 98401

Arco Products Corp.
Englewood, NJ 07631

Black & Decker
Towson, MD 21204

Bostik Consumer Division
U.S.M. Corporation
Reading, PA 19605

Coastal Abrasive & Tools Co.
Trumbull, CT 06611

The Connecticut Valley Mfg. Co.
New Britain, CT 06051

Disston, Inc.
Danvill, VA 24541

Electro Engineering Product. Co.
Chicago, IL 60647

Henry L. Hanson, Inc.
Worcester, MA 01606

The Irwin Auger Bit Co.
Wilmington, OH 45177

Portable Appliance & Tool Group
McGraw-Edison Company
Columbia, MO 65201

Millers Falls
Greenfield, MA 01301

Milwaukee Electric Tool Corp.
Brookfield, WI 53005

Montgomery Ward & Co.
New York, NY 10019

J.C. Penney Company
Chicago, IL 60684

The 3M Company
St. Paul, MN 55101

Remington Arms
Bridgeport, CN 06602

Rockwell International
Memphis, TN 38138

Sears, Roebuck and Co.
Chicago, IL 60684

Skil Corporation
Chicago, Il 60646

The Stanley Works
New Britain, CT 06050

The Thompson Tool Co., Inc.
Norwalk, CT 06850

Wen Products, Inc.
Chicago, IL 60631

The plans on pages 128 to 149 originally appeared in a different form in *Popular Science Magazine*. Their use here is courtesy of American Plywood Association.

Index

8.32728301320